GROUNDWORK FOR COMMUNITY-BASED CONSERVATION

Strategies for Social Research

Diane Russell and Camilla Harshbarger

ALTAMIRA
P R E S S

A Division of Rowman & Littlefield Publishers, Inc.
Walnut Creek • Lanham • New York • Oxford

ALTAMIRA PRESS
A Division of Rowman & Littlefield Publishers, Inc.
1630 North Main Street, #367
Walnut Creek, CA 94596
www.altamirapress.com

Rowman & Littlefield Publishers, Inc.
A Member of the Rowman & Littlefield Publishing Group
4501 Forbes Boulevard, Suite 200
Lanham, MD 20706

PO Box 317
Oxford
OX2 9RU, United Kingdom

British Library Cataloguing in Publication Information Available

Library of Congress Cataloging-in-Publication Data

Russell, Diane, 1950–
    Groundwork for community-based conservation : strategies for social
    research / Diane Russell and Camilla Harshbarger.
        p. cm.
    Includes bibliographical references (p.   ).
    ISBN 0-7425-0437-9 (cloth : alk. paper)—ISBN 0-7425-0438-7 (pbk : alk. paper)
    1. Nature conservation—Social aspects—Research. 2. Nature conservation—
    Economic aspects—Research. 3. Nature conservation—Citizen participation—
    Research. I. Harshbarger, Camilla, 1954– II. Title.

QH75 .R87 2002
333.7′2—dc21
                                                            2002004999
Printed in the United States of America

♾™ The paper used in this publication meets the minimum requirements of
American National Standard for Information Sciences—Permanence of Paper
for Printed Library Materials, ANSI/NISO Z39.48-1992.

GROUNDWORK FOR COMMUNITY-BASED CONSERVATION

For KNT
You said you would be nowhere,
but here you are

For Geneva and Lulu
My grandmothers who taught me to love nature

For all the people who shared their lives with us

Contents

Photos, Figures, Maps, and Tables   vii

Acknowledgments   ix

1   Introduction   1

2   Conservation as Human Behavior   15

3   Social Elements of Conservation   27

4   Resource Management Systems   40

5   Economic Systems   57

6   Population and Social Systems   77

7   Belief and Knowledge Systems   102

8   Ethics, Targets, and Planning   111

9   Partnership   125

10   Organizing the Research   143

11   Regional Studies   169

12 Interviewing   189

13 Ethnographic Approaches   207

14 Surveys   224

15 Action Research   235

16 Learning and Communicating   257

Resources   277

References   295

Index   308

About the Authors   321

Photos, Figures, Maps, and Tables

Photo

4.1. Example of a multistory agroforestry system
in Indonesia   46

Figures

5.1. Declining terms of trade to farmers   68
11.1. Dendritic market structure   184
13.1. The five primary ethnobiological ranks and their
respective taxa   213
13.2. Example of kinship diagram indicating four generations   218
15.1. Monitoring change in nontimber-forest-product species   252

Map

11.1. Tshopo subregion within the Democratic Republic
of Congo   172

Tables

4.1. Types of control and ownership of resources   44
5.1. Economic indicators at the household level   72

5.2. Economic levels, investment strategies, and
     conservation initiatives   74
6.1. Evolution of institutions   85
6.2. The importance of social categories   92
8.1. Paradigms in conservation and development projects   123
9.1. Residents' Development Committee (RDC)
     historical time lines   138
10.1. Research management as a system   167
12.1. Questions for different instruments   198
15.1. Benefits and risks of PRA versus surveys   245
16.1. Monitoring impacts of conservation enterprises   259

Acknowledgments

Major thanks for help in preparation of this manuscript go to Hank Cauley, G. William Aalbersberg, Nick Salafsky, Martin Olson, Jessica Stabile, Diane Goodwillie, Jennifer Collier, David Wilkie, Torie Osborne, Eduardo Brondizio, William Burch, Aline Martinez, John Parks, Rosalie Robertson, Grace Ebron, Steven Franzel, James Booth, Joan Kariuki, James Yuma, Christin Hutchinson, Michael Brown, Judy Oglethorpe, and an anonymous reviewer.

Our work is based on sharing and dialogue with our local partners living at conservation sites, colleagues from CARE, the University of Florida, the International Institute for Tropical Agriculture, the staff and partners of the Biodiversity Conservation Network, the Biodiversity Support Program, the Central African Regional Program on the Environment, the United States Agency for International Development, the International Centre for Research in Agroforestry, Yale University School of Forestry and Environmental Studies, and the American Anthropological Association's Anthropology and Environment section/Conservation and Community working group. We have learned so much from these colleagues and friends, but we must take full responsibility for this book.

* * *

This book was prepared using funds from the Biodiversity Conservation Network (BCN). BCN was a program of the Biodiversity Support Program (BSP), a consortium of World Wildlife Fund (WWF), the Nature Conservancy, and World Resources Institute, funded by the United States Agency for International Development (USAID). This publication was made possible in part through support provided by USAID, under the terms of Cooperative Agreement #AEP-A-00-92-00043-00. The opinions expressed herein are those of the authors and do not necessarily reflect the views of BCN, BSP, WWF, or USAID.

1

Introduction

Nature is a temple where living pillars
Sometimes let out confused words.
Man passes there through forests of symbols
Which observe him with a familiar gaze.

—Baudelaire, *Les Fleurs du Mal*

This book is about using the insights and methods of social science—particularly anthropology and related disciplines—to improve the practice of conservation. It is neither a textbook nor an academic treatise but a conversation about the authors' experiences and lessons from around the world—a practical "idea book." We present no easy paths to research and implementation: It was tempting to write a book that claims "do it this way and you will achieve success" or "this is the appropriate model to follow" because this is the style of much literature oriented to conservation projects. Instead of defending a particular approach or model, this book encourages exploration. We tread lightly around hot anthropological debates and avoid jargon, walking a fine line between academic rigor and accessibility to non–social scientists. We believe that social research for conservation is a learning process that changes at it matures, as the partners grow in understanding. There are many choices to be made, many potential pitfalls, and no recipes for success. This book features a range of research methods, indicating where each may be appropriate to specific conditions, scales, and research questions. We ground the discussion on social research in examples drawn from our own field experience.

THE CONSEQUENCES OF POOR COMMUNICATION

The villagers around the large protected area in central Africa seemed to be amenable to its plans for expansion. Authorities had discussed the plans with village elders and distributed some rice and wine to the population. It was explained that jobs would be created when tourism started up. In a group meeting, the elders agreed that it was a good idea to make people request permission from authorities before hunting or moving to another village. A small survey revealed that the vast majority did not at all understand the purpose of the protected area, but the authorities were not concerned by what they perceived as apathy and lack of education. It came as a surprise, then, when during a period of civil conflict the ranger station was attacked, looted, and burned to the ground, apparently by young men from the surrounding villages.

Human behavior is highly complex. Human culture is ever changing and vital. There are no easy or quick ways to understand and work with people in the process of conservation. This book presents challenges in social research for conservation and strategies and resources to craft sounder, deeper social research. We believe that overreliance on rapid appraisals, superficial surveys, and pseudo-participatory group interviews is partially responsible for the failure of conservation initiatives. The overuse of these methods reflects a paucity of accessible guidance on a range of approaches to social research for conservation, a focus on quick "results," and emphasis on gathering data for models rather than as reflections of social realities.

Methods grounded in ethnography, agrarian studies, and human/ political ecology transform research for conservation practitioners. Rapid methods have their place, and we discuss them as well. But let us put them, indeed all methods, in the context of improving the quality and effectiveness of social science research. Our aim is not just generating "data" but using insights and conceptual tools from these disciplines to craft better conservation initiatives based on richer understanding of humans in nature.

POOR PROJECT PLANNING IN ASIA

An Asian conservation organization had the idea that providing benefits to local people would increase buy-in to its activities to create a community-based forest reserve. The idea that they came up with, in concert with a women's committee, was to produce rattan baskets for sale in the provincial market. Some older women were expert weavers and would teach the younger women. After a year, however, the project was abandoned because it turned out that the provincial market was saturated with baskets. The older women wanted to be compensated for the training, but there was no revenue. The conservation organization paid the older women out of its budget, and this created jealousy because no one else was getting any benefit. The resulting hurt feelings caused the conservation organization to get a bad name.

Why We Need Better Social Research for Conservation

Lack of genuine buy-in to conservation by local populations is one of the problems that social research addresses. Research and planning has to be collaborative and grounded in local realities. Partnership with and integration into local institutions can substantially increase effectiveness if it involves a deep understanding of lines of power and communication within and among institutions. Participant observation, key informant interviews, social mapping, and censuses are some of the methods that reveal perception and lines of power.

Insufficient attention to the sustainability of conservation efforts, whether they are integrated conservation and development projects (ICDPs) or protected areas, is another widespread problem. Lack of sustainability can arise from weak financial, institutional, and political bases. Few viable alternatives may exist for livelihood and income when land and resources are taken away or restricted. Existing markets may be saturated or dominated by certain commodity chains or monopolies. Jealousy over benefits or perceived benefits can destroy the best-intentioned efforts.

THE POLITICS OF SAVING MAMMALS

A well-funded and managed program to conserve a threatened mammal was determined to do it right. They worked closely with local institutions, held numerous participatory planning sessions, and created a largely successful ecotourism enterprise that provided substantial benefits to local people. The program received a major setback, however, when provincial authorities gave out a large logging concession within the habitat of the protected species. Pleas to the national authorities were unsuccessful because a much-heralded decentralization initiative had given the power of assigning concessions to the provincial administration. Failure to make contact with the provincial authorities resulted in defeat for the initiative.

To equip conservation practitioners to deal with these situations, the social researcher has to present factors in the analysis of the local and wider economic and political systems. This analysis has to include many components that may not fit the standard definition of economy: the social economy, the division of labor, and the hidden (or underground) economy. Political power manifests at all levels, from the household to the global, and also takes many forms. None of the levels can be neglected. In most cases, a "project" will replicate local power and economic dynamics unless it builds coalitions and taps in to wider reforms.

This defeat could have been avoided or mitigated if a sound political and social analysis had been carried out. Social research is not limited to the village or the site—it encompasses arenas such as political struggles, policies, and even global commodity trends. For example, the history of commodity extraction and land expropiation, the fate of previous conservation and developmental projects, and policies and practices of taxation are key areas to be explored.

Integration of social science data and information with biological information is not just a matter of putting together an interdisciplinary team or even of writing joint reports. It involves creative problem solving that hones in on key bottlenecks and solutions. Different disciplines use different boundaries, scales, knowledge bases, meth-

---

CASE STUDY

CHALLENGES OF COMMUNICATION ACROSS DISCIPLINES

An interdisciplinary team of scientists was sent to a site to assess the status of a rare and highly valued palm species and to get some insight into how the local population uses this species. The botanist created several plots in the forest to measure size class distribution and determined that, because of the rarity of seedlings, there was little if any regeneration of the species going on. The social scientist meanwhile discovered that people were encouraging the growth of this species in areas near their homes but had little control over the deep forest area, where they did not have legal rights to restrict access. There was conflict about how to report the status of the species, and the end result was a recommendation for further research.

---

ods, and communication modes with local people; they also have varying prestige and resources. But the bottom line is how well applied research solves problems. Sometimes problems are technical, often they are social and political. In the case study below, addressing the "open access" situation in the forest takes precedence over technical plant conservation efforts, such as replanting or domestication.

We need to work with different units of analysis, methods at different scales, integration of biological and social data, and approaches that merge scientific and indigenous knowledge. Defining the research question is the most challenging and creative step.

Failure to define the conservation problem holistically and see links between conservation and other social problems, such as poverty, inequality, human rights abuses, conflict, governance, health, and reproductive rights, can lead to serious ethical and practical dilemmas. It is not reasonable to think that "pure" conservation can take place anywhere, abstracted from social forces and problems. But how to understand these problems? How to attack them with limited resources and restricted mandate? Conservation is embedded in society—it is a social process—and as such we need ways to examine conservation and other social problems together in research and in practical partnership (for

HEALTH CONSEQUENCES OF CONSERVATION

A large conservation organization on a small Pacific island was concerned to protect coral reefs. Its strategy was to create a marine protected area where the harvesting of certain species was prohibited. The protected area was set up and functioned well for a number of years before a team came to evaluate the effort. By chance, they went to the local clinic and looked at the health records. They were astonished to find a decline in birth weights and an increase in cases of malnutrition among girls between the ages of three and five years. The health worker reported that the intensive logging on the island had led to a steep decline in soil fertility and thus harvest failures over the past few years. Further inquiries led to the finding that since reef fishing and shellfish gathering had been restricted, fish were given primarily to senior men and eaten by others only on feast days.

excellent summaries of this point of view, see Brechin et al., 2002; Wilshusen et al., 2002).

These Problems Are Widespread

In rural regions of the tropics where we have worked, we have seen a number of conservation and natural resource management initiatives fail because of a lack of understanding of social dynamics and poor-quality social data. The previously presented stories are loosely based on real cases. It is our experience that conservation programs often send out researchers and development workers with little knowledge, short time frames, and externally driven agendas to try to effect change in deeply tangled and charged situations.

Conservation is a complex human activity, requiring that people of different cultures, beliefs, needs, and statuses work together toward a common goal. The social dimensions of conservation range from understanding priorities of different "stakeholders" at a site to crafting international policy. Yet in many institutions devoted to conservation and natural resource management, social science research amounts to spotty GIS (geographic information systems) maps, household surveys with no clear focus, collection of demographic data for inadequately conceived models, participatory rural appraisals (PRAs) done at the initial stages of a project and never followed through, or monitoring and evaluation that amounts to the collection of success stories. In part, this limited menu of options and low quality is because of the dearth of social scientists in decision roles in international institutions. It also reflects a bias that "quantitative" research based on surveys is more scientific or broadly useful to institutions working at a large scale. More realistically, rapid research tends to be research that meets "data needs" of institutions while not challenging assumptions or modes of work. Project managers may think that academic-quality social research is too expensive and time consuming and risks being off target or irrelevant. There is the possibility that the social researcher might turn up information that is contrary to project design or to assumptions underlying that design. Therefore, it is often the practice to use secondary data in planning or to send out a smart but relatively untrained (and junior) person to carry out some surveys, do some "participatory" exercises in order to collect "socioeconomic data," and motivate the locals to get involved. Another common pattern is to use consultants or students rather than project staff. However, in many villages today, the locals flee when they see people approaching with notebooks because they are tired of being studied with no benefit. Even if the social research is completed, it may not be sound or scientific. Finally, it may be well crafted but ignored by decision makers (for a discussion of development research in the same vein, see Pottier 1993).

The social researcher needs to know how to do high-quality research and how to ground it in solid social theory and time-tested concepts. On the practical level, representing local communities is fraught with contradictions and pitfalls (Brosius et al. 1998). Institutionally, the social researcher needs to know how to hold out for resources and for a space at the table within the institution and initiative. The research has to be used.

What can be done to improve the quality of social research within organizations focused on conservation and natural resource management? Specifically, how can we encourage ethnographic approaches and more nuanced sociopolitical and historical analyses? Ethnography and history need to go beyond descriptions of "indigenous knowledge" that provide an attractive annex to reports: They have to provide operational guidance on dealing with cultural and power differentials through deep understanding of institutions, economic patterns, resource management strategies, networks, and modes of communication.

Creatively Critical Approaches

The challenge is broader, however. It has to do with the role of a "constructively critical" perspective and a rethinking of investments in research, conservation, support for local institutions, and other essentials of conservation initiatives. Many initiatives discourage or downplay a critical perspective, essential to the conduct of science, because it interferes with collecting "success stories" that are felt to be necessary to garner donor support. (Donor support in itself is part of a complex political process involving multiple constituencies, often far removed from the problem or from understanding scientific and development issues.) On the other hand, anthropologists and other "social scientists" are renowned for the critical perspective, such that many institutions are wary of collaboration with them. Anthropologists are constantly touting the exception to the rule, showing how plans cannot work, how actions are potentially dangerous or unethical, and how project-related research does not get to the heart of the matter. Thus is born the "socioeconomist," whose task is clearly data collection, not critique.

We want to show how a critical perspective is linked to wiser investments rather than to rhetoric and inaction. Investments are being made and will continue to be made in conservation around the world. A great many people are passionately interested in supporting conservation. Most are convinced that their investments are and should be targeted to safeguarding exotic animals and "wild" areas and are not well enough aware of the importance of maintaining and improving livelihoods, land security, and ecosystem processes. We think that people can fully understand these concepts.

Conservationists can understand also that local populations are complex. Without a local constituency, conservation efforts will inevitably fail. Yet finding or creating this constituency is fraught with pitfalls. Analysis of local politics, subpopulations, divisions, and factions is critical: unpacking the idea of a unified "community" without throwing out the package. Conservation is typically about some people not getting their way and about others finding a common way. Sanctions and regulations that play an important role in conservation may reinforce political and social divisions or create new conflicts. Hence, social analysis has to help delineate these lines of power and draw out consequences of different rules, sanctions, and regulations. This kind of analysis cannot be done adequately without participant observation and understanding of local social categories and perceptions.

Operationally, we find that the top-down approaches common to many donor-funded and government initiatives have not been effective in institutionalizing conservation. Elaborate project designs and plans with short time frames and shifting priorities emanating from distant capitals generate frustration, dependency, and anger in local communities, governments, and nongovernmental organizations. Many programs budget little support for local researchers and their institutions, further limiting the capacity for understanding and local ownership. When the initiative is faltering, planners and project implementers often ask social researchers how to change local people or get them to adopt what has been planned for them. These untimely interventions rarely lead to significant insight or change.

The micro-approach of many ICDPs, working with a few communities in a small area, also has limited effectiveness in meeting higher-order conservation challenges (the World Wildlife Fund's experience is well documented in World Wildlife Fund 1995a, 1995b, 1996, 1997a, 1997b; See also Rhoades and Stallings 2001). Yet research into management of common-pool biological resources finds that local, self-organized, resource-user groups and community-based organizations do a better job at conservation than government agencies and other large-scale institutions (Margoluis et al. 2000; Ostrom 1998c). These groups can be the foundation of strategies to conserve species and habitats across broad ranges. Resource users and communities affected by environmental degradation are able to learn scientific monitoring methods and use them for management and policy change, as we discuss in chapter 14.

The linking of local systems and social structures that can effectively manage resources at socially viable scales into strategies that can meet wider threats is our greatest hope for sustainable and equitable conservation strategies. There are many political and economic challenges to the empowerment of local resource users and in creating these wider linkages. We present tools to facilitate these linkages and show relations among scales and levels.

To understand the constraints to and opportunities for local partners in conservation, the first step is for conservationists to learn how to understand and work with institutions that are significant to local people. We also need to devise concrete strategies that emerge out of better social research for how to deal with the power of extralocal actors. This is perhaps the most important challenge for social research in conservation.

There Was No Resource Like Our Book

There is a wealth of manuals on how to implement a conservation initiative from technical and managerial standpoints, many of which discuss social and institutional elements (see e.g., Borrini-Feyerabend 1997; Brown and Wyckoff-Baird 1996; Byers 2000; Salafsky and Margoluis 1998; The Nature Conservancy 2000). These do not go far enough toward the quality social research needed. On the other hand, books on anthropological methods, specialist books, and journal articles are not accessible to conservation practitioners.

Conservation practitioners need a guide to social research tailored to conservation concerns. To meet that need, we have written this book. Our book presents concepts and methods used by social scientists studying natural resource management and human ecology and by development practitioners who are engaged in work with local communities on conservation issues as well as lessons from social research in conservation initiatives.

This book emerged from social science research, monitoring, and evaluation within the Biodiversity Conservation Network (BCN), a program funded by the United States Agency for International Development, and focused on analysis of a community-based enterprise approaches to conservation in Asia-Pacific (www.bcnet.org). In turn, BCN was part of the Biodiversity Support Program, a consortium of the World Wildlife Fund, The Nature Conservancy, and the World Resources Institute. These institutions, as well as the local BCN projects, provided many of the examples for this book, but the authors also draw on their own experiences in Africa, Southeast Asia, Latin America, and the Pacific.

Social research means not just understanding people but interacting with them as well. Unlike research in the biological and physical sciences, our "subjects" are our partners. Hence, social research demands "emotional intelligence" as well as logic and sound methodology. Social researchers have to be able to challenge assumptions and document on-site conditions from different viewpoints. This delicate role involves dealing with the hard realities of elitism, factionalism, poverty, political power, and conflicting visions for the future. In application, it means finding paths to partnership among many social actors. A balance of insider and outsider knowledge is critical. Local people have important knowledge of species, habitats, practices, and social systems but may not necessarily have access to information on wider political, demographic, biological, and economic trends that threaten ecosystems and livelihoods.

This book describes social research concepts and methods that can be used to increase understanding of human behavior, social structure, culture, institutions, and key trends. We look at research holistically: from understanding humans within their habitat to conceptual approaches to data collection and analysis toward learning and insight. Social research for conservation should employ the most appropriate con-

---

Box 1.1.   Pet Theories in Conservation Initiatives

Pet theories are ideas about what should work or not work based on
assumptions and beliefs rather than testing and validation. Some examples:
    Formal projects are the best ways to foster conservation
    Nongovernmental organizations should be the primary implementers of
       community-based conservation initiatives
    Market-based approaches provide incentives for local communities to
       conserve biodiversity
    Participatory workshops are more appropriate to community research than
       surveys

---

cepts and tools, whether academic, applied, indigenous, or scientific,
and not be framed by pet theories (see box 1.1 for some recent examples).

We show how research and information gathering must flow into
planning and decision making. The design of a conservation initiative
should proceed in tandem with research as all partners learn and decide what steps to take. Hence, we include sections on targets, planning, and partnership. We emphasize the ethics of research and the
importance of testing assumptions made during the research process.
Research choices can directly influence project planning and therefore
affect people's lives. All methodological approaches are subject to misuse. For example, both "scientific" survey methods and "participatory"
methods are used to march into a community and begin work that has
already been planned in distant capitals.

This book is targeted to people who will carry out or supervise research and social development activities at conservation sites or would
like to learn about the social dimensions of conservation. It is aimed at
people with a college or university degree or who are in a degree program. We know from experience, however, that people with little formal
education can be trained in appropriate research methods, given the time,
the encouragement, and the resources. But we want to stress that we do
not think that social research is easy or can be quickly learned by anyone
who wishes to collect data or interview folks in a village. We have seen
too many dreadful questionnaires and research protocols to believe that.

This book can be a guide for individual or group study, but it is not
a training manual. We think that formal training is not the best way to
learn the practice of social research. The hypothetical nature of training
builds artificial confidence—it is devoid of the complexity of the social
reality of the field. Understanding the experience of others, listening to
their narratives grounded in social and historical contexts, and then

striking out under the supervision of a mentor is how one best learns the practice of social research.

While perspectives from many fields such as rural sociology, rural development, social forestry, and conservation biology are incorporated into this book, human ecology and institutional approaches are highlighted. Within human ecology, we address the issues raised by political ecology, an approach that illustrates how local patterns of land use are related to larger political/economic conditions and to historic patterns of inequality.

Human and political ecology provide important tools and insights; however, we also want to link research to action. Thus, we need to use tools to show not only how people manage resources but also how people organize themselves to take action and how local and wider institutions are linked. The study of institutions for resource management has advanced significantly in recent years because of the work of common-property theorists such as Elinor Ostrom, Bonnie McCay, and James Acheson (recent references include Acheson 2000; McCay 1998, 2000a, 2000b; Ostrom 1998a, 1998b, 1998c; see also the International Association for the Study of Common Property under "Institutions for Natural Resource Management" in the Resources section). Much is known about the characteristics of groups that manage resources under an array of circumstances, including what makes for more successful institutional arrangements.

The institutional approach goes far in helping explain factors that govern the formation of groups involved in natural resource management, but there are other tools as well that are more action oriented. Conservation has to be based on engagement and building constituencies. Scientific research can be a vital part of this engagement. It can help link local communities to wider networks. In this book, several promising action research approaches are discussed, such as participatory mapping, community monitoring, and appreciative inquiry.

We caution that participatory action research for planning and local management needs to be complemented with scientifically sound social research; otherwise, the "community" effort risks being centered on the outspoken, the men, and the elites. We believe that this more "formal" research can in most cases be participatory and become a learning experience for all partners, and we discuss that premise with respect to ethnographic and survey research.

How We Organized This Book

Chapters 2 and 3 discuss how knowledge of human evolution and history informs social research for conservation. They present concepts that underlie our understanding of human behavior. Humans are seen as a species, among other species on earth, and as populations with distinct histories and cultures. These chapters bring up provocative issues about population growth, territorialism, knowledge systems, and diversity to challenge conservationists to think broadly about the human behavior and history.

Chapters 4 to 7 present concepts and tools for understanding scales and corresponding social dimensions of a population: resource management systems and trends, the local economy, social systems and institutions, beliefs, and worldview. These chapters look at conservation and resource management from the point of view of the local resource user, thus providing an important balance to conservation approaches that emphasize large-scale processes and areas.

Chapters 8 and 9 examine how conservation initiatives get started: how target populations and locations are chosen, how initiatives might be designed, and the ethics of working with particular groups and social categories. We emphasize the importance of working within flexible strategies and reject top-heavy programming and planning. We discuss why partnership is important to conservation activities, including the benefits of authentic collaboration and the value of merging local and "outsider" skills and knowledge. The pros and cons of partnering are described along with a strategy to select partners.

It is only at this point that we begin to discuss research! We start with defining research questions, scales, levels, and units of analysis. The interplay of quantitative and qualitative approaches is reviewed, as are sampling procedures appropriate to different conservation research questions and units of analysis. Chapter 10 raises practical considerations about putting together interdisciplinary research teams and research management.

For reasons discussed earlier, it proved challenging but essential to provide an overview of regional approaches to research. First, how are regions defined? Conservation organizations have been quick to use spatial studies and rapid appraisals but may not be aware of the study of regional economic and social networks, which are not so easily mapped yet provide deep insight into how and why resources are used in a given area. Here we draw on economic anthropology and social geography.

A guide to interviewing, from initial protocol to forms of interviews appropriate to different research questions, is presented in chapter 12. Interviews are at the heart of social research. While you cannot really learn to be a good interviewer from this book, we think that you can learn to identify the pitfalls and the appropriate steps to take in the process.

Chapter 13 highlights ethnographic methods that are essential to conservation research, such as participant observation, ethnobiology, kinship and genealogical research, and land history, indicating resources for further study. Ethnographic methods are often seen as time consuming, costly, and small scale, yet they provide unparalleled insight into local dynamics and practices. We show how ethnographic methods answer questions that other methods cannot, get beyond normative responses to questions, and provide a culturally appropriate framework for interacting with local communities. The vexing issues of scale and duration in ethnography are addressed.

Chapter 14 presents different types of surveys and discuss when they are appropriate. Experience teaches that household and group interviews are not sufficient to identify subpopulations and interest groups. Without that knowledge, planning and implementation are incomplete; key groups can be left out. Surveys can be participatory and build skills of local partners, and they can use data collected in decision making and negotiating with authorities. The main issues are when to implement surveys, how to scale them down to collect data on variation (not general questions), how to make them appropriate and useful to local actors, and how to integrate them with data obtained through other methods.

Chapter 15 concerns action research, a category of research that places community development in the forefront. Action research has evolved since the emergence of participation rural appraisal (PRA). We present new approaches that build on PRA and related methods. In particular, we present ideas from appreciative inquiry, an approach that gets away from the "problem-solving" approach to focus on the strengths and vision of a community.

Chapter 16 shows how data and information can be integrated and analyzed across scales and sites with the imperative to compare data and experiences. "Scaling up" beyond ICDPs and pilot sites is becoming an increasingly important factor in conservation. We show how cross-site analysis can be participatory and built into any research effort. The chapter includes a discussion of monitoring, evaluation, and communication. Monitoring and evaluation have received a great deal of attention in conservation projects because of the need to document impact and results for donors. We argue above all that monitoring and evaluation should be a learning tool. Communication strategies need to focus on the appropriate means to reach target audiences.

The Resources section at the end of this book is an extensive documentation of the topics discussed in the book, including Internet links, groups, articles, and books.

2

Conservation as Human Behavior

> We can sustain ecosystems across boundaries only if we understand how humans behave with respect to the places they claim as territory.
>
> —Brunson (1998: 66)

This chapter gives a context for the role of social research in conservation from the point of view of the human species. It examines certain human behavior patterns, such as territoriality, reproduction, and consumerism. These are among the most critical and hotly debated human behaviors that shape our interaction with nature and our views on conservation. We sidestep the major battles over genetic versus social learning views of human nature. While our primate and mammalian heritage plays a role in behavior, the human brain has evolved the capacity to create and implement totally new forms of behavior. The aim is to show that human behavior is part of nature even as it increasingly becomes a major shaper of nature.

The Nature in Human Nature

In order to understand the relationship between humans and nature, we must look at human evolution and history. Human evolution is the long story written in genes, bones, and artifacts that shows how humans are linked to all life on earth and how we adapted to changing circumstances over the ages. History is the shorter story of human relations and adaptations as recorded in various ways by humans themselves.

Humans are one species (American Anthropological Association 1998b: 3). Most scientists believe that race is largely a social construct, not a biological determinant. (However, racial categories as socially constructed affect many aspects of life, including exposure to environmental hazards and participation in conservation activities.) As a species, we are all together in one habitat: the earth. The more we spread out and made use of ecosystem variation, the greater our success as a species has been. But as we inhabit and transform a multitude of ecosystems, so can we endanger them.

The Long Story

Humans share certain traits with all species, certain others with all mammals, and many with our cousins, the primates. What we share with all species is a set of strategies for survival and reproduction. Each species has a different set of strategies. While we reject the stance of some scientists that human behavior is closely controlled by genetic imperatives, we think it is important to show how elements of human behavior are grounded in our heritage. Most behaviors we discuss are shaped largely by culture, which we define in this chapter. The important point is that behaviors do not consist of isolated actions but rather are part of complex social and cultural systems with long histories.

To Kill or to Cooperate?

As mammals and primates, cooperative social life is part of our strategy because our babies need intensive protection for a prolonged period of time, which requires that individuals other than the biological parents protect the offspring of the group. But the human species is also intensely competitive—so much so that we have contributed to the extinction of many other species, perhaps even closely related ones in the not-so-distant past, in our quest for survival and dominance. Cooperation and competition are thus the twin engines of human behavior.

Understanding the roots of competition may help us explain why humans are fast destroying their habitat; learning how cooperation works will give us insights into how to build resource management rules that work. There is new evidence that humans and other primates cooperate *through* competition, giving signals about who is dominant while at the same time appearing to be cooperative and helpful (Dugatkin 1999).

The human species' complex mix of competitive and cooperative survival strategies shapes institutions that are flawed, contradictory, and often ineffective in tackling social problems. Human behavior is messy, and no one is exempt from the game of status and competition for power. To think otherwise leads to simplistic and unworkable initiatives.

Pathways in the Forest

Another key behavior for conservation is territoriality. Humans share this trait with other species. Individuals and groups set boundaries around territories and defend them by social, legal, physical, and other means. These boundaries structure access to resources that people use to survive, trade, and in general make a living. We discuss how conservation initiatives need to map human territories and boundaries together with ecological ones.

Human boundaries stretch beyond the physical to include cultural, social, and economic boundaries. Human geographer Melanie Hughes McDermott suggests that we might better speak of "pathways" rather than boundaries because the ways that people get access to land and resources often wind through physical and social boundaries (McDermott 2000). For example, in negotiating a land claim in a society where lands are held in common, a person might call on kin, state authorities, or patron–client relations (see chapter 6) to get access to the land. The land that a person or family claims—its physical space—may be fragmented, comanaged, or contested by other families.

Human ecologist Emilio Moran points out that the size of a population's territory may depend on ecological factors, such as food and type of vegetation (Moran 1993). Where food and water are scarce, such as in deserts, or where key nutrients are scattered over large areas, such as in some forests, the territory or range of a population is larger. Colonial and modern policies, as discussed in chapter 3, attempted to settle migrating or shifting populations along roads for easy collection of commodities and taxation; the justification given was better access to health care and education. This policy damaged or destroyed the ability of many populations to meet their basic needs from their territories. Migration also alters the relationship between local groups and their territories with implications for conservation planning at a regional level (see chapter 11).

The Cultural Animal

To explain human behavioral variety, we must learn about human adaptation to specific habitats. To understand human adaptation, we use the concept of *culture*. Culture is multifaceted behavior in intricate patterns, including language, symbols, music, art, social institutions, and technology. This behavior is learned rather than transmitted genetically. Our cousins, the great apes, are now said to display cultural differences among their groups, but highly complex long-lasting cultures are a human phenomenon (for an extended discussion of apes, humans, and culture, see de Waal 2001). Chapter 13 shows how the concept of culture is central to conservation and can be used in conservation research (for a detailed definition of culture, see "Ethnographic Approaches" in the Resources section and chapter 13).

The Population Question

Understanding human reproductive strategies helps us see why humans grow in numbers, damaging ecosystems on which their survival depends (for an extended discussion of population and conservation, refer to Cincotta and Engleman 2000). Human reproductive strategies are as complex as culture. Having many children can be a key survival strategy for a family at one stage of development and counterproductive at another stage. Men and women may have different reproductive strategies and different goals in terms of family size, child spacing, and gender of offspring. Raising the standard of living and creating government-level social safety nets makes it both expensive and unnecessary for families to have large numbers of children to achieve security and status. In fact, in many countries of the developed world, birthrates are below replacement level.

Yet many countries and cultures continue to have high birthrates. The population explosion of the past fifty years threatens species and habitats. But this threat is not a simple equation of more people equals more destruction. The equation is in fact hotly debated. The many viewpoints on population and environment reflect the complexity of human behavior: how we base our actions on differing notions of evidence and proof, belief systems, our position in society, and our dreams and wishes for the future.

If men have different reproductive strategies than women do, can changing the balance of power between men and women have implications for the size of families? The World Bank has claimed that educating girls is the single best investment that could be made in the environment (World Bank, n.d.). Why? Because education allows girls and women to secure their own incomes and have more control over the number of children they bring into the world. This control translates into smaller families and better care of the household and its environs. Access to contraceptives has also been found to be a key to smaller families.

THE POPULATION—ENVIRONMENT DEBATE

In some cases, there may be a clear link between population growth and migration into fragile habitats and loss of species. In other cases, logging roads and mining could be opening up fragile lands. Population density can in many cases be related to degradation, while in other cases there is no direct relationship or the patterns are very complex. In the Amazon, for example, Moran (1993) documents how cattle ranching causes deforestation but may in fact have decreased population. Some religious groups contest the need for limits to population growth and consequently the fact that population growth is a prime factor in environmental degradation. Feminists also decry a simplistic relationship between demographics and environment. Progressives point to evidence that rich consumers and multinational corporations, rather than poor folks with high birthrates, do the most damage to the environment. Libertarians and students of technological change argue that population growth is a boon for technological and financial innovation, fostering innovations that relieve environmental pressures. Some techno-optimists go so far as to say that technology created by an increased number of scientists will get us out of the fix we are in. We can preserve all the lost species in gene banks. Some evidence points to higher biodiversity in areas of higher population density.

Why Do We Need So Much Stuff?

With economic development, we may have fewer people who are more educated with higher standards of living and gender equity. Does that mean that they will become mindful of the need for conservation? Many thinkers believe that consumerism and materialism—attachment to products and goods—are key drivers for species and habitat destruction. Why are humans so driven to acquire material things, especially when their basic needs are fulfilled? Yes, they make life easier, but perhaps there is a deeper reason: competition for status and prestige. *Status* means position or rank in society; *prestige* is a mark of high status. High status is not useful unless others know you have it. Acquiring material objects that symbolize high status shows others that you outrank them: If there is conflict over resources, you will win. You are armored and protected against threat. Thus, the sports utility vehicle squashes the Volkswagen Beetle on the highway.

Advertising and the structure of Western economies in general play into competition for prestige. We will be seen as low status if we do not have certain products. We are told that we cannot stop consuming, or the economy, which is now equated with our whole world, will collapse. The waste and destruction around us is largely ignored because we are so focused on our species-level and social-group competition. In Victorian times, people worried about getting ostrich feathers for their hats to show off at social gatherings and pianos with ivory keys to grace their living rooms. Just as now, very few wondered about the fate of the species that provided these items.

Cultures have ways of displaying status that interact with the way natural resources are used. Among the peoples of the Pacific Northwest, accumulating and giving away large amounts of food and goods in ceremonies called potlatches expressed status. In India, status can be expressed by the size of a dowry that accompanies a woman in marriage. Prestige can come from a feather headdress, a yacht with teak interiors, a water buffalo, or a green lawn full of chemicals. It seems that, among humans, one can never have enough prestige, and so there is always a hunger for the things that display high status. In some cultures, having many children is still seen to confer prestige even after a high standard of living is attained.

What Brings Us Together

Cooperative strategies are complex and changing. Small, cohesive groups may adhere to rules and punish cheaters—or misfits move on to another group. But fewer and fewer people in the world today live in these kinds of groups. Some create or refashion forms of cohesiveness within the context of ethnicity, religion, or neotribalism. Many community-based conservation initiatives are based around ethnic groups' territories (see the many examples of ethnically oriented conservation in the Resources section). Powerless people have little choice but to unite to fight for their rights, and ethnicity is a powerful principle relating to one's personal identity. Yet there are dangers in this strategy. Anthropologists have long known that ethnic groups are internally complex and that their composition changes over time. Tribalism in the extreme can lead to genocide.

Ethnicity can be one basis for cooperation in conservation, but it will not be the answer to stopping global destruction. For that, we must turn to the creation of partnerships, coalitions, and information-based action. Multiethnic social and political action based around issues rather than identities is critical for conservation and general reform, but it cannot succeed unless inequality and cultural differences are addressed within coalitions and partnerships (see chapter 9).

On the other hand, people must see concrete benefits from conservation and work together within their territories. A sense of place linked to social identity is often the motivation for conservation action (Gallagher 1993). People care deeply about their landscapes and the resources that nourish them.

Thus, locally perceived benefits to social groups are critical, but these must be placed in the context of a wider strategy. As a community leader from Solomon Islands remarked, "For years I worked with this large conservation organization, and I thought conservation was only about the economic benefit to our tribe. Then I took a trip to New Zealand and saw conservation areas in the service of all the people. I realized then that I had not understood the full meaning of conservation."

The Big Question: Balancing Conservation and Development

The relationship between human welfare and conservation is central to the work of social research for conservation. Like the population equation, it is a complex issue. The relationship is often presented in a simplistic picture that improving the economic welfare or advancement of people at a conservation site will promote conservation or, conversely, that people at a site being isolated and less materialistic will serve conservation. Some theorists believe that local development and conservation are inextricably linked because poverty is the driving factor in degradation, while others see the two as valid social goals but not necessarily linked. Different levels of development (local, national) must be distinguished, along with modes of development. Still others see conservation and development as diametrically opposed or do not see any conservation benefit from investments in development (see "Critiques of Community-Based/Sustainable Use Approaches" in the Resources section).

We believe that development and conservation can be complementary parts of a rural support strategy that focuses on diversifying community assets and options. But in crafting these strategies, let us return to our central idea that human behavior is complex. We need to look at changing values and aspirations, ambition on the part of some community members, disappearance of cultures along with the natural resource base that support those cultures, co-optation of some group members by more powerful outsiders, and also the possibility for new forms of cooperation. But above all, understanding the struggles for power and status—both within communities and between communities and outside agents—has to be an integral part of any strategy.

Technology: Appropriate or Overrated?

Will science and invention ultimately solve conservation problems by creating new technologies that use up fewer resources, use energy sustainably, or perhaps even mine the resources of the solar system for human use? Humans are ingenious. Technology has been used historically both to solve social problems and to intensify competition. The arms race during the Cold War was no accident of history. It was completely in line with human group strategies to outcompete other groups through intensification of technology. In the past, the technology might have been better chariots, guns, or ships; now it is information systems and genetic modification. Technology created for war has peace applications (e.g., the Internet), while technology created for conservation can be used for destruction (e.g., a geographic information system [GIS] used for tracking animals discovered on the Web by poachers).

Development practitioners learned long ago that technology in itself will not solve social problems—and conservation is a social problem. Technology provides tools, some of which are useful, many of which are more trouble than they are worth. "Appropriate" technology can translate into "labor-intensive" technology that the poor cannot afford to adopt because their returns to labor are so low. And technology cannot replace ecosystem functions. We can channel water and filter it—though it is far better to conserve the watershed—but we cannot replace water. Germplasm in gene banks is not the same as species in their habitats.

There are equity issues in the use of science and technology. If local partners cannot access or understand the technology we use, how do we share information? If our conservation planning is based on expensive machinery, patented software, highly complex models, and huge amounts of data crunching, how will local planners adopt it? On the other hand, is it ethical to restrict our use of technology because we believe that local partners could not or should not use it? This problem has emerged in relation to genetically modified crops that may raise yields and lessen pesticide exposure of poor farmers but pose a risk to biodiversity.

A History of Diversity

The debate over human nature and the impact of humans is affected by our beliefs and knowledge systems. Ancient religions used and valued a multiplicity of wild species and habitats and saw people as part of nature. The sacred grove is a manifestation of ancient religions' construction of in situ gene banks and protection of watersheds and water sources (for discussions of sacred groves, see "Spirituality, Ethics, and Values in Conservation" in the Resources section).

When the written word supplanted oral tradition, religious experience was disembodied from nature and became an abstraction, according to theorists such as David Abram (1996). The view of humans as "above" and "apart" from nature was passed on to European Christians who destroyed most traces of the ancient religions in Europe. The Bible ordered, "Though shalt not plant thee a grove of trees near unto the Altar of the Lord" (Deut. 16:21). Mystical Christians, however, continued to find inspiration in woods—the cross of Jesus as a tree of life, the forest as a place of renunciation, the world tree as a source of salvation, and Anne (the mother of the Virgin Mary) sitting under a laurel tree (Aburrow 1994). Again we see that human behavior presents no simple patterns.

Some millenarian religions encourage people to use resources intensively and not worry about the consequences because "Jesus will provide." Status within many religions is linked to acquisition of and control over resources as evidence of a person's "destiny." In other religions, however, materialism is discouraged or downplayed, at least in theory or during certain stages of life (see "Spirituality, Ethics, and Values in Conservation" in the Resources section).

The extreme dominance of one knowledge/economic system over others is highly risky. Those who wish to dominate the world, from the Romans to multinational corporations, have prized uniformity, but it is not good for the survival of life forms. Ecosystems depend on a variety of species for food chains and genetic material and as buffers against climate change. Because of the dominance of one system—Western market capitalism and its associated values—human cultural diversity is as threatened as biological diversity. Cultures have features such as language, rules, rituals, and norms that enabled them to adapt to particular habitats and to patterns of climate change and variation learned over long spans of time (see chapter 13).

Market capitalism is an incredibly powerful human artifact—the most powerful the world has ever known. It is able to link buyers, consumers, and commodities in financial transactions involving cooperation and trust throughout the world. But it is a human artifact and thus fragile and contradictory. While on the one hand it destroys communities by undermining their local economies and value systems, on the other it provides the means to create a diversity of global communities centered on global issues and addressing global threats.

Environmental Governance to the Rescue

To compete in global capitalism, corporations externalize their costs—seek subsidies and free or cheap access to natural resources—and expropriate resources without paying their full value, such as the value of alternate uses and ecosystem functions of the resource (Korten 1995). When the public, through government, subsidizes extractive private-sector activities, the public doubly loses out. As consumers and citizens, we let this happen when we fail to consider the real costs of using natural resources.

Conservation is thus an issue of governance, the struggle to put the needs of the whole above the needs of special interests. The drama is played out at every level, from households to global institutions. Environmental governance has to do with how decisions are made with respect to natural resources. It deals with the central question of balancing conservation and competition for access to resources.

In the past fifty years, survival has become easier for some people and more difficult for others based on their role in the markets of capitalism, access to power, and living in the "right" neighborhood or country. Much of the world's recent "progress" is built on petrochemicals, which ironically may be contributing to declining fertility among humans and other animals (Colburn et al. 1996). The opening up of previously inaccessible areas to gain access to timber or minerals may also bring tremendous risk of disease in addition to the destruction of biological diversity.

Unfortunately, institutions to deal with global threats, such as conventions (e.g., the Convention on International Trade in Endangered Species and the Convention on Biodiversity) and monitoring agencies, are weak and national and local governance systems inadequate to cope with these challenges. The vast majority of the world's leaders are fully committed to high-growth development models—not to be is political suicide.

Growth with inequality provides at least some hope that the wealth will spread. Conservation, on the other hand, is seen as an end or limit to growth and therefore a direct threat not only to powerful and wealthy individuals but also to poor folk who believe that an end to growth is an end to their chances. Conservation is seen to help the future at the expense of the present. How can this view change?

Recent thought in environmental governance shows that inefficiencies in the way that resources are used waste both economic and natural capital. These inefficiencies are often a result of corruption and power relations creating "perverse incentives." Identifying perverse incentives and attacking them is an important first step in environmental governance (for further information, see "Environmental Governance" in the Resources section).

What Does It All Add Up To?

But how do we deal with large-scale policy strategies, population issues, the roots of inequality, and the rapid intensification seemingly inherent in capitalist markets in the context of specific conservation initiatives? First, by incorporating an informed and nonsimplistic view of

CASE STUDY

PERVERSE INCENTIVE: FOREST CHARGES IN THE PHILIPPINES

Perverse incentives are policies or practices that favor overexploitation of a resource while at the same time generating very little benefit from that exploitation to the local population. In the 1990s, the Department of Environment and Natural Resources (DENR) of the Philippines placed a tax on forest products such as rattan as they came out of the forest. This taxation system encouraged traders to underinvoice rattan and bribe local officials to avoid or reduce the tax. This system thus benefited local officials by providing them with revenue, but the national DENR and wider tax base were shortchanged, and the rattan monitoring system was severely compromised. The DENR found it hard to change the system, as it was entrenched in local power relations and it compensated for the low wages of local DENR officials.

human behavior into our thinking. Second, by building alliances across disciplines and scales—from the local to the regional, national, and global; and, finally, by linking large-scale environmental governance strategies with concrete benefits of conservation, such as clear rights to resources, cleaner water, and greater agricultural productivity that can accrue to local communities.

As conservationists, we need to think broadly and deeply about the human species in its habitat. In carrying out practical social research at a conservation site, we can expand our horizons and those of our partners beyond the immediate questions to address wider issues on a wider scale. We can reach out to others working on the same or similar questions, with science as a bridge. In this way, we make a small step to common solutions.

3

Social Elements of Conservation

The rain forest, far from being an evolutionary Eden, is a dangerous, bandit-ridden place, perhaps as violent as any inner-city in the West. . . . There is an urgent need to fill this gap in knowledge, and to take account of new social realities in these supposedly "pristine" environments, where automatic weapons and crack cocaine may be as common as on the streets of Liverpool or Detroit.

—Guyer and Richards (1996: 8)

Let us move now from the very broad arena of human behavior to address the more specific topic of human activities that affect ecosystems. First, we look at the historical and social context of conservation, concentrating on the critical importance of understanding commodities and social institutions. Then we turn to a discussion of community-focused conservation and describe the challenges to social research stemming from this discussion.

Resource Management through the Ages

What are the key human activities that destroy species and their habitats? Local populations clear forest for farming, overhunt certain species, or pollute areas with waste. Locals or outsiders can be involved in logging, mining, or the creation of plantations. Invasive and alien species resulting from human movements can also degrade native biodiversity. But these activities are often driven by the following:

- Migration into previously unsettled or marginal areas
- Increase in demand for resources (technology driven or more consumers)
- Land speculation that increases the price of land so that it must be "used"
- Economic incentives to maximize short-term profits for investors and speculators
- Warfare and other conflicts resulting in migration, use of destructive chemicals, and resource degradation

We talk more about the history of these trends in this chapter. Though they have taken on a new intensity, these trends are, in fact, ancient. Conservationists have studied species extinction and habitat loss extensively. But what do we know about conservation? When have human populations been motivated and able to protect or even enhance biological diversity? From historical and archaeological research, we find that there are lower rates of species extinction and environmental degradation when the following occur:

1. There is low human population density because of ecological conditions such as poor soils, disease, swamps, steep slopes, or historical circumstances (war, famine, or disease).
2. The level of technology limits destructive practices. It is now clear, however, that "low" technology, such as fire making and stone tools, can be quite devastating. For example, the large-scale extinction of large mammals in Europe took place before metal tools were crafted. The technology of the ancient Egyptians and Greeks was sufficient to deforest the Mediterranean basin and destroy many species. The prehistoric extinction of land birds at the hands of Polynesian colonists is another example. Nevertheless, when bulldozers and chainsaws enter an area where the highest technology has been the machete, destruction intensifies.
3. Sanctions are enforced against destroying species or habitats, including community-based sanctions such as using totems (a group is forbidden to kill a certain species), tabu (off limits) areas, seasonal restrictions, and sacred groves. These sanctions are enforced by chiefs or priests, and, in the past, offenders could be forced to leave the community or even put to death. These types of sanctions persist to the present but in weaker forms than in the past. Externally imposed sanctions include killing poachers in the "the king's game preserve" or putting forest guards around large-

scale conservation areas or "government forests." These sanctions were enforced by outsiders to the local resource-user community and could result in death. Today, conservation officers in parks and protected areas in the tropical world find themselves constantly at war with "poachers" but lack the means to guard large areas without the involvement of local communities.

4. Incentives exist for maintaining diversity, such as the following:

- Financial incentives: People receive cash payments for products that grow only in the wild, or people such as ecotourists pay to see unique habitats and species or use the area for recreational purposes.
- Cultural heritage: People take pride in habitats with high levels of unique biodiversity as part of cultural and spiritual heritage (e.g., sacred forests or mountains that are revered by an indigenous culture or national parks that provide recreation).
- Insurance: Communities realize that long-term economic and health risks are associated with resource degradation and band together to protect watersheds, rivers, lakes, shorelines, or other key habitats through direct purchase and enactment of regulations concerning use.
- Investment: Governments or private organizations purchase or obtain land and protect species to maintain biodiversity and ecosystem functions.

In chapter 2, we mentioned that human diversity is linked to biological diversity. Throughout most of human evolution, humans survived by spreading out into small, mobile groups that depended on a wide range of resources. People recognize and use a wide range of biological resources when they have lived in a place for a long time; thus, there is great value in basing conservation initiatives around local knowledge.

The density and social structure of a population is shaped in part by soil quality, water availability and quality, topography, and density of domesticable flora and fauna (Butzer 1990; Diamond 1997). In complex, or stratified, societies, those with hierarchies of power and authority, castes, or other occupational groups (e.g., basket weavers or fishermen) may depend on sustainable use of certain habitats and species. Other social groups do not depend directly on exploitation of biological resources but rather on trade and the wealth generated by exploitation and trade.

The impact of humans on ecosystems has been profound. We have evolved together. There is evidence that in some circumstances human occupation enriches the habitats of other species. For example, archaeologist Liz Graham finds that abandoned building materials and waste disposal practices encouraged biodiversity at Mayan sites in Belize (Graham 1998). Williams (1994) has compiled a bibliography on how Native Americans managed forests with fire to shape ecosystems that favored a diverse array of tree and game species. When this management system fell apart, the results were interpreted as "wilderness." Oelschlager (1991) traces the history of the concept of "wilderness," while Adams and McShane (1992) expose the "myth of wild Africa" and how this myth affected conservation strategies and ideologies. Anthropologist Serge Bahuchet, who has worked with forest peoples of central Africa for decades, states boldly, "Present equatorial ecosystems are the result of human activities. There are no such thing [sic] as virgin forests" (Bahuchet n.d.). James Fairhead and Melissa Leach find that, contrary to long-standing narratives of deforestation, villagers in their study area of western African actually created and nurtured forest islands—forest area was in fact increasing rather than decreasing (Fairhead and Leach 1996). Schwartzmann et al. (2000b: 1371) claim that "the 'pristine forest' [of the Amazon] is in fact a recent artifact of the demographic collapse of indigenous populations after 1500 brought about by introduced diseases" (for further discussion of the Amazon's anthropogenic nature, see Raffles 1999; Roosevelt 1989).

But these findings do not imply that in general human activity results in enhancement of ecosystems and increased diversity of species. Actual changes in land use have to be determined empirically (for a critique of Fairhead and Leach's findings in West Africa, see Nyerges and Green 2000). Overall, the balance between humans and other species has undergone a titanic shift in the past fifty years. Population growth increases exponentially in some areas, while in others superconsumerism drives unprecedented levels of resource use. Sanctions of old are unenforceable, and many incentives are overrun by survival needs or greed. Why did this shift happen?

Commodities Are King

Let's look at the role of commodities—raw or semifinished natural resources packaged for sale in distant markets—in changes in land and resource use. Virtually all tropical areas that harbor a high number and density of species (as well as most "charismatic" species, such as lions, elephants, and gorillas) were or are part of a colonial or indigenous empire or state that extracted natural resources to produce commodities.

The extraction, processing, supply, and trade of commodities can support many levels of social elites who do not have to work the land to make a living. Commodities fuel the ultimate in human dominance/status behavior: warfare. Commodity extractors must coerce or convince us, the consumers, that we require their goods for survival or prestige. Commodities such as timber, metals, coffee, tea, cocoa, copra, sugar, bananas, and rubber, together with food crops, now form the backbone of the rural economy and consequently shape land tenure, infrastructure, political relations, social relations, and even religious beliefs (on the history of sugar, for example, see Mintz 1985). The micro-commodities of biochemical and genetic material are increasingly contested—with critical ramifications for equity in use conservation.

Commodity production fed the need of ancient and modern empires and states for cash and also provided opportunities for the rural elite to earn cash as traders or middlemen. Primary producers or extractors of natural resources were taxed to "encourage" them to produce and become dependent on the cash economy. Commodity production dominated or replaced small-scale sustainable agricultural and husbandry systems as well as economic systems based on barter and exchange involving goods such as shells, feathers, pigs, or iron rods, whose extraction and trade left subsistence production relatively intact.

Although some communities remove themselves from the market economy in part to promote religious beliefs, stewardship, and sustainability, for the vast majority there is no turning away from commodity production because rural people have few other sources of cash. Rural people need cash for taxes and education—in many cases the only sure path to upgrading social status—or for investment in technologies that enable them to compete with others. The growth of consumer classes in all parts of the world is fueled by and in turn fuels the demand for commodities.

So what can we do? There are options to diversify local economies by promoting commodities that are extracted sustainably—nuts, parts of trees and plants, and fibers—thus spreading risk and potentially lessening the ecological impact of extraction, adding value to commodities locally, and introducing non–commodity-based activities such as ecotourism (see "Sustainable Use of Natural Resources" in the Resources section). Social researchers have criticized these small-scale economic solutions as neglecting the wider patterns of economic exploitation and the real causes of environmental degradation, which go beyond the local community. They may even exacerbate local inequalities (on nontimber forest products, see Dove 1993; on wildlife tourism, see Hughes 2001). Yet under some circumstances, these activities can motivate local people to move toward conservation (see Biodiversity Conservation Network 1997, 1998).

Commodity production could harmonize with the protection of biodiversity if land use zones were clearly demarcated according to the tenets of conservation science, an ever stronger thrust of large-scale conservation initiatives. But political realities intervene, including a lack of clarity about who owns land and other resources and who should make decisions on land use. There may be conflicting systems of land tenure or complex systems of use and access to land where one "resource" can be used by many different groups or individuals with overlapping rights and responsibilities or private property where owners feel that they may do as they please.

In many developing countries, all "empty" or commonly held land became the property of the state and thus available for resource extraction or high levels or "conservation" at the expense of local resource users. Where this full-scale alienation of land did not take place (e.g., Melanesian areas, such as Solomon Islands, Papua New Guinea, or Fiji), landowners face many economic pressures that cause conflicts over land use and control. Today, as in the past, "land-use planning" exercises tend to leave the rich richer and the poor with less land.

Lack of clarity and conflict means many interest groups jockeying for access to and control over land and valuable resources, hence precipitating the "tragedy of the commons" (Hardin and Baden 1977) (see box 3.1). This situation comes about when individuals maximize their use of common-pool resources rather than cooperating to conserve them. Thus, the common resources are destroyed or degraded. An example might be fishing groups around a lake that do not cooperate in managing the lake. Perhaps the government has taken control of that function but does not have the resources or will to carry it out. The size

---

Box 3.1.   Tragedy of the Commons?

An important dimension of social research for conservation concerns how resource-user groups organize to prevent overuse of common-pool or common-property resources, such as fisheries, forests, and lakes. The study of rules, sanctions, and communication within groups is critical. For more information, see the International Association for the Study of Common Property under "Institutions for Natural Resource Management" in the Resources section.

of nets decreases so that ever smaller fish are being taken. At some point, there are no fish left.

Please note, however, that since Hardin and Baden's book *Managing the Commons* (1977) came out, numerous examples of cooperation and efficiency in common property resource management have been identified that belie the assumption that the tragedy of the commons is the "natural state" of common property resource management without state control. Indeed, it is often state control that creates conditions of misuse and degradation (see references to the International Association for the Study of Common Property under "Institutions for Natural Resource Management" in the Resources section).

Where planning for conservation is most urgently needed, it can become infinitely more difficult because of this lack of clarity on ownership and because of inequalities among stakeholders, or claimants to a resource. To make matters worse, local populations living in areas of great biological wealth are among the poorest on earth, according to standard economic measures (Peluso 1992).

Most of the remaining areas of significant biodiversity are in remote locations. These are areas where there are a large percentage of endemic (unique to a specific location) species, breeding grounds for key species, or significant populations of species that require certain habitats. Populations in remote areas of high biodiversity are on the fringe of national political and economic systems, far from policy and development planning (Tsing 1993). They suffer the direct impacts of resource extraction and reap few of the benefits. They are often blamed for the destruction of biodiversity, even as they have nurtured it over time. They may be called on to protect it—with few resources to do so.

From this historical context stem at least three critical issues for social research in conservation:

1. Describing the social, economic, and political forces that shape resource use
2. Mapping the trends in resource use by both local communities and outsiders
3. Tracing the evolution of institutions for management of resources

What is meant by institutions? We discussed in chapter 2 how, as social animals, humans are constantly balancing competition over resources with cooperation in raising families, finding resources, and providing security. We endeavor to survive as individuals, but we need other people to survive. Humans devise rules for security and protection as well as ways of disputing, sharing, and dividing up resources. Over the millions of years of human evolution, social rules and structures have been devised that enable people to live and work together, albeit imperfectly. The rules and social structures that endure become "institutions." Institutions are not inherently good, bad, or even "functional" in the sense that they are in the members' best interests. They are as complex and contradictory as human behavior itself.

Institutional theorist Norman Uphoff (1986: 9) describes institutions as "a complex of norms and behaviors that persists over time by serving some socially valued purpose." (Valued by whom? we may ask.) He notes that some institutions are also organizations, or a structure of recognized and accepted roles, while others are abstract systems of rules and norms, such as legislation or resource tenure. Institutions span economic, social, religious, and political life and provide the framework within which people act and make choices.

Actions that affect biodiversity are not just the result of individual choices but are "mediated" through institutions. Institutions such as kinship and religious groups, markets, and schools shape our actions and our very thinking. Institutions shape our worldview, the lens of beliefs and values through which we make decisions. Investment in people, in enterprises, and in infrastructure is channeled through institutions.

As we will see in chapters 4 to 7, many different kinds of institutions operating at all levels affect conservation action and resource use, not just institutions devoted to conservation. We have talked here about the role of very high level institutions, such as corporations, empires, and states, in extracting commodities. At the local level, rules that govern status and respect behavior directly affect lines of communication within resource-user groups and thus affect the efficiency and effectiveness of resource management. For example, a leader may decide to sell rights to a logging company without consulting the community, and there is no institutional process within society to challenge this decision.

Where Is the Community in Conservation?

Increasingly, local communities, in partnership with government and nongovernmental organizations are being asked to play a major role in managing biological resources. Why? In many cases, it is because the resources are already significantly depleted or the land is no longer as valuable as it once was. Take the case of joint forest management in India and community forestry in the Philippines or Cameroon (see

"Community-Based Natural Resource Management/Collective Action" in the Resources section for numerous examples).

Other motivations include the high cost of government-supported conservation, pressure from donors and international institutions, strong incentives on the part of local resource users, the importance of local knowledge, and the desire for social justice. The complex motivations of "outsiders" make for a mix of approaches and attitudes that are often very confusing to local communities struggling for control over their own resources and with their own internal contradictions (for discussions of communities' exasperation with conservatism projects, see Brosius et al. 1998; New Zealand Overseas Development Association 1998 discusses ecotourism projects in the Pacific).

Whatever the motivation of "planners," the long-term success of conservation will involve extensive struggle, strategic partnerships, and institutional evolution. For those who want to do it right, the process requires astute knowledge of institutions affecting the populations involved at different scales and how they might grow and change. It involves devising medium- to long-term strategies rather than discrete "projects" that must be based on knowledge of historical trends and human behavior. Conservation initiatives, which by their very nature entail long-term value retention, have no choice but to support the institutional and partnership approach. Chapter 8 addresses strategies and planning.

Conservation efforts in different countries are working with community management approaches (see box 3.2). There are many different forms of community management, from total community control to temporary, experimental efforts in joint management between government agencies and local people. Several excellent resources present lessons on community management, including *Common Property Resource Digest; Forest, Trees and People; Asia Forest Network;* and *Indigenous Knowledge and Development Monitor* (see the Resources section).

Box 3.2. Examples of Community Management

Joint forest management (India)
Community forest users' groups (Nepal)
Community forestry stewardship agreements (Philippines)
Landowners' rights recognition (Fiji, Solomon Islands)
Community marine parks (Palau, Micronesia)
CAMPFIRE program for community wildlife management (Zimbabwe)
Land trusts (United States)

There are tremendous risks, however, in the community partnership and management approach. Consider the historical trends described previously, particularly the dominance of commodities in the rural economy and the political marginalization of rural people. If these risks are not anticipated and met head on with effective strategies, community management will become just another fad that failed. Already, many conservationists have become sharp critics of community-based approaches, including integration of conservation and development, and advocate a turn toward stricter protectionism (see "Critiques of Community-Based/Sustainable Use Approaches" in the Resources section). Rejecting community-based approaches would be a tragic outcome given what we now know about the relative effectiveness of local resource-user groups and the need to forge closer links between governance and environmental issues. We must also realize that 95 percent of land is not "protected" and never will be.

Community-based strategies for agricultural and inhabited areas, such as land trusts and "Landcare," are gaining ground in richer countries, and experiments in similar approaches are now in full swing in developing countries (Campbell 1994; Catacutan 2001; Kennebeck Highlands Project, n.d.). In addition, we can draw on the numerous historical and modern examples of sustainable use (see "Sustainable Use of Natural Resources" in the Resources section).

The challenges of community-based conservation discussed in the book include the following:

- How the concept of community hides complex social formations and power relations that need to be mapped and understood by both external and local planners.
- Ways in which livelihood or development activities involve different social formations than conservation activities. Attempts to integrate livelihood and conservation must look at how different interest groups interact and share benefits.
- Forging a partnership approach that includes sustainable financing so that communities do not carry the weight of the whole conservation effort, with few resources to do so.
- How conflicts over benefits can sideline an initiative that focuses too much on providing "aid" to communities.
- The backlash against community control, particularly when valuable resources are involved. It is naive to think that people in power will easily cede valuable resources to community management.
- Conservation planners' emphasis on land use on a large scale that may neglect local boundaries that communities can under-

stand and work within. Large-scale ecological maps are critically important, but they must build in local land use patterns, tenure systems, boundaries, and local institutions to be effective. Conversely, a community focus can overshadow attention to serious threats at a higher level and the need for linking institutions and processes.

- The danger that community-based conservation will proceed without testing assumptions about incentives, the unity of communities, and the roles of other stakeholders.

The Challenge of Social Research for Conservation

Conservation initiatives face pressure to move quickly, yet understanding the local situation and its wider context at a conservation site takes time. Conservation initiatives are pressed for time because destruction of species and habitats moves at a rapid pace. And many initiatives are funded by donors that want to see results quickly in order to justify the expense of the initiative to their taxpayers or benefactors.

Moving fast increases the risk of failure. Failure of an initiative, when people become discouraged or resentful, can have serious consequences. The idea of conservation may be rejected, conflict may break out, and rates of destruction can even increase. On the other hand, if partners in the initiative see no tangible results in a reasonable time frame, they may lose heart. Conservation is a long-term benefit to all people, but in the short term people directly affected need to see benefits and need to deal with their own risks. The balance of producing locally valued results and reducing the risk of failure is the conservation challenge.

Social research can play a major role in improving the odds for conservation. Good social data at different scales; insight into cultural and social systems; knowledge of history, politics, and the local and wider economy; and a learning atmosphere within the initiative are invaluable resources. The success of the conservation initiative could rest in the sensitivity of the researchers, the appropriateness and rigor of the research, and the usefulness of that research to conservation planners.

But social research faces its own challenges. There are ethical and practical issues about which scales to research, which methods to adopt, and how to analyze and share findings. Important conservation sites, where biodiversity is rich, are often remote and inaccessible, meaning that social and behavioral data are very precious. Such resources should not be wasted in poorly designed research. Because of the rush to produce results, the social research carried out may not be scientific or build on previous work. Decision makers may never use it because it is not valued. It might be wrapped in conflict as a result of competing agendas.

Scientists from other disciplines may undervalue social research because they believe that it involves little more than collecting data. People feel that they understand human behavior because they themselves are human. They may not see the need for developing skills or for learning from history, human evolution, and the experience of others. Let's be realistic—anyone with basic field experience can collect data. But to get good data on human behavior linked at different scales takes a great deal of patience, skill, and practice. Social research is as much a craft as a science, and knowledge generation goes beyond collecting data.

There is a connection between the way you collect data and the kind of analysis done as well as the way the research is presented to others. Trends that emphasize quick-and-dirty social research and extractive data collection may address immediate "data needs" of large-scale organizations or outside researchers, but they do not move the local conservation agenda forward. The information may never get back to those who need it most.

Using complex models and technologies may limit the local partners' ability to understand and participate in the research. Model-driven approaches to research are attractive for those who seek to predict rather than "simply" describe. There is urgency to the need to predict behavior so as to plan and prioritize conservation activities and a desire to apply scientific approaches to conservation. But model-driven approaches to social research often lead us down false trails, particularly when the basic parameters and measures are unclear or even unknown, which is often the case for social phenomena in many parts of the world. "The real world is almost always a great deal more complicated than our models," warns conservation biologist David Ehrenfeld (2000: 110) with respect to dealing with the challenges of globalization and other social forces.

Human ecologist Emilio Moran (1993: 192) argues, however, that modeling is "particularly useful in the preliminary stages of an investigation . . . [it] helps to identify knowledge gaps, and to formulate relationships to be investigated. . . . Another advantage of modeling is that systemic relationships rather than detailed content receive special attention." Common property researchers, for example, have looked at game theory models in an attempt to understand cooperation and competition strategies (Ruttan 2000; see also the critiques of game theory in the same issue of *Common Property Resource Digest*). Local partners may wish to learn and use models for their own advancement and planning (for more on models, see chapter 10).

Models are not the only comparative tools we have. There are other ways to link data at different scales and compare and contrast the situation and issues at one conservation site with others working on similar issues. Consequently, in chapter 16 we take you through the steps of gathering information to formulate many kinds of case examples, stories, and analyses for different audiences.

There are many choices to make in social research and no "right" answers to complex problems. Studying human behavior and history, learning and experimenting with different methods, and being open to new approaches provide a foundation for your work.

4

Resource Management Systems

> There are two predominant paradigms for conservation. One advocates locking up as much pristine forest as possible in parks protected by government agencies. Here on the Malinau River, local officials point out that 30 percent of the district is already listed as a national park, and that so far it has brought no benefits to local people. The second paradigm attaches greater importance to the value of forests to local people. We should work with them, mobilizing their knowledge to manage forests sustainably, while setting aside a relatively small network of key areas for nature alone. I belong unashamedly to this camp.
>
> —Sayer (n.d.)

This chapter provides some background on how social researchers view the human use of natural resources. Biological resources are the organisms—humans use for food, fodder, fuel, shelter, and other needs. The vast majority of organisms are not used or managed directly by humans, of course, and humans do not even know about them. Yet humans have a huge impact on them through practices such as farming, damming water, dredging, waste disposal, or extraction of commodities—even in areas set aside for conservation. Ignorance of the dynamics of species and ecosystems does not prevent humans from using and managing resources. They can be aware of the pieces of the picture that concern them and not aware of other pieces. They can also choose not to be aware.

Humans use biological resources for direct survival needs and for longer-term goals such as gaining status. Resource management refers to the practices that humans use to shape biological and nonbiological resources to meet their needs and goals. Although some conservationists dispute this idea, conservation is part of resource management because it is a human activity involving human choice and management. Conservation that involves preserving species and habitats in large areas that may not be used by humans is alien to the vast majority of peoples. Conservation of specific species and habitats for a period of time, on the other hand, is a common practice found in virtually all cultures to promote regeneration.

Conservation planning typically looks at what should be conserved from the point of view of the policymaker, forester, biologist, or fisheries agent. This chapter works toward conservation by taking the point of reference of the resource user and how she or he manages resources to make a living. Both viewpoints are needed if we want to foster the partnership of conservationists with local resource users/managers. There is a vast literature on each of the subjects discussed here, so this chapter points out only key areas of concern or interest to conservationists regarding different aspects of resource management.

The Many Ways of Using Resources

Subsistence Strategies

When social scientists first studied the relationship between humans and the environment, their study centered on how people make a living from the natural resources around them. They soon realized that there was no simple relationship between climate and natural resources on the one hand and type of social structure on the other. Complex stratified societies, those containing many occupations and statuses, and tiny foraging (hunting and gathering) groups could exist in the same natural environment.

Scientists did learn over time, however, how making a living from the earth shapes the way people organize themselves. There is no straightforward causal relationship between nature, livelihood, and social structure, however: Tools, technology and historical circumstance mediate this relationship. A society can change as well—sometimes drastically—by adopting new technology or adding or losing knowledge and skills.

Modes of subsistence include, but are not limited to, the following:

- *Foraging.* Hunting animals and gathering plants involves moving around the landscape exploiting seasonal and microclimatic variations to obtain a wide variety of food, medicines, trade objects, and fibers. Foraging typically involves small, mobile groups, but in areas of abundance it can support semipermanent groups.

"Foragers" may be marginalized remnants of larger populations (Wilmsen 1989).

- *Swidden agriculture and multistory agroforestry.* These systems involve burning, clearing, crop rotation, and intercropping (planting together) of trees and food crops (Posey and Balée 1989). Swidden systems are characterized by long fallow (soil resting) cycles. Population pressure, cash crops, and migrants turn relatively sustainable swidden systems into unsustainable slash-and-burn systems. Swidden involves small semipermanent social groups with extensive common land for regrowth of forest, hunting, fishing, and gathering of forest products. Institutions for sharing labor and the fruits of common property, such as hunting, are important. Note that slash-and-burn agriculture involves cutting and burning forest or bush to plant an array of crops or one crop. Fallow cycles are short, from two to six years. Both swidden and slash-and-burn cropping systems can exist in the same area.

- *Irrigated agriculture.* This can range from one or two small hand-planted plots to the use of mechanization over a vast area. Irrigation can be embedded in ancient social systems such as found in Bali or the rice terraces of northern Luzon, the Philippines. Water-user institutions, such as temples and irrigation management boards, are an important component of irrigated systems (for an intriguing example, see Lansing 1991).

- *Pastoralism.* Pastoralists can be nomadic, seminomadic, or settled, subsisting on various combinations of agriculture and herding. Traditionally, pastoralists have competed with agriculturalists for land and water (Harshbarger 1995). Many authors attribute state formation as a partial outcome of resulting conflicts, as pastoralists used sheep and cattle to occupy lands. Over time, because of population pressure, degraded natural resources, shrinking lands, and increased competition, pastoralists are increasingly settled and in some cases disenfranchised. Even seminomadic lifestyles can be dangerous because of wars and the introduction of guns among herders in some parts of Africa. Herders have become an important part of local cash economies, consistently providing protein for communities by selling beef and milk and selling livestock to local farmers. Sedentary pastoralists raise crops to become less dependent on nearby farmers. In some areas, with the use of cow dung as fertilizer, agropastoralists have an edge on agricultural production.

- *Marine and freshwater subsistence.* These systems inherently involve the management of common property, although inshore areas and resources can be controlled and "owned" by individual families or clans. Anthropologists have carried out extensive research on the resource management systems of fishing societies (see, e.g., McCay and Hanna 1998). Like pastoralists, fishing people often exchange with farmers within their own or other societies to obtain food crops and other goods.

All these subsistence strategies have been drastically reshaped in most parts of the world by wider economic and political systems. Those with greater power may either take land and then rent it out to producers or simply remove local people and render them landless. They may also control the economic system such that people must have cash and must earn it from commodity extraction or production. Then producers have to intensify production to meet these demands as well as their own needs (see chapter 15). Migrants move into an area and change the mode of subsistence, for example, by practicing slash and burn rather than swidden or introducing cash crops. New opportunities, such as plantation agriculture, mining, or working in logging camps, can drastically affect labor supply and the emphasis on getting cash.

Anthropologists have learned not to assume that people living in small-scale societies with simple technologies are remnants of more "primitive" times or have always lived in the same fashion. All peoples have a history, marked by contact, conflict, disease, ecological change, and their own internal development.

The Ground on Which We Walk

Land represents a resource, a habitat, and a territory. These are overlapping and often contradictory functions. Land is owned or controlled by the state, individuals, or groups and used by others directly or indirectly. Land as territory is bounded by human inhabitants, as habitat by species and ecosystem boundaries, and as resource by users and owners. Mapping these different categories of land gives a sense of how the social, political, economic, and biological dimensions interact and conflict.

Table 4.1 shows nine forms of control over land and some of the issues raised with respect to each type. Close study is needed because what people say about who controls and uses resources is often contradicted by actual practice. For example, at a site in sub-Saharan Africa, preliminary interviews revealed that a specific tract of land was "chief's land," but observations uncovered that outsiders actually farmed large sections of this land. Further interviews indicated that the chief leased the land for cash.

Table 4.1. Types of Control and Ownership of Resources

Type	Example	Issues for Research
Private ownership (individual or family)	Yards staked out near the house; registered lands	Taxation; guidelines for registration and delineation; usurpation of other resource users
Corporate ownership or long-term lease	Dole pineapple plantation; land leased to sugar farmers in Fiji	Taxation; usurpation of other resource users; leasing mechanisms
Family or clan control	Land controlled by Melanesian clans	User zones; conflicts over boundaries and land use; tenure over resources such as trees and minerals
State ownership	State parks and government forests	Policing; use rights of different groups; history of land expropriation
"Customary" tenure/ Indigenous people's domains	Ancestral domains in the Philippines; biosphere reserves on Inuit lands (Canada)	Regulations; enforcement; conflicts over boundaries; security of tenure; concessions and other economic activity on the land
Use/access rights and traditions	Harvest rights of special castes in India; reef fishing rights in Fiji	Multiple users; conflicts between different rights
Communal, *ejido*	*Ejidos* in Mexico	Rights of individuals and households; use of land as investment; pressure to privatize
De facto tenure/ control	Chief's rights to lands or resources	Appropriation of control and use of some "common" resources by individuals or groups
Other	Mixed tenure: community, forestry, common-property hunting grounds	Guidelines, access, control, and history/evolution of the user group and its regulations

Access to and use of land tightens up with increasing pressure from the cash economy. Borders and rights can also freeze or even be created when development or conservation efforts attempt to find out who controls land and resources, for example, in creating a management plan or targeting beneficiaries of an initiative. Changes in land use change habitats—typically by shrinking, fragmentation, and degradation through loss of key nutrients and species.

Many societies have rules that provide for overlapping rights to land and other resources. For example, an individual may be allowed to plant a garden in land "owned" by another group or harvest certain products from a tree, but the same person would not be allowed to plant a tree because the planting of trees on land indicates ownership. Sometimes there are many conflicting "owners" and users of a piece of land because the land might have been loaned out or used in a debt or a family line may have died out.

Land contains resources whose use and ownership may or may not be linked to ownership of the land itself (box 4.1). Claims to resources on a given piece of land can be highly complex and can shift quickly. An *open-access situation* is one where there are weak or nonexistent resource management institutions or where management systems are in flux or so complex that rules are not followed. This type of situation contributes to intensification of resource use as exploiters compete to use up the resource before others can get to it. An example is found in the exploitation of *almaciga* resin on the island of Palawan in the Philippines. When regulations were in flux about whether indigenous communities or the previous concession holders controlled the trade, after control of the land itself had been granted to local communities, there was a marked increase in extraction and unsustainable practices that ultimately killed many trees.

Making a Living on the Land

Virtually any conservation effort will deal with agriculture. This is how people make a living and feed themselves. Agriculture, be it

---

Box 4.1. Encouraging Plants and Trees in the "Wild"

People who live in the forest "manage" wild plants by planting or depositing seeds, by setting fires to encourage certain species, or by pruning wild trees, clearing bush, or depositing compost around them. Valuable "wild" trees are often managed and controlled by individuals or families, even if on "communal" land.

sustainable swidden systems within the forest or large-scale irrigated rice systems, largely defines (from the local point of view) land use and culture. Thus, conservationists need to understand the cropping systems that are in place and learn how they interact with harvesting from forests, marine, or freshwater areas.

Conservationists may view agriculture as a key threat to biodiversity. Yet some agricultural systems can contain a high degree of diversity and even foster diversity with long and complex fallow systems and cropping cycles. It is the expansion of agriculture into marginal lands, use of chemicals, and simplification of cropping systems that create a threat. If a logging road opens up a piece of forest, the agriculture around the road and the logging camp will tend to be slash-and-burn, simplified farming carried out by recent migrants or laborers.

Soil fertility is one thing that local people desire to conserve. Yet often they do not. Why not? The answers are complex. Soil improvement technologies, such as mounding, mulching, composting, and crop rotation, are labor intensive, and often agriculture in poor countries does not pay enough or yield enough to justify the investment in labor or materials. It is easier to move to a new patch of forest and clear it.

There is thus an intimate relationship between soil fertility and forest conservation. Swidden and multistory agroforestry systems conserve soil and forest (photo 4.1). When these are replaced by more "primitive" slash-and-burn or clear-cut techniques, a cycle of degradation sets in.

Photo 4.1. Example of a multistory agroforestry system in Indonesia. (Photo by Bernd Cordes; courtesy of World Wildlife Fund)

When fallow times drop below about six years, the soil is not regenerating. Pests and weeds proliferate. More forest has to be cleared to produce crops (see http://www.asb.cgiar.org).

Food Crops

A food crop or variety can define a culture and shape an ecology. Irrigated rice is one example of an intensive system that creates microhabitats of flooded terrain, fallow or abandoned rice fields, and border areas with fruit trees and other crops (Elphick 2000). Cassava, or manioc, is an example of a lead crop—a crop around which a farmer's field will be structured—that has many different varieties adapted to different soil conditions, uses, tastes, and timing. Irrigated rice transforms the land, whereas farmers typically use and breed cassava varieties in relation to different soil conditions.

Food crops become cash crops when there is little else to sell or when there is a surplus. But selling food crops does not mean there is a surplus. Food crops can be sold, and people in the household can go hungry. There may be a debt to pay, an investment in an important purchase, or simply the desire to get money to buy a pack of cigarettes.

An important conservation focus for local people is the preservation of traditional food crop varieties. Virginia Nazarea of the University of Georgia has promoted a promising in situ conservation approach called "memory banking" to preserve heritage and traditional varieties (Nazarea 1998, 1999). There is worry that, without these varieties and wild relatives to common food crops, disease and pests could significantly affect the germplasm of the world's key crops, as the varieties used commercially are built on a very narrow genetic base.

Different varieties are adapted to different habitats, and connections can be made between loss of habitat and declining food availability. For example, in a mixed savanna-forest area, loss of forest means that the shade-adapted varieties or crops will no longer grow well, if at all. In a forest-farming area, declining fallow times will mean that some crops do not grow at all, while increased weeds and pests and overall decline in soil fertility weaken others.

Cash Crops

Cash crops are commodities that define the economy of an area, as discussed in chapter 3. Cash crops and food crops often overlap but may be grown in different ways for different uses. For example, fruit trees for home consumption are grown around the house or on the borders of fields, while tree crops for the market will be grown on a plantation. Cash crops such as rubber, cocoa, coffee, tea, palm oil, and coconut meat (copra) are grown both by smallholders (family farms) or on plantations that can range from a dozen to thousands of trees.

Understanding the ecology, economics, and social structure of crop production is essential in an overall conservation strategy. The pesticides and other chemicals used on plantations and in family farms affect surrounding plants and animals. For example, copper-based fungicides used to prevent rot in cocoa trees can destroy fungi (mushrooms and mycorrhizae). The plantation economy shapes labor patterns: It may encourage in-migration of laborers and encourage dependency on the plantation infrastructure of stores, roads, and schools (see chapter 11 for a discussion of commodity market systems).

Forest Exploitation

Logging

Logging is found throughout tropical as well as temperate forests. Logging can be highly selective (high grading or low grading) or involve cutting all trees in a selected area (clear-cutting or shelterwood system if natural forest regeneration is planned). Logging species can also be important species for food, medicine, or other purposes. Local people rarely receive substantial benefits from logging, unless they own the firms, but the benefits they do receive can be larger than those obtained from cash crops, fishing, tourism, or other activities during the period of logging. Isolated forested areas may have few economic alternatives. Hence, the temptation to participate in logging or to cede land for logging is great. In areas where land belongs to the state or to large private interests, local people have little say in the allocation of logging concessions. In Melanesia, local clans control access to forests but are often manipulated and divided over benefits of logging.

Many conservation groups are concerned about logging. Some work directly with logging companies to improve practices (e.g., sustainable logging, certification, and ceding of concession area to conservation), while others work with communities in order to protest logging or obtain greater benefits from it. Logging roads, albeit often temporary, bring settlers, guns, and other threats to forest ecosystems. Yet governments around the world support logging because it brings in large revenues. Small-scale logging, such as chainsaw logging or portable "walkabout" sawmills, have been seen as one compromise: Local people can do it and get benefits, but it is not as destructive.

Problems of this approach include the inability of small-scale enterprises to compete on the world (or even local) market and a lack of skill and experience in running machinery and managing funds. Community logging in some communities in Mexico presents successes (see the Resources section).

Nontimber Forest Products

Is promoting the harvesting and processing of valuable plant and tree products from the wild likely to be a catalyst for conservation? Many believe this to be the case because the benefits go to local people and the harvest of these products is seen to be less harmful than logging or agriculture. Others are skeptical. It is extremely hard to monitor, much less ensure, the sustainability of nontimber forest products (NTFPs), but not impossible (for guidance on community-based monitoring, see Biodiversity Support Program 1998a; C. M. Peters 1994, 1996, 1999). When one forest product becomes scarce, people typically turn to a substitute or attempt to domesticate the plant or tree, thus diminishing the incentive to conserve its habitat. In addition, NTFPs are usually scattered around the forest and so can be difficult to collect and to get to market.

Gatherers of NTFPs throughout the tropical world tend to be marginalized—the poorest of the poor—such as "tribals" living around forest areas in India, rubber tappers in the Amazon, and indigenous rattan gatherers in the Philippines and Indonesia. When given the opportunity, these people often prefer to take up or expand farming or animal husbandry, both of which provide more secure benefits.

The benefits from marketing NTFPs are not received directly by the government; hence, governments typically do not see NTFPs as a replacement for logging revenues. Financial benefits from NTFPs such as honey or medicinal plants may be small, seasonal, and uncertain. However, subsistence benefits of NTFPs can be important to poor households. When NTFPs become commercialized, poorer households can lose out because the cost of access increases and they lack skills for processing.

Many conservation and development groups have tried to set up or encourage NTFP enterprises in the hope that they will foster or at least complement conservation efforts. The Biodiversity Conservation Network (BCN) was created in part to test claims about NTFP enterprises. The BCN found that these enterprises are only one part of a conservation strategy but can rarely if ever be "the solution" to conservation. However, NTFP enterprises may have other effects, such as catalyzing people's interest in conservation, creating stakeholder groups, and promoting resource monitoring (for resources on NTFPs, see "Sustainable Use of Natural Resources" in the Resource section).

Creatures Wild and Wonderful

Domestic Animals

Domestic animals are "created" by humans through breeding (and now genetic engineering) for specific functions. Domesticated animals use up vast plant and water resources in developed countries, and there is concern that increased meat consumption could create immense ecological problems for developing countries. On the other hand, some conservationists believe that substituting domestic meat production for hunting could reduce pressure on wild animals.

In poor communities, animals are used as security or investments, for gifts, and for special occasions. For example, among the indigenous Lumad of Mindanao, the Philippines, the carabao, or water buffalo, is their bank. The domestic animal is an investment that families make that can be cashed in at feasts, at funerals, to pay debts, or as a gift to important visitors. Pastoral peoples have complex management strategies in terms of their use of different habitats, interactions with farmers, trade, migration patterns, and investment strategies. The monetary value of their herds can be very large even as these peoples appear to be "poor."

Commercial husbandry, such as chicken ranching, is often risky for isolated peoples because of disease, market insecurities, and the social risk of displaying wealth. Yet cattle ranching is popular in the Amazon because it is a way to save and invest at the individual or family level rather than the group level. So one must be careful to look at how limits placed on savings and investment (e.g., land may be communally owned) might explain why people adopt and expand animal husbandry.

Wild Animals

Who owns the animals of the forest when the forest is owned by the state or is common property? In many societies, hunting grounds were demarcated for specific social groups, with rights to these territories being borrowed or traded as appropriate. Animals hunted in a group become the property of the group, with rules spelling out how the animal is divided and who gets each piece. Seasonal restrictions on hunting were enforced.

The situation changes when guns and cash come into the picture. No longer is the animal shared, but it may be carved up for smoked meat or for its skin, tusks, body parts, or horns. As an inhabitant of a village near the Dja Reserve Forest in Cameroon commented, "The BaAka [pygmies] used to hunt with nets, bows and arrows and only take what they needed for food and local trade. Now they don't even know how to use bow and arrow anymore—only guns." Another villager remarked that hunters set large numbers of traps not to catch bushmeat (box 4.2) but for the occasional leopard that would command far higher prices. The intensification of hunting is not new. For example, pressure on wildlife was intense during the colonial period in Africa, even in "remote" areas, such as the eastern Congo.

Wildlife management areas (WMAs) or "hunting domains" (*Domaines de Chasse*) are attempts to formalize who can hunt in specific areas. Typically, people are allowed to live in a WMA, *Domaines de Chasse*, or biosphere reserve but not in a national park (for a complete classification of protected areas, see IUCN, the World Conservation Union, at www.iucn.org or the World Conservation Monitoring Centre at www.wcmc.org). These areas may be demarcated with local people, but local involvement does not mean there is a uniformity of opinion. There can be significant conflict among pastoralists, hunters, and agriculturalists or even among those who hunt for a living and those who do not.

Preserving the ranges of top predators or other keystone species is a goal of many conservation efforts. But how do these ranges interact

---

Box 4.2.   Bushmeat

Conservationists claim that there is a crisis in west and central Africa: wild animals, including great apes (gorillas, chimpanzees, and bonobos), are being overhunted for food (bushmeat) and in some cases trophies. This overhunting could lead to disastrous species declines or even extinction (Bushmeat Crisis Task Force 2000).

How can social research help?
Provide historical understanding of hunting practices
Identify key actors in the trade and their motivations
Examine implications of proposed solutions such as animal husbandry for
    local people and their likely reactions
Assess relative costs and benefits of different solutions
Integrate local knowledge into analyses and solutions

with human settlements and hunting and collecting areas? Is it ethical to move people out of the way, to zone their activities, or to compromise their subsistence in order to preserve these animals? Is it ethical not to, given that much of the danger to animals that are important to local subsistence might actually be coming from "outsiders"?

What about community-based wildlife programs such as CAMP-FIRE in Zimbabwe? These programs are touted as increasing livelihoods and wildlife at the same time. Analysts point to the huge donor investment in CAMPFIRE (making it a model unlikely to be replicated), the attraction of migrants from poor neighboring communities, and potential loss of land to white-owned tourism operations (see the CBNRM and CAMPFIRE websites under "Community-Based Natural Resource Management/Collective Action" in the Resources section; for a comprehensive overview of ecotourism, see Honey 1999).

Indigenous societies have intimate relations with wild animal species. Some clans or groups are said to be able to control certain species (e.g., lion, shark, and hippopotamus) that guard territories and pose a risk to humans. Other groups do not eat certain species because of tabus and totems (see chapter 2). As Western peoples anthropomorphize animals (make them seem humanlike), non-Western peoples tend to see human individuals and groups as having "animal-like" characteristics. Sorcerers and "witches," who are commonly recognized to exist and play active roles in virtually all societies, are able to bridge the human and animal worlds by transforming themselves into animals.

Is this all nonsense that any sensible conservationist should ignore? Perhaps not, argues David Abram in *The Spell of the Sensuous*. He finds that food gifts "for the spirits" in Java are eaten by ants that might otherwise ravage the household stores. Hunters' psychological attunement to animals makes it easier to track and locate them. Conversely, the inability to "read" nature makes people see it as entirely instrumental, either for quick extraction or for sterile preservation (Abram 1996).

Water: The Last Frontier

The crisis in marine and freshwater systems stems largely from an intensification of production by industrialized countries, but even in small-scale fishing communities there can be serious problems. Stream fishers in the tropical world use poisons to stun fish. This technique can be overused and fish populations destroyed. The use of finer meshes in nets means that smaller fish are caught, perhaps those that have not yet reproduced.

Many resource economists claim that the fundamental problem in fisheries is too many fishers. In other words, limiting fishing effort would go a long way to maintaining fish supplies. But this solution raises ethical issues, as the cost of permits and licenses rises and perhaps can be monopolized by large corporations.

What about the family-owned business and traditional fishing communities? Anthropologists argue that community-based fishing can be sustainable when communities maintain control over their fishing territories and are able to enforce rules and regulations about who fishes, when to fish, and what species and size to catch. It is not easy to maintain community control, however. In Fiji, where local communities do have a great deal of control over land and inshore resources, the government can still issue fishing licenses, and chiefs can also approve licenses without consulting their constituencies.

In Solomon Islands, conservationists became concerned about large-scale bait fishing and shark fishing (for shark fins) as well as overharvesting shellfish. Confusion over community versus government control can contribute to overharvesting of inshore resources. The Samoan fisheries department attempted to resolve this problem by giving control and technical assistance to communities to make their own management plans (for more information, see the SPREP website under "Community-Based Natural Resource Management/Collective Action" in the Resources section).

Biodiversity

Biodiversity means richness of species and genetic variation. Humid tropical forests are the most biodiverse places on earth, followed by coral reefs. Some areas of high biodiversity may be "created" either by human practices (e.g., depositing garbage or creating edges and ecotones), by the fact that they are "no-man's-lands" on the borders of territories or in areas that are highly inhospitable to humans, such as swamps. In Bolivia, for example, it was found that an indigenous groups' no-man's-land and game reserve was relatively isomorphic with a conservation area designed by scientists. In some areas, there are low population densities for historical reasons where, for example, indigenous populations were wiped out by conflict or disease. Schwartzmann et al. (2000b: 1371) argue that "the 'pristine forest' [of the Amazon] is in fact a recent artifact of the demographic collapse of indigenous populations after 1500 brought about by introduced diseases."

Conservation planners are concerned with preserving areas of high biodiversity. It is important to learn the history of an area and its

CONSERVATION OR COMMON SENSE?

One conservation organization working in Papua New Guinea placed a project in an area of high biodiversity, which was a no-man's-land at the border of three tribes that were typically hostile to one another. Working out relations among these tribes took up so much time that ultimately the project bogged down. Project personnel living in the no-man's-land became sick or died, confirming the indigenous belief that it was not a healthy place.

surroundings. Archaeology can help where written or oral history is inadequate (see chapter 13).

Human habitation and use can also simplify ecosystems and destroy species. But who is to blame? Local people and their food crops and guns? Local hunters, loggers, and traders? Distant consumers, logging CEOs, and government officials who see biodiversity as commodities? Often the targets of projects are local people who are virtually powerless to halt large-scale economic and ecological change. Yet they have motivation to conserve if their resource base is degraded to the extent that they cannot get food, clean water, or medicines. In chapter 9, we discuss how local people organize and build partnerships across social and economic strata.

Protected Areas

A policy paper by the Panos Institute on conventions, protected areas (PAs) and people says that despite conflict regarding local people and use of resources, PAs are growing in area and type:

Parks once covered a few national biological "treasures," such as supposedly pristine rainforest areas. Now a wider range of ecosystems is gaining protection. More than 500 wetlands are officially designated as conservation sites under the Ramsar Convention on Wetlands Important as Waterfowl Habitat, currently adopted by 96 countries. Mountain and desert parks also abound. The world's largest protected area is Antarctica, an entire continent designated by signatories to the Antarctic Treaty as a "world park." WWF [Worldwide Fund for Nature] recently agreed terms with the Russian government to establish a series of large national parks in the Siberian Arctic. (Panos 1997: 10)

This book sidesteps the debate over maintaining and expanding protected areas (see Brosius and Russell, 2003) by pointing out that conservation is not what is planned to be conserved but what is actually conserved. Hence, many parks and protected areas do not conserve designated species and habitats, while private or communal areas may conserve within the context of other uses. Chapter 8 addresses the ethics of planning parks and protected areas, while chapter 15 discusses non-biological measures of conservation within a given territory.

CASE STUDY

INTENSIFICATION IN RURAL AFRICA

The "registered farm" is a type of land use that was growing in Cameroon and Zaire in the 1980s and 1990s. This farm, which is registered to an individual or family, may be carved out of lands formerly governed by a much wider social unit ("customary land"). Typically, a family with some resources registers several hectares as a farm. The owners could be local leaders or chiefs or could have had access to cash and political connections through salaried income at some point. The farm tends to use more intensive agricultural technologies, such as fish ponds, animal husbandry, and plantations, than the gardens of "customary" landholders. The aim of the farmer is often to produce crops or animals for sale or perhaps for barter or family use. The implications of this trend for conservation will depend on how much land is taken up, whether forests or marshy areas are being cleared, or whether chemicals are being used that harm plants and animals.

Resource Management Systems Evolve

Change in resource management systems can be very rapid, and these changes often have serious negative consequences for biodiversity. Key changes include the following:

- *Changes in land ownership and use over time.* What new types of land or resource use have emerged? Which ones are declining in use (see case study above)?
- *Changes in technologies used.* A simple lamp for night fishing can increase intensification of fish harvesting and threaten livelihoods and incomes.
- *Social trends that affect resource management.* Changes could include policies that directly affect resources, such as change in tenure laws or new regulations for trade in forest commodities. Powerful social trends include immigration into an area and out-migration or migration out of the area because of lack of opportunity or perceived oppression (see case study below).

Chapter 15 discusses how to describe and monitor resource management systems and trends with local people through community monitoring and mapping. The Resources section on "Human and Political Ecology" presents several good references to learn more about subsistence and land use strategies.

CASE STUDY

TRANSMIGRATION: AN EGREGIOUS POLICY

The Suharto government in Indonesia had a policy of transmigration that relocated people from areas of high population density to areas of lower population density. The migrants were given a plot of land and some start-up capital for a house and small business. This system meant that people enter the new area with little or no knowledge of its ecology. They could have very different farming and resource management practices from long-term inhabitants.

5

Economic Systems

At the level of the rural village, with its associated markets and exchange networks, the "local economy" is the web of activities that link producers to consumers through the production and distribution of goods and services. Even if little or no cash is exchanged at the local level, the local economy is embedded in a regional, national, and global economy that uses its goods and services in some way.

Among societies, there are various kinds of distribution networks and different values for goods and services. In some societies, animals from a hunt are distributed to the whole community, and tradition dictates how to divide up and distribute the meat. In other societies, *bridewealth* (money or goods given by a groom to the bride's family at the time of marriage) or *dowry* (money or goods given to a groom's family at time of marriage by the bride's family) are significant sources of distribution, and payments can stretch over long periods of time. Different ways of valuing or distributing goods or services may depend on relationships. For example, a young man will get wages for work done for a company, but for family members, the same work might be minimally paid.

We do not assume that a person's main goal at any point in time is to maximize cash income—life is not that simple. Although this is certainly a very important goal for many people, there are other outcomes that people simultaneously pursue, such as security and insurance from risk, spiritual purity, good relations with neighbors and kin (social safety net), respect and prestige, power and the desire to put others in one's debt, and adventure.

The priorities of these goals fluctuate, depending on circumstances. For example, because of the tradition of social equality in some Melanesian, African, and indigenous cultures, it is often necessary for individuals to give relationship stability and reciprocity (see the following discussion) priority over accruing cash earnings and savings. In addition, studies in Africa have shown that young people do not migrate to cities just to earn more money: They want to get away from the oppression of elders or garner the experience and prestige of having lived in a city (e.g., Rempel et al. 1970). Goals and strategies change with age, status, and gender.

Here we look at certain components of the local economy and show how these are linked to the wider economy. The importance for conservationists of understanding these components is also indicated through case studies that illustrate the linkages.

Pieces of the Economic Puzzle

Just Subsisting, or Living Well on Local Means?

Subsistence agriculture is often characterized by low-technology practices, such as swiddening (see chapter 4), extended fallow periods, and the use of simple tools, such as hoes. Increasingly, subsistence farmers are under pressure to sell food for cash or to put subsistence land into cash crop cultivation. Cash is then used to purchase imported food, such as rice, and for other needs. The net result of this shift is often loss of food security because of unstable markets and prices. This lack will cause people to "mine" (extract without renewing) resources for cash. Examples of subsistence elements include household gardens, domestic animals, and small-scale fishing.

Implications for Conservation

When the subsistence economy weakens because there is not sufficient land or labor, there are important impacts on households and communities. Women are often more concerned about maintaining a subsistence base than men are because they are in charge of food, firewood, water supply, and family health and may not control cash that could be used to buy resources. In any conservation initiative, activities that encourage time and effort away from subsistence need to be monitored.

There Is More to the Economy Than Cash

The social economy refers to transactions made by people in order to build social capital (trust and confidence among people working

NGALI NUTS FOR SUBSISTENCE OR CASH?

Conservation planners on Makira Island, Solomon Islands, were concerned about commercializing *ngali* nut *(Canarium indicum)* oil. This nut is used in "kastom feasts" (ceremonies) and in the diet. The project presses the nut oil to sell to overseas companies such as the Body Shop. The nut could become overharvested and/or diverted to the commercial sphere, thus reducing its importance in the diet. The project tried community monitoring of the nuts to track biological impact (see chapter 15).

together), social safety nets (insurance against loss), or in general cooperate with kin and neighbors in order to survive. These transactions may have a monetary element. For example, in Africa, bridewealth is paid to the bride's parents in cattle, cloth, or other goods, and increasingly there is cash involved. But the key is that paying these costs establishes a long-term relationship between the parties involved, unlike strictly cash transactions. Examples of the social economy include bridewealth and dowry distribution, "custom feasts," sharing of meals, gift exchange, and volunteer activities.

Implications for Conservation

People's social identity and status (see the next chapter) are tied up with their role and level of participation in social exchanges. Social identity can equate to survival in times of crisis. Consequently, people may invest time and money in funerals and other social functions more readily than in development or conservation efforts. "Custom feasts" are often ways that people use to gain access to resources—to formally request use of land or other resources.

Mutual aid and development funds are funds of cash that individuals contribute to in order to have a safety net in case of death or illness. A church group, a neighborhood group, or a kin group can

LOGGERS MANIPULATE SOCIAL ECONOMY IN NEW GUINEA

Conservation activists in New Guinea described how loggers manipulate the social economy by presenting gifts in such a way that a social debt is incurred. This kind of debt is much more serious to local people than a cash debt and cannot be ignored.

manage these funds. In some societies, significant sources of funds are raised in "informal" groups that are used to seed enterprises. What are the terms of entry into these groups? Typically, being a member of a certain ethnic group or clan and having the right family connections play a role. What can we learn from indigenous modes of development that can inform conservation initiatives?

The Bamiléké are an ethnic group in western Cameroon with a strong entrepreneurial tradition. To gain entry to a credit group, one has to have the right family connections, and to get access to credit, the new member must develop a business plan. The plan can be subject to much debate and refinement before approval. Failure to repay the debt to the group or other infringement may ultimately result in harm to a family member of the debtor or the debtor him- or herself. Therefore, compliance is high. This system is tied to respect for ancestors and honoring people who make significant investments in their own communities.

Markets Have Many Functions

Markets are centers of social as well as economic activity. They also can be where people trade natural resources used for food, medicine, seed stock, or relaxation. Markets can open on a daily, weekly, or periodic basis. Merchants and traders typically control markets, although producers and farmers may have their own stalls. Town and city markets are usually more diverse than rural markets, but some rural areas can be quite privileged if they have valuable resources (for more on markets, see chapter 11).

Shops and stores are often where people go to pay debts and gossip as well as to buy consumer items. They may be one of the only avenues the local elite have to invest money, and some families invest just in order to have a mechanism for savings. These local stores are tied in to the world market; in some countries, they sell few if any local goods and are major suppliers of liquor and tobacco as well as imported food, cola beverages, and snacks.

Informal Markets and Barter

Examples include intrafamily rural–urban exchanges (a bag of cassava to a relative in town in exchange for a place to sleep), flea markets, "forest trade" markets (see the case study below), and merchandise for commodity swaps. There are stated and unstated rules about hospitality, exchange value, and appropriateness of exchange. These systems are often used for forest products.

CASE STUDY

"Forest markets" located on smuggling routes in the Congo (formerly Zaire) are the locus of clandestine trade in bushmeat (wild animals) as well as other valuables such as gold and diamonds. Many of the traders are local military who have access to guns.

DOUBLE THREAT TO CONSERVATION

In a local store in a "Dayak" (indigenous) area of Kalimantan, Indonesia, Chinese medicines containing substances made from endangered species are sold to impoverished rubber tappers. These ineffective potions waste the money of the local people while they waste precious biological resources.

Labor Markets

Labor markets define the number, identity, skills, and availability of workers for specific jobs. The wage rate (payment per unit, such as day, week, or task for a specific job or category of laborer) and labor recruitment (method of obtaining labor) patterns can reveal how the specific tasks fit within larger social patterns and also say a lot about gender and ethnic differences in labor. What is the daily or per hectare rate for clearing land? Does it change depending on social identity or on the extent of forest to be cut? Do outsiders come in and do certain jobs?

Even at the household level, there are "markets" for labor. Women within a household can receive compensation in kind or in cash for their

FORBIDDEN BARTER

In carrying out research on trade and markets in a cash-poor area of Congo, the researcher wondered why no one reported barter exchanges. After probing, she discovered that barter was officially forbidden by the state because it was impossible to tax barter transactions. Nevertheless, it occurred to a great extent.

CASE STUDY

MEN AND WOMEN WORK DIFFERENTLY

In many countries, men work in temporary gangs on specific projects, while women work in more stable long-term work groups that encompass many tasks. These groups can form the nucleus of a resource management group, such as the Mahila Mangal Dals in Garhwal, India, who manage forest fodder resources (Bhatt 1998).

work in family plantations or fields. Different tasks and incentives draw different kinds of labor. Opportunities to work in plantations, logging camps, or animal husbandry can draw people from outside an area. These people may settle or make other claims on the land. Sometimes the market for the product they produce crashes, and they have nothing to do but grow food crops or in other ways use the land to make a living.

Services and trades. These include carpentry, tailoring, and hairstyling that people do for cash or barter. Many people in rural areas have skills but no way to practice them. These skills represent significant social capital. How can a conservation initiative use these skills?

CASE STUDY

SOCIAL CAPITAL IN A FIJIAN VILLAGE

On Viti Levu in Fiji, a man took over an important chiefly title from his deceased father. As he was also a trained demographer, the chief decided to do a survey to learn about his people. He discovered many skills in the population that he had not known about. The people possessing these skills had few opportunities to use them. He developed a plan for improving the village using the skills of these people.

Transportation Systems

These include paths, roads, taxis, trucks, buses, airplanes, and boats. When did these routes get mapped out? Who determines transport routes and fares? Is negotiation with the transporter possible, or are the fares fixed? Understanding the transport system for both humans and goods is critical. Roads are among the most significant threats to biodiversity, but they can represent "modernity" and progress to local people. How can a conservation initiative work to minimize the impact of roads while meeting local needs? When is a road imposed on people in the name of "national progress" and to provide access to resources for elites?

Credit and Savings Systems

These include banks, church-based schemes, rotating credit systems, credit unions, and micro-lending programs. Researchers can look at interest rates, payment schedules, relationships between debtors and creditors, and the stigma of indebtedness. Debt can lead to selling or leasing land, which may lead to confusion over ownership or conversion of the land to cash crops (Biodiversity Conservation Network and Institute of Environmental Science for Social Change 1997).

CASE STUDY

TRANSPORT AND ECONOMIC DEVELOPMENT

High transport fees and transport monopolies are often the reason why rural micro-enterprises fail. Transport routes are often linked to the evacuation of key commodities. In many rural isolated areas, logging roads are the only roads around. Logging roads can bypass formerly important trade routes, causing them to decline in importance. River transportation, which is smaller scale and less destructive, can be neglected.

CASE STUDY

SAVINGS IN KIND

Many rural people prefer to save in kind rather than keep cash around the house, where it will be borrowed or perhaps used for nonessential purposes. That means they will invest in animals; in prestige items, such as traditional money or jewelry; or in creating or expanding plantations. Enterprises that produce significant amounts of cash require mechanisms for saving and investment. Formal- and even informal-sector credit schemes can be inappropriate for remote dwellers.

The "Underground Economy"

When people have few ways to earn a living legally because the laws are draconian, keep shifting, or ban the most lucrative enterprises, people carry out these activities clandestinely and/or pay off officials to continue the activities. In some countries or areas, most of the economy is "underground" for these reasons and because of conflict, a weak government, or isolation. Officials can be deeply involved in these "illegal" activities. Tracing the informal or underground economy is difficult but crucial. Its shape will often determine many aspects of local behavior (see studies of smuggling and poaching in MacGaffey 1991; Manning 1993; Thompson 1975).

Tracking Economic Change

Here are four concepts—commodification, terms of trade, transaction costs, and coping strategies—that can reveal trends in the local economy. These concepts can be used during the collection of baseline information on the economic situation at the site. In addition, you can explore what indicators (signs) people use to gauge trends in the local economy (see chapter 16). Men and women may differ significantly in their assessments of the situation, depending on the impact on food security and children's well-being. People with different statuses and

THE MOST VALUABLE NONTIMBER FOREST PRODUCT

At a village meeting in central Africa to discuss livelihood options, a researcher asked, "What is the most valuable nontimber forest product?" After a silence, a villager who knew the researcher well remarked, "You know that we grow marijuana here, and it makes a lot more money for us than any nut or seed." This response explained a lot about a puzzling aspect of resource management—that some people were planting their fields far from the house.

roles are very likely to have different assessments of the economic situation.

Commodification

The subsistence economy works within a world of social complexity where resources often have multiple "owners" and users. People share and trade resources on the basis of relationships with the aim to maximize the density of relationships. The commodity-based economy encourages uniformity and simplification in order to better control and regulate trade. People acquire resources to get cash for multiple purposes.

The transition from subsistence to commodity production means that the value of resources in themselves becomes more important than the value of social relations that provide access to resources. This trend means that social institutions that in the past regulated people's behavior in relation to role and status (see chapter 6) are no longer effective for management and new institutions based around key commodities predominate. Thus, a village council may become an agricultural or marketing cooperative but in this transformation will struggle to compete with traders with much more developed business skills. There is an overall decline in reciprocity and other sharing behaviors with increased commodification, or at least people imagine that this is the case (Taussig 1980).

Measuring Commodification

As demand increases, certain resources come to be bought and sold in markets as commodities. Some commodities are ancient (timber); others are new (*ngali* nut oil). The quantities sold and the amount of income derived from a commodity are relatively straightforward measures of the importance of commodities, although note that prices can be significantly manipulated by market structures such as monopolies (one seller, many buyers) and monopsonies (one buyer, many sellers) or cartels that act like monopolies. In addition, some commodities come with subsidies, such as cheap agricultural inputs, or other benefits that make them more important than other commodities. Prices and market volumes can be obtained from local suppliers, traders, or government agencies charged with commodity trade (see chapter 11; see also "Market Analysis and Conservation Enterprises" in the Resources section).

To estimate the level of commodification within the local economy, list the major commodities sold in markets. Find out which ones were not sold or rarely sold in the past (the time frame depends on the pace of change). Look at the amount of land taken up by plantations and the amount of time taken to produce or process key commodities compared to other activities with the population (for different groups and genders, this equation may differ significantly). The overall level of commodification can also be estimated by looking at the percentage of food purchased by households within groups or wider populations. Examples follow:

- Food crops that were not sold in the past are now being sold.
- Gardens for high-value vegetables are replacing subsistence gardens.
- Women are spending time on basket weaving for the market rather than making traditional mats for ceremonies.
- Traditional crop varieties are disappearing.

Terms of Trade

"Terms of trade" refers to the relative price trends of imported goods and local commodities. Local producers may produce more or sell more but still slip behind in profits because of pricing structures, lack of technology, or political barriers. This indicator can show whether the local economy is improving or declining. Seasonality can play a role, and sometimes the trend can be very different, depending on location (access to transport), world market situation (e.g., cocoa experiences periodic booms and busts), and other factors, such as civil unrest.

Gauging Terms of Trade

Declining terms of trade to producers means that prices for commodities sold by local producers rise at a lower rate (or do not rise) than prices for consumer items. Improving terms of trade to producers means that commodity prices rise at higher rate than prices for consumer items that the producer must buy. The importance of this concept is that it measures economic change using the economic resources most valued by people.

To gauge trends in terms of trade in a simple way (there are highly complex models for complex economies), pick one or two key commodities sold by people in the area. Also choose a few goods typically sold and purchased by households that are easy to price (e.g., sack of rice or a measure of cloth). Graph the prices of these items over time (see figure 5.1). What do the trends show? Are there seasonal trends? Note that the same set of merchants may control both trades.

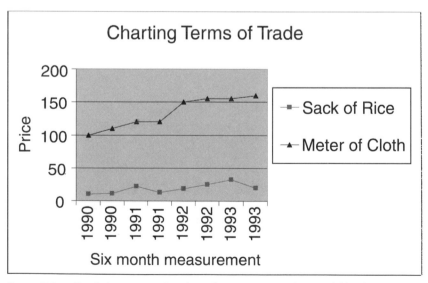

Figure 5.1. *Declining terms of trade to farmers (price of rice sold by farmers goes down, price of sack of cloth bought by farmers goes up).*

The Cost of Doing Business

Taxation and Other Rents

Head tax, registration taxes, and salary or wage taxes are official taxes. "Hidden" taxation can be more significant than these official taxes. These hidden taxes include "fees" that have to be paid to officials in order to get documents, do business, travel, or otherwise make a living in some countries. This factor contributes to perverse incentives (see chapter 2) and also to mining resources because locals cannot sustain their livelihoods (see "Perverse Incentives" and "Environmental Governance" in the Resources section). Rural people under repressive or corrupt regimes must pay fees for even the smallest government task and face fines and even imprisonment for small infractions. These costs add to household expenses. Taxation can also cause people to migrate (see box 5.1).

Stagnation or decline in a local economy can be the result of low producer prices and transport costs, but it can also be the result of the numerous transaction costs (time and social costs of doing business) imposed on rural producers and traders. These transaction costs involve normal costs of doing business, such as getting access to resources, transportation, and collaboration, but often there are much steeper transaction costs for disempowered and marginalized people.

Assessing Transaction Costs

The costs of doing business or making a living in many nations involves multiple informal "taxes," fines, permits, bribes, and other seldom-documented social costs. Some people or groups may try to control ownership of land or other resources by charging fees for use or access or manipulating laws, rules, social structures, and assets to gain ownership of significant resources. These undocumented costs are transaction costs. An aspect of transaction costs is the manipulation of laws that make a substance or activity legal or illegal, thus rendering the producers outlaws in the name of conservation (Neumann 1998, 2000; Thompson 1975).

Assessing trends in transaction costs is difficult but not impossible. One proxy or indirect measure of transaction cost is the average amount of time it takes to accomplish tasks, such as registering a business, getting a permit to trade, or registering land. People may even be able to enumerate the cost of a typical bribe—some are standardized. Knowledge about this trend is vital to setting up any project. Are major income-generating activities legal and open, controlled, restricted, or illegal?

Box 5.1. Hidden Taxation and Its Social Costs

"Futa Wino ya Leta" in Zaire

In Congo, the former Zaire, the government charged citizens for their own arrest and imprisonment, which often occurred for very minor infractions. "Futa Wino ya Leta" means "pay the state's ink" in Lingala, a local lingua franca. It implies that prisoners had to buy even paper and ink to write up reports on their "crimes." This system meant that there was no cost to the state of charging and imprisoning people and quite a bit of incentive to do so. Prisoners worked for chiefs and local authorities.

Soli in Fiji

Villagers in Fiji are constantly being called on to give a "contribution," or *soli*, toward development projects and church and chiefly functions. These contributions keep social life going, but they can be a burden for poorer families.

No Logging Concession for Locals in Indonesia

Despite—or perhaps because of—sponsorship by a major U.S. university, the U.S. government, and the national forestry department, a project was not able to get permission from the local forestry department to grant a former logging concession to local communities. The project worked intensively for three years, but, being a U.S. government–sponsored project, the staff was not able to provide "incentives" to local officials. This long delay in getting permission led to high degrees of staff and local community frustration and at one point an increase in illegal logging.

Assessing transaction costs is also important in gauging the costs and benefits of participation. How much time is expected from individuals and groups? Is this time away from subsistence and cash-generating activity? Are there political and/or economic risks involved? Often, outsiders assume that local people should participate because it is in their interest to do so. But have the whole array of interests been understood? Do the transaction costs rise or fall with increased involvement?

Coping Strategies

Coping strategies can be defined as those activities that enable individuals and communities to survive declining access to resources and reversals of fortune so common in rural areas of developing countries. Coping strategies may have a long-run negative effect on sustainability, as by their nature they are actually responses to crisis or negative trends in the economy and environment rather than strategies for increasing well-being. Monitor them and assess their impact on participation and management strategies.

Coping strategies characteristic of reactions to economic stress include the following:

1. The creation of larger, less well-managed agricultural fields using the work of women, children, and old people (able-bodied men have migrated)
2. A cycle of breakdown and reformation of group efforts to work/invest in agriculture or marketing ventures as when able leaders have migrated, and there is a lack of trust among community members
3. Expansion of production by bringing marginal lands under cultivation, including the use of swamp forests, higher mountain slopes, and shorter fallow lands
4. Increased collecting and eating of wild plants or food with less nutritional value, including the shift to cassava and away from plantains or yams
5. Increased reliance on nonfarming (extractive) activities for revenue and young men engaging in "risky" ventures with potential high payoff, including the cultivation of drug crops, processing home brew and whisky, artisanal gold panning and mining, hunting with rifles, or manufacturing homemade rifles
6. Town-to-village "straddling" and increased tension between town and village, as when people maintain land in the village by cultivating a garden, support a relative to look after their land, or send young women to the town to prostitute themselves

Savings and Investment

Table 5.1 examines two economic indicators at the household level that affect how people cooperate with development and conservation initiatives: savings and debt and food security.

Table 5.1. Economic Indicators at the Household Level

Indicator	Implications
Level of savings and debt	If people are putting away cash in a safe place for a period of time or participating in an in-kind or cash payment savings group and use credit, cash, and savings to make consumption, social, or productive investments, the initiative can build on these savings traditions for enterprise or other investment, taking care not to damage them (see table 5.2).
	If people are getting into debt to buy goods and services, the initiative has to tackle debt as a primary concern because it will cause mining of the resources. Measures such as interest rates, repayment terms, and amounts can indicate level of indebtedness. People may be taking credit but not paying it back.
Level of food security	If land or other resources become scarce, there is drought or conflict, the hungry season leaves families without food resources, cash for food is used for other purposes, or women have little or no access to cash or garden space, the initiative must tackle food security issues at the outset.
	By contrast, if food security improves, the initiative needs to examine possible intensification of agriculture and plantations at the expense of conservation. Improvements could be a result of subsidies such as remittances from overseas migrants or government handouts. Differences among households with respect to food security can be great.

Saving and investing cash is very difficult in many rural and isolated communities. First, there are no banks or other secure places to put cash. Second, relatives and neighbors borrow money for immediate needs if they know it is around. Finally, having a lot of cash is often seen as being greedy. For these reasons, people invest cash socially, either individually in consumption or communally through feasts, bridewealth payments, and religious donations. However, when appropriate savings mechanisms are put into place, poor people respond avidly. For example, Jayshree Vyas, managing director of Sewa Bank in India, a bank that serves self-employed women, claims, "Savings from our clients just pour in. As long as we design attractive savings schemes tailored to their needs and provide them with easy collection mechanisms, we see that poor women are great savers" (www.sewabank.org). Chao-Beroff (1999: 2) confirms, "For those who assume that the poor cannot save, there are now numerous examples demonstrating the contrary."

Investments in social goods help provide a social safety net and thus may pay off better in the long run than would economic investments. Formally educated and entrepreneurial individuals tend to balance their individual and family cash needs with these social investments. Some migrate in order to distance themselves from the redistributive pressures at home or convert to religions or sects that allow them to accumulate and share within a more affluent group.

Investment strategies are how people use their resources to maintain or improve their welfare. Table 5.2 shows several types and levels of investment. It reflects the complexity and situation of the economic environment at the local level and provides some ideas for how conservation initiatives can cope with each level.

Before there was cash, there were systems of exchange and barter that continue to be used and valued:

- Reciprocity. All people in the group share labor, gatherings, and harvests according to specific customs and active membership in the group. Foragers use this principle to distribute game meat and other products for the subsistence of the whole group. This system still exists in places where women exchange meals among households, women and men share work in work groups, and families participate in gift giving. This system helps us understand how the nonfinancial benefits from common-pool resources should be shared.
- Redistribution. People contribute harvests and prestige goods to a chief or other leader who distributes them within the community according to specific customs. Small-scale farming and fishing communities used this system. This system still exists in the form of bridewealth distributions, church contributions, and taxation. Conservation initiatives can build on this principle by finding out about prestige goods in the community, how they are distributed, and who is trusted to distribute them. Does this redistribution help retain social unity, or does it create conflict?

Globalization Is Not New

With respect to the extraction of natural resources, globalization is not a new phenomenon. Few areas of the world were isolated a hundred years ago, and most felt the effects of trade and colonization hundreds of years before then (Nash 1981). Many if not most local populations have been under the economic and/or political domination of

Table 5.2. Economic Levels, Investment Strategies, and Conservation Initiatives

Economic Level	Investment Strategy	Implications for Conservation Initiative
No surplus—crisis, refugee landless, or subjugated population	No cash; limited ability for in-kind investment; no land or assets	Essential needs must come first; trust may be low; no buy-in to conservation
Subsistence—very small holdings, widows, poor	Cash is used for small items; no cash for larger purchases	Need for low-risk projects that build on in-kind investments and economic security
Average rural families with some holdings and assets, little or no access to banking facilities	Some regular source of income or products that can be sold to pay school fees, medical bills, or clothes	Projects that provide extra income that does not risk regular income sources
Upper average, local elite households	Build family house; invest in family business; have plantation and animals	Build responsible entrepreneurship and stewardship of resources
Community level (church, kin, or village group)	Build community house and church; savings group and communal field	Work with youth and men and women community leaders; check for inequities
Institutional level (town dwellers, strong institutions)	Put money in savings account; manage community funds for development	Work within networks of local institutions: church, school, and kin groups located in town
High levels of non-productive investment	Spend money on alcohol or tobacco; pay exorbitant interest rates (money not reinvested in community)	Work with women
Tribute—coercive social investment	Taxation without benefit to those taxed; high levels of bribes and other transaction costs	Take care with any project

empires for centuries. Some areas of the world are experiencing new pressures because of the importance of new commodities (e.g., increased pesticide use from growing of "off season" vegetables in the Caribbean and Central America), the scarcity of an old commodity (e.g., increased sale price of rhino horn for Chinese medicine), the expanding importance of a commodity (e.g., preferences for shrimp-promoting aquaculture in fragile mangrove habitats), or shifts to new locations resulting from exhaustion of previously important sources (e.g., expanded hardwood logging in central Africa). What is new is the (still very limited) ability of local populations to benefit from the global economy. Serfdom, slavery, and indentured servitude still exist, but they are no longer the "natural state" of a large proportion of the world's peoples. And awareness is focused on global problems, such as global warming, the spread of synthetic hormones, the loss of forests, and the destruction of fisheries.

Thus, research on the impact of globalization has to take into account the ecological effects of shifting global markets but also both the social costs and the social gains of being part of global networks. In the past, the plight of marginalized people and ecologically vulnerable areas would be unknown to all but a very few, and there would be no way to affect the outcomes short of revolution or prolonged nonviolent struggle such as Gandhi and followers waged in India. Today there are hundreds, if not thousands, of websites devoted to the plight of "rainforest peoples" and other poor and marginalized communities (see "Community-Based Natural Resource Management/Collective Action" in the Resources section)—not that this Internet traffic translates automatically into improved conditions, but it is a dramatic expansion of awareness and concern.

Consumers play a pivotal role in the global economy. Often we see globalization as a juggernaut that will destroy all local economies and replace them with McDonald's and Wal-Mart. Yet folks in many parts of the world now have at least some choice in where they shop, what they buy, and how much they buy. In the richest countries, there is a growing movement toward "voluntary simplicity" that encourages consumers to pare down their wants and needs and replace consumer goods with social and spiritual community. There is a steep rise in the consumption of organic produce.

The strength of anti-corporatism and anti-globalization has been sorely underestimated by leaders who run the World Trade Organization, the World Bank, and the International Monetary Fund. People want to participate in the running of their economy, not be passive pawns in a vast game of profit maximization and debt formation. Citizen activism tapped for anti-globalization is rooted in concern for the environment but also concern about people marginalized by the global economy. Bringing these two concerns together is critical for the reconciliation of conservation and human rights (e.g., environmental justice and labor rights).

Conservation initiatives benefit from globalization when they are able to put pressure through consumers on a whole economic sector. Timber certification, such as that promoted by the Forest

Stewardship Council and practiced by Smartwood, is one example (see "Sustainable Use of Natural Resources" in the Resources section). Certification is no panacea: There are many definitional and practical problems to be worked out. But it is one step toward spreading best practices throughout the world.

6

Population and Social Systems

> Humans exploit resources for social purposes and in the context of competitive, often hierarchical social arrangements. These purposes, and the cultural goals and values behind them, create the conditions in which individuals use and modify resources as they attempt to meet their basic needs.
>
> —Nyerges and Green (2000: 1)

A conservation initiative cannot just deal with individuals. It has to deal with groups and populations, a whole social world. To have impact, population, groups, and stakeholders in relation to a habitat, species, or piece of land have to be involved. Many people must be influenced to change behaviors and practices. An initiative wastes resources if only a few people benefit or get involved in change. The best way to maximize impact is to understand social realities and tap in to local networks. This does not mean that an initiative has to work with the whole population, but it does mean that it must be strategic in working with institutions that will make a difference.

Initiatives that work at very broad scales (e.g., ecoregions and landscapes) need tools to relate wider trends over large areas with specific social groups and institutions. Getting a broad-brush overview of demographics and population in an area is only the first step in social research. It is not going to help move the conservation agenda forward on the ground. That can be done only by working with local groups and institutions.

A major theme of this book is that both the regional and the micro-scale, what we will call the "social impact" scale, are needed. Chapters 10 through 15 provide methods appropriate to different scales and to integrate scales and units of analysis.

People in Diverse Settings

Society, nation, and state are large political units. Population, ethnic group, community, clan, village, household, and stakeholders are terms for groups of people found at a conservation site. Let us look at these terms and the role of different types of groups and institutions in using, controlling, managing, or degrading resources and how they are units of analysis in social research for conservation.

Societies are made up of many local units. This term can be used more specifically to refer to ethnic or territorial groups ("Javanese society") or even countries ("Filipino society"), and it means that these people share customs, symbols, or language from common history, territory, or kinship. Research on broad social trends, attitudes, or discourse (public discussions or statements that shape opinion) often takes place at the level of society. The "state" refers to the unit of governance within a country and typically is the unit of analysis for policies, economic trends, and research on environmental governance, although one can study these at a provincial and municipal level as well, particularly with the trend toward decentralization.

"Nation" is a term that used to denote the physical and social territory of a state or country and now is being used to distinguish distinct cultural groups, such as indigenous peoples, within a larger population, society, or state. Hence, "First Nations" is an appropriate term for Native Americans.

A population is all the groups residing in a given locality or site; they may or may not speak the same languages or have other common identity. For example, various ethnic groups, both "indigenous" and recent migrants living at or near a conservation area, are the population of the area.

High- or moderate-quality demographic information is often hard or impossible to come by in remote areas and even in populous areas of many countries. National censuses may be outdated or inadequate, and the data collection categories used may be of little use. However, it is imperative to get any census material available. It can be tested in some locations to see how widely it varies with reality. Some key information to be obtained about a population includes the following:

- Total population
- Age distribution (this will show population trends)
- Population densities (note that these can vary greatly even in small areas—get the most disaggregated data available)

LORE LINDU NATIONAL PARK

The population around the northern part of Lore Lindu National Park, Sulawesi, Indonesia, where the Biodiversity Conservation Network funded a project of The Nature Conservancy (TNC), included several different ethnic groups, some of them very recently arrived and some of them indigenous to the area. TNC and its partner CARE worked with all these groups, as it is this population that uses the resources in the park. TNC and CARE's social research focused on the population around the park (Biodiversity Conservation Network 1997).

- Gender distribution
- Information on infant mortality and overall on morbidity and mortality
- Migration trends, if possible

"Community" is a term used for everything from one small hamlet to a very large area and often includes nonresidents who are part of the same ethnic group. Today, the term can refer to those who are part of the same religious group or other common affiliation regardless of where they live. In research, use the more specific terms that are given here when describing a population (for discussion of the diversity of community and misuse of the term, see Gujit and Shah 1998).

A settlement or village is a group of people living together who have close relations and whose lives are linked to the extent that actions affecting one family or individual will affect the others. A village can in turn be made up of hamlets, where specific clans, families, or just a group of neighbors live. Sometimes large villages have many hamlets, and these might be correlated with different livelihoods (fishing, hunting, pottery making).

Households

The term "household" is a catchall phrase that is used in common language as well as in censuses, socioeconomic surveys, and monitoring.

THE IMPORTANCE OF UNDERSTANDING SUBVILLAGE FORMATIONS

"A significant finding that emerged from the Asia Forest Network meeting was that while most countries in the region delegate governance authority down to the administrative village level, actual forest management practice often occurs among smaller, subvillage-level hamlets. Administrative villages are often arbitrary groupings of many smaller settlements. The larger, wealthier communities, often situated on the road, tend to control government projects and are the seat of administrative decision making. In other words, formal authority stops at the end of the road where operational forest management begins. . . . Where countries are devolving power to those administrative villages . . . the central government assumes that these administrative village leaders understand local forest needs and management priorities and will effectively reflect the interests of local user groups. . . . [But] from a sociological perspective, administrative villages are often government-defined constructs dominated by the most powerful socioeconomic groups within the cluster of communities" (Asia Forest Network 1997: 44).

Each society defines a household differently. Governments also define households in censuses. Households can be made up of people living in one house or one compound, or they can be related people not necessarily living in the house at the same time. Take care to have local people define the household and do not assume that the household is the proper unit of analysis for understanding incentives, economic activities, or resource management. There can be significant differences between the genders and among generations in terms of behavior, and there are always many important links between "households" to other kin, neighbors, and outsiders.

Households, villages, and other social groupings change in size and composition over time. After conflicts, epidemics, or other major social disturbances, there will be significant change. Other changes can be brought about by public health measures, changes in access to

INVISIBLE HUSBANDS

Widows in southern Cameroon may have "husbands" who live with them for many years. These men have no rights to land and are "invisible" in the household unless one asks very pointed questions. However, they care for the fields and forests and chase away those who might want to snatch the widow's lands. Interviewing these men is critical for understanding resource management. But when asked, people will say they are not part of the household.

transportation, or access to schools. At the household level, changes in generations bring changes in resource management, depending on education, the number of people remaining in the household, subsistence strategies, and types of marriage alliances.

Kinship Groups

A clan, tribe, or ethnic group has family ties and a common identity (self-identified and identified by others) expressed through language, dress, beliefs, and shared knowledge. A clan traces ancestry from a common, often mythical, ancestor. Several lineages may be found within clans—these are groups of people related either through the male line (patrilineages) or female line (matrilineages) with elders at the head of the group. Clan membership can sometimes cross ethnic boundaries (see box 6.1).

A tribe or ethnic group is often associated with a specific language, territory, or even occupation. Clan and lineage elders or leaders are major decision makers in many rural areas. People of the same tribe, clan, or village are not all the same; they may belong to different religions, have different values and status/economic levels, and be linked in many ways to "outsiders." Members of the group may reside temporarily or semipermanently away from the larger group yet retain rights and responsibilities within the group.

Clans, tribes, and ethnic groups are not limited to only one territory—city people can still be part of a rural community. People living

---

Box 6.1.   Fijian Social Structure

Vanua TRIBE/social identity unit (*vanua* also means land)
↓
Yavusa CLAN/policy decision unit, administrative unit
↓
Mataqali LINEAGE/land holding unit
↓
Tokatoka HOUSEHOLD/EXTENDED FAMILY/investment unit
↓
House FAMILY/residence unit

---

in the same village may or may not be part of the clan, tribe, or ethnic group—that depends on how they define it themselves. The spatial dimensions of clans, tribes, and ethnic groups can vary considerably and is often difficult to discern because of overlapping territories, migrations, and other historical and social factors. Clans or castes can also be associated with occupations such as fishing or basket making. Castes are often much larger than clans or lineages, but because they are endogamous, meaning that people of one caste traditionally marry only within that caste, they have a lot to do with regulating kinship and marriage relations. They also may have many other functions that clans and lineages do not necessarily have, such as indication of status and occupation.

In many societies, membership in a specific clan or lineage gave access to certain resources and also prohibited members from certain behaviors, foods, and animals. This system was a way of dividing up resources—both human and biological—and conserving some. Elders determined when certain areas and resources were to be avoided and when they could be exploited. For the most part, this ancient system, which is found in many parts of the world, has weakened if not broken down considerably. Some conservation initiatives, however, build on this system with some success.

Stakeholders

What many conservation practitioners call stakeholders are found both within a community or population and/or outside it. Stakeholders are those with a claim or interest in the resources at the site. These claims may be "legitimate" or "illegal," and they may be conflicting or mutually agreed on. Be aware of the common error of interchanging the terms "stakeholder" and "community." The term may legitimate all

LUMAD AND DUMAGAT

The Lumad of Bendum in Mindanao, the Philippines, are part of an ethnic group of indigenous people who are different from the migrants in the area because of their historical occupation of the territory, their use of the land, language, customs, and social status (lower than the migrants). Some Lumad are Catholic, and some are evangelical Christians. There is intermarriage between Lumad and the Dumagat migrants. A project run by the Institute of Environmental Science for Social Change (ESSC), a partner of the Biodiversity Conservation Network, focused on the Lumad ethnic group, as they are the main users/managers of the forest, but they also worked with the migrants whose land purchases and intensive agriculture can be threats to the forest. The ESSC's social research focused on documenting the history of the lineages within Bendum and other villages in order to prepare for the Certificate of Ancestral Domain Claim.

claimants to a resource when it is often important to distinguish those who are dependent on the resource, longtime inhabitants, traditional users, and more recent claimants. There can be advantages in using the term "stakeholder" if it shakes out all the interested parties, including those who may be hidden or distant.

Urban constituencies are now seen to play a very important role in conservation because of their consumer choices and their understanding of conservation issues that affect the wealth and patrimony of their countries. Mobilizing these groups is the focus of some innovative initiatives for building constituencies for conservation.

Institutionally Speaking

We said in chapter 2 that institutions are the rules and social structures that endure. They can take similar forms across cultures but have significant differences because they emerge from particular

STAKEHOLDERS IN KALAHAN RESERVE, THE PHILIPPINES

Powerful politicians own land within or near the Kalahan Reserve, where the Kalahan Educational Foundation (KEF) is located. They have a stake in developing the land in the reserve. KEF's research has looked at the impact of different stakeholders in developing policies for use of the land in and around the reserve.

historical circumstances. Other characteristics of institutions are the following:

- They endure after changes in leadership and membership.
- They are of a higher order than local groups; that is, they mediate relations among groups.
- They have rules that structure how people get access to resources and adapt to new challenges and incentives (as well as "rules for breaking rules").
- They adapt to new circumstances and evolve.

CONSUMERS OF BUSHMEAT

The Tropical Forest People's Program (APFT) based in Europe has studied the importance of urban consumers on wildlife (bushmeat) and on nontimber forest products. They conclude that understanding the tastes and goals of urban dwellers is key to forging sustainable conservation strategies. Indeed, many supporters of conservation live in urban areas (Trefon and Defo 1999).

Table 6.1 shows how institutions can evolve in response to incentives and challenges. There is much evidence to show that poorly designed initiatives can badly damage or destroy local institutions, while others may be able to strengthen them.

In order to promote stewardship—actions that conserve biodiversity—it is necessary to understand and work through institutions that shape how people use and value resources. Some institutions and groups that conservation initiatives may not consider as partners but should include the following:

- Church congregations
- "Old boys" and "old girls" alumni networks
- Clans and other kinship associations
- Guilds and other work associations
- The police and military
- Market associations
- Savings and credit groups

Table 6.1.   Evolution of Institutions

Early Stage
Leaders develop "proto-institutions" or adapt existing institutions to deal with new challenges or opportunities.
Original leadership guides the group by force of charisma (e.g., by promise of incentives and/or sanctions).
Incentives and/or sanctions begin to play a role in shaping people's behavior.
Conflicts over benefits and access to resources begin to occur as incentives come on line (conflicts can happen even before benefits flow to those participating in the institution, depending on how potential benefits are perceived).
Conflicts lead to dissolution of group/end of effort—individuals pursue own strategies.

Midstage
Institution survives conflicts and challenges to and changes in leadership.
Institution grows: Contact is made with other, similar institutions; rules and regulations become formalized.
Institution grows too big, exceeds its mandate, loses touch with its constituency (e.g., the tendency toward "federations" of local groups), benefits flow only to leaders, and leaders are not doing the work.
Institution may survive but is not effective (may actually survive on donor funds).

Mature Stage
Institution becomes deeply rooted in communities, is part of daily life (e.g., church and school), or integrates into such deeply rooted institutions.

CASE STUDY

FOREST USERS' GROUPS

Working with a forest users' group to get them to use the forest resources sustainably may not have long-term impact if the institutions governing access to and use of resources do not change their rules. If the forest users' group has been given no power to keep outsiders from taking the forest resources, they may have little incentive to harvest sustainably. Therefore, it is important to also work with institutions, such as the forest department and other governing agencies, on wider reforms.

An institution comprises a set of rules that links people and resources; these rules are often but not always embodied by specific groups and organizations, such as government agencies and ministries, churches, schools, and family and kin groups. Local-level groups—for example, a specific enterprise group, cooperative, or tribal council—can be formed or dissolved with little impact on wider institutions.

Greater impact can be achieved by working through and with institutions rather than just with local groups (institutions are by definition sustainable), but institutional change is a much longer, more intensive process than the formation or reorientation of groups to work on specific projects.

Institutions regulate the transactions of different local groups either horizontally through mutual agreement or vertically through top-down control. Some institutions are not amenable to change from outside pressures. For example, the Forest Department in India is not likely to grant local users permanent tenure to forests anytime soon, but working with local officials has been found to yield locally appropriate solutions.

The following institutions may or may not be associated with conservation but typically have a profound impact on behavior, motivation, and values—all of which affect resource management practices and conservation efforts.

Marriage and Kinship Institutions

In many societies, these institutions govern who can marry whom, the rights and responsibilities of husbands and wives in marriage, control over children, status of different family groups, obligations of family members, and inheritance of assets. Examples include clans, lineages, and castes.

Implications for conservation. The status of a woman is shaped by marriage. It may structure a woman's access to land and trees and shape resource management behavior. The level of bridewealth or dowry can be an important factor in the local economy. Social investments in kin connections and marriage are often equally or more important than economic investments.

Political and Legal Institutions

These allocate resources and resolve conflicts and disputes according to precedents and rules. Examples include courts, tribunals, tribal councils, and municipal government agencies. In some societies, these institutions can overlap in function with customary institutions, or there may even be two or more sets of rules. Related groups include political party cells, local unions, and local advocacy groups (see the discussion of civil society institutions later in this chapter).

Implications for conservation. Conservation is not possible without a deep understanding of relations of power and influence. People or groups with significant resources—money, land, and education— typically shape decisions and rules to benefit themselves. People without significant resources will try to shape rules and decisions as well but have less chance of succeeding and take more risks in trying. Understanding how political institutions are chartered and how they are funded is critical.

Note that decision-making "groups" can be informal yet quite powerful. For example, the local elite can meet informally in social situations or for business and come to consensus about how to handle situations. Similarly, poor people often meet informally and, through networks of "gossip" and discussion, control a situation or make a decision.

Tenure institutions are an important subset of political/legal institutions. They regulate access to and control of natural resources based on status, such as gender, location, ethnicity, need, wealth, or other rules (private ownership, clan ownership, marriage, history of arrival). Examples include the Forest Department, landowners' associations, and tribal councils.

Implications for conservation. Understanding the level of jurisdiction and legal status of tenure institutions is essential. User groups may be formed or self-organized to manage land or resources, such as irrigation water or wells. These are not institutions unless they are part of a regulating agency or have permanent or long-term legal control over the resource. Yet they can be more efficient and effective under certain circumstances than larger-scale institutions at managing resources. On the ground, tenure relations can be very complex, involving overlapping rights and responsibilities to different resources.

Economic Institutions

These institutions regulate production, distribution, and valuation of goods and services. The rules for barter and exchange of goods and services are often found within kinship or religious institutions, although in the past in many societies barter and exchange were part of the formal economy (e.g., exchange of marriage gifts, prestige gifts to chiefs). Examples include companies or firms, small enterprises, markets, banks, guilds, traders' and market associations, the Securities and Exchange Commission, and cooperatives.

Implications for conservation. Understanding both local and wider markets for key commodities is critical for any conservation and development initiative. In addition, planners need to know how trade is structured and controlled. Power relations shape economic institutions to the benefit of the elite. For example, cooperatives may look like they are horizontally organized, by farmers' or producers' mutual consent, but often they are vertically organized, as farmers or producers are given little say in how they are run or in access to competitive market outlets. Rules for export and trade in a forest commodity can be complex and daunting, whereas agricultural commodities are relatively easy to market. In many countries, the sale of forest products is under the jurisdiction of the forest or environment department rather than an agency that regulates other market activities.

Local-level economic activities can be organized in groups, such as

- Production groups, such as harvesters or agricultural labor groups that extract natural resources (either wild or planted) for subsistence or exchange for other resources.
- Processing groups, such as weavers' groups or pottery cooperatives that make products for themselves or others out of resources.

- Credit and savings groups that hold common savings for group or individual projects or provide credit or credit guarantees for members. Examples are rotating credit groups that hold members' funds and provide a large sum to individuals on a rotating or as-needed basis.

Social and Civil Institutions

These are ostensibly designed to pass on and adapt/enrich learning, knowledge, and rules; increase well-being of society; and provide a social safety net. But they can also be means for increasing or cementing social status of certain individuals and groups at the expense of others. Examples include charitable organizations, schools, apprenticeships, clinics and hospitals, and the Red Cross. Related local groups include youth or sports clubs, religious organizations, title and secret societies, mutual aid groups, teachers' or medical associations, "old boys" and "old girls" networks of alumni, and neighborhood groups.

Implications for conservation. Focus conservation activities on schools, centers of worship, mutual aid, and alumni groups as the centers of social action: Often teachers, church elders, and caregivers are community leaders. These institutions are typically where local people turn for guidance, and as such the conservation message must be embedded in them.

Civil society institutions, such as the League of Women Voters, unions, Rotary clubs, and political parties are another important subset of social institutions. They give people a voice in the wider society, mobilize and pool resources, build social and national identity within a mass society, and lobby for particular causes. Local groups include advocacy nongovernmental organizations (NGOs), such as environmental NGOs, chapters of international groups, and associations of like-minded people. These institutions can also be used by elite members as patron-client networks. There is significant overlap between civil society and social welfare institutions. But typically, social welfare institutions have no overt political agenda. As in social welfare institutions, civil society groups can be important loci for conservation initiatives, either directly or in partnership with a conservation organization. In fact, they may be the most important institutions in creating agendas for wider reform that are necessary to attack broad problems over large scales.

Conservation institutions are set up to manage areas or resources that people wish to conserve. These include parks and protected areas, land trusts, indigenous sacred area management units, and ex situ conservation institutions, such as gene banks and zoos. Note how conservation institutions are integrated with other institutions, who leads and promotes them, and who is included and who is not.

THE SOCIAL IDENTITY OF CONSERVATIONISTS

In many parts of the developing world, major conservation institutions are run by westerners, if not at the country level, then with control of larger budgets and programming.

The Military and Refugee Camps

Conflict and war are emerging as key threats to biodiversity (Hart and Hart 1997; Shambaugh et al. 2001). These crises cause vast migrations of people and put them in places that quickly get degraded. The military can use their guns for hunting game as well as carrying out their official duties. Refugee and military camps can damage resources and ecosystems around them even after they are disbanded, but they may also be places for conservation education, reforestation, or sustainable livelihood activities.

Who's Who

Role and Status

A role is what you do in society—healer, pastor, teacher, or mother. Roles are complementary. If you want to know about "women's roles," then you have to also learn about men's roles. Healers relate to patients or clients, teachers to students, and so on. In short, roles do not stand alone. Roles are not about individuals but about important social categories. Learning about roles helps the researcher understand how people think and aids in an institutional analysis. For example, many societies have special groups or institutions for those playing key roles in society: women, youth, chiefs, or healer. Role can relate to occupation or skill, but there can be roles that do not correspond to occupation.

Status relates to who you are in society with respect to access to resources and decision making: chief, senior wife, landless laborer. Rights and responsibilities are linked to status. A person can have several roles but usually only has one status—this is more ambiguous when it comes to

Box 6.2.   Hierarchy of Statuses in a Maasai Community (Kenya)

Lineage head
Elder man
Elder woman
Married junior man
Married woman with children
Married woman
Moran (warrior: adolescent and young man after initiation)
Unmarried woman
Male child, uncircumcised
Female child

women, who may have high status in society but be subservient to husband and male relatives in the household. Status expresses social hierarchy (e.g., box 6.2). There are often written and unwritten rules related to status: who eats first, where a person sleeps, or who may talk in a meeting. As discussed in chapter 2, gaining or keeping status is a crucial element of all human survival strategies. "Formal" status is not the only thing that determines power. Education, personality, and luck also contribute.

The categories shown in table 6.2 are important to any social research at the level of the individual or household because they have an impact on the status of the individual or household. Status affects access to and control over resources. Make sure that you find out what people actually do, however, and not what people say they should be doing based on these social categories. Social categories can be more flexible than people think, and social stereotypes are common.

Organizing for Power

Some political institutions, such as courts and political parties, have been discussed here. Political systems describe patterns of authority, power, decision making, justice, and law. These systems evolve and change (witness the dramatic transformations in many of the formerly communist countries and the variation in those changes). The following categories are used by anthropologists to characterize the structure of political systems:

- *Egalitarian.* There is little or no hierarchy within society. Conservation initiatives have to deal with all people. An example is the BaAka "pygmies" of central Africa.

Table 6.2. The Importance of Social Categories

Social Category	Reason for Importance	Implications
Gender	Men and women have different rights to, control over, and access to resources.	Data must always be gender disaggregated; interview men and women separately in most cases.
Generation/age	Access to "formal" schooling differs; elders have power that younger people do not.	Views of generations may differ radically; interview separately.
Education or skill level	Occupation and training leads to different knowledge and status.	Interview specialists and understand categories.
Religion	Religions demand adherence to certain practices.	Will affect attitudes and behaviors as well as networks.
Locality (e.g., remoteness)	Different opportunities and constraints/lifestyles.	Get out and interview the really remote people.
Status (e.g., leader, chief, or commoner)	Each status protects different interests and may have different life goals.	Learn the relevant categories and have key informants in each group.
Ethnicity, tribe, or caste	Different access to resources, status, and belief systems.	Understand each one and their interactions with one another.

- *Redistributive (clan-based, "big man" structure).* Men gather resources, such as pigs or shell money: Now consumer items or access to patronage networks may substitute for these traditional gifts. These resources are distributed to others in ceremonies or as bargaining chips. The status of "big man" is not hereditary. Conservation initiatives need to deal extensively, but by no means exclusively, with big men and elders. Factionalism is rampant and can inhibit communal action. An example is the peoples of Solomon Islands.
- *Chiefly.* A hereditary chiefly class exists that distinguishes itself from commoners and other classes. Sometimes this is highly formalized, while in other cases people from chiefly classes are hardly distinguishable from commoners. The chief and his or her allies can play a crucial role in mobilizing people or can be a serious impediment. Other classes, such as traditional fishers, farmers, or merchants, need to be included in an analysis.

Samoan islanders and peoples of highland Cameroon fall into this category.

- *Feudal.* A high chief or lord takes tribute from other classes and from subject chiefs. A paramount chief may play this role as well if other chiefs are subject to him. Understanding alliances, factions, and the decision-making structure is critical. An example is Somalia.
- *Bureaucratic/nation-state.* There are many and diverse statuses reflecting social, political, and economic hierarchies. Entering a professional service class is a key route to higher social status. Education plays an important role in determining status, and thus appealing to the educated and wealthy is an important conservation strategy. European states are examples.
- *Authoritarian.* An individual, party, or oligarchy makes virtually all major decisions and controls key aspects of social, economic, and political life. Mobutu's Zaire was an authoritarian state with pro-conservation policies in terms of the creation of protected areas. Yet the country was also plundered by Mobutu's family and close allies.

Remnants of earlier political forms, the influence of colonialism, and the construction of a modern state mean that many if not most societies today have elements of several of these six idealized political systems. We caution that conservation researchers need to learn the reality and not the textbook model of political systems: They are flexible, changeable, and complex.

The State–Society Struggle

If we want to understand resource management from the point of view of the local resource user, it is essential to look at how different empires, states, and nations have attempted to control the actions of local people and extract resources. The fight for control between local people and the state brings several important consequences for conservation (see references to agrarian studies under "Land History" in the Resources section).

As an example, in order to more easily tax people and use their labor, colonial states forced populations to live along a road rather than in the forest. This means that there is no one in the forest to guard it against outside incursion. What was once "communal" land became the property of the state. Again, the original owners or users lose the right to patrol or police an area. The agents of the state have often not been able to do the job either because there are not enough of them or because they are corrupt and ill trained.

Many practices used by local people to earn a living are made illegal, while much more damaging large-scale practices receive major investments. For example, villagers are prohibited from distilling whisky in their backyards, but the state allows imported whisky to be sold in the local shops owned by local elites; locals are prohibited from using chainsaws, while the state sells off major logging concessions. Efforts to "improve" the locals involve changing their lifestyles—sometimes forcibly—to resemble the dominant groups. This shift often involves conversion to "world" religions or adoption of more extractive lifestyles (Tsing 1993).

Often, rural people are taxed at different rates or subject to different kinds of hidden taxes (see chapter 5). For example, they are expected to maintain roads and bridges at their own expense, while these expenses are taken care of by the state in urban areas. Thus, there is a disincentive to work with the state. Rural people are usually keenly aware of their disadvantages and become demoralized. These factors contribute to out-migration of able people, leaving behind the weak and powerless. Taxation can be pegged to income, thus providing a disincentive to entrepreneurialism (e.g., rural cocoa farmers in Cameroon were taxed at a higher rate than urban dwellers). These actions lead to the creation of the "underground economy"(see chapter 5) that involves people in activities and transactions that are technically illegal. This means that there are few formal, "visible" institutions that can be effective in mobilizing people.

Thus, we need to understand the nature of authority, power, and the role of elites at conservation sites and within the wider region as we enter into partnerships with local institutions. Bachrach and Baratz's (1970) classic work describes three mechanisms of elite dominance: agenda control, anticipated reaction, and false consciousness. According to this theory, elites dominate by defining potentially contentious issues as nonpolitical or illegitimate, thereby excluding them from the political agenda. Anticipated reaction is present when potential opponents do not raise complaints out of fear of repercussions, while false consciousness can arise from the close contact between elites and nonelites in rural areas, which allows elites to influence the perceptions of nonelites so that they are more obliging. This theory allows us to understand why certain topics that might be central to our understanding of resource management are never brought to light.

Some aspects of the discourse, or social conversation, about communities, conservation, and resource management that reflect important power relations include the following:

- The premise that community-based resource management is sufficient to counter threats to resource depletion even though virtually no resources are allocated to communities to counter wider threats
- The idea that the conservation of biodiversity is a technical subject and can be understood only by specialists
- The drawing up of management plans with very little if any local input despite lip service being paid to community conservation
- The debate over the role of NGOs as intermediaries between communities and government or the private sector as they are increasingly drawn into acting as service providers to donors and governments
- The controversy about how funds set aside by donors and governments for conservation go to large conservation organizations rather than local- or community-level groups
- The idea that degradation of resources is caused by lack of knowledge or understanding of ecosystem dynamics and can thereby be addressed through "awareness" campaigns and environmental education
- Discussion of the appropriate roles for indigenous and scientific knowledge
- The difficulty of publicly addressing struggles over control of land and other resources (Olson 2001)
- The very "nature" of nature (Cronon 1995) as debated among conservationists, social scientists, indigenous people, and the state (Scott 1998)

Sociopolitical Realities Affect Resource Management

Factionalism

A faction is a group of people within a village, clan, or population with certain social ties that influence their decisions and actions. A faction can be headed by a leader who distributes resources on the basis of loyalty or service or a kinship group that mutually manages resources. Factions change over time: Clans split up, leaders die or lose prestige, and individuals find common interests. Factionalism—the tendency for a community to split into ever smaller decision-making units—intensifies under times of stress.

FACTIONS FIGHTING FOR
RATTAN CONCESSION

At one conservation site in the Philippines, there were two factions vying for control over a rattan concession. The conservation effort had to negotiate with both of these factions. All the people involved were related, but a powerful, articulate man who was also the former head of the board of directors of the local partner organization headed one faction.

Patronage Relations

Relations of mutual dependency with built-in inequality (called "patron–client" relations by social scientists) are a fundamental component of societies. Local officials are often patrons, with clients who do their bidding in return for protection and favors. Patronage is the cause of much corruption in the world as people bypass formal and legal means to obtain access to resources and draw on patronage networks to achieve their aims.

PATRONAGE NETWORKS IN THE PHILIPPINES

At one site in the Philippines, a local official sponsored several young people for scholarships in return for support to build a road through their small village. This road was opposed by the sector of the community allied with the conservation initiative, and the resulting division of the community created problems for sound resource management.

CASE STUDY

DEBT AND DEPENDENCY IN THE RATTAN TRADE

Rattan harvesters in Palawan, the Philippines, go into debt to traders before they trek out to gather rattan. The money borrowed is used to pay for supplies for the trip. The debt is subtracted from the amount given for the rattan, often leaving little or nothing for the harvester. Debt is considered to be one of the key factors in intensification of resource use (Biodiversity Conservation Network and Institute of Environmental Science for Social Change 1997).

Another common type of clientage is the debtor–creditor relationship. The trader–supplier relationship is complex: Credit may or may not be offered by traders, and there may or may not be other services provided in the context of long-standing ties.

A key social relation is that between landlord or owner and renter or lessee, where the landlord or owner fixes a rent or a fee for use of land or other resources (animals, trees). In remote areas, where access to land is relatively open, better-off migrants may rent from poorer local people but be in a more powerful situation because they have much greater access to cash and to the political elite.

Fission

Clans, lineages, and other social structures break into smaller pieces, and some fragments move away from the larger group, often because of conflicts in access to resources or a desire to acquire new resources. A related trend is conversion to a new religion or sect. This means the leadership is in turmoil.

Migration

More assertive or talented people migrate to towns and cities where they are less constrained in their ambitions; migration also occurs because

LAND LEASING IN FIJI

Fijian *mataqalis* are landholding groups, controlling 83 percent of the land in Fiji. Some of this land is leased by Indo-Fijians (Fiji islanders of Indian descent) and other investors for periods of up to ninety-nine years. Although the *mataqalis* get rents, much of the benefit is controlled by chiefs or government agencies. The insecurity of tenure on the part of the lessee and lack of benefit to local villagers can result in resource mining.

of degradation of resources and lack of opportunity. This means that there may be few talented or skilled people around.

Conversely, an area can attract migrants, either because it has resources to exploit, and these may have been opened up by a new road, or because there are pressures outside the area that move people in (or both). Migrants are seen to be a threat both to local populations and to the ecosystem, as they may use more intensive technology and not know the natural systems. Yet determining who is or is not a "recent" migrant is not easy (Giles-Vernick 2001; Hardin 2000). And there is no guarantee that migrants are by nature more destructive than indigenous

RELIGIOUS SECTS SEPARATE COMMUNITY MEMBERS

One village at a conservation site in Solomon Islands converted to a millenarian religion. They bought a chainsaw to build a church and removed themselves from the conservation initiative. In western Kenya, some denominations are so small that they comprise only one household.

CASE STUDY

OUTMIGRATION DEPLETES SOCIAL CAPITAL

At a socioeconomic workshop, Fijian leaders remarked that young people leaving the village was one of their most serious social problems and one that made it hard to start conservation initiatives.

populations. Migrants can also bring important skills and opportunities to indigenous populations. There can be intermarriage and exchange of skills just as there can be conflict and sharp differentiation. Sometimes, migrants will get along in their new homes for extended periods of time until there is a land dispute or other issue that arises. The point is that assessing the role of migrants, and even determining who is a migrant, requires careful research (Giles-Vernick 2001; P. Peters 1996).

Differentiation

Some families are getting significantly richer than others by selling assets or products, through entrepreneurial activity, or by establishing contacts at higher levels; they are hiring labor and making capital investments. Other families are becoming impoverished and/or landless.

CASE STUDY

THE MIGRATION ISSUE IN THE UNITED STATES IS HIGHLY CONTENTIOUS

In 1999, the majority of members of Sierra Club in California voted for a proposition claiming that immigration was a major cause of environmental destruction. This vote created a serious division within the Club.

CASE STUDY

INTENSIFICATION LEADS TO DIFFERENTIATION

A new harvesting technology is introduced that only the better off can afford. A town-based family purchases this technology and puts the smaller harvesters out of business.

Even in very poor small-scale societies, differentiation takes place, and a new "class" is born. In Solomon Islands, access to education changes a person's status dramatically, even with the traditional leveling mechanisms, such as discouraging displays of wealth, gossip, and sorcery accusations. Ecotourism, which requires English-speaking guides, can accelerate the process (Russell and Stabile, in press).

Stratification

In the past, stratification was associated with the creation of a class of chiefs or other elite groups whose status was inherited. Today, stratification can come about with access to education or salaried positions. The status is "inherited" when investment is made to ensure that children get similar access to education. This means that the gap in status among families is widening.

CASE STUDY

GOVERNMENT JOBS LEAD TO A NEW CLASS OF PEOPLE

In Nigeria, access to a salaried position will mean automatically that one is a "patron" who can command respect. That person would get status and even be given a title in order to encourage him or her to invest in the village.

From these few examples, we can see that there are multiple social and political institutions and behaviors that conservation practitioners need to understand in order to be effective, not just ones associated with conservation or natural resource management. Many people have studied these dimensions in disciplines such as anthropology, political science, history, human geography, and political ecology (see "Human and Political Ecology" and "Institutions for Natural Resource Management" in the Resources section). As a practitioner, think about how to bring an understanding of this research on social and political institutions, behaviors, and trends to partners, particularly local partners. What social formations and changes are being observed in the area where you work that others have documented elsewhere? How can an understanding of institutional change help guide the conservation initiative?

7

Belief and Knowledge Systems

Chapter 2 introduced the topic of belief systems with respect to conservation. In this chapter, we probe a little deeper into the underlying values and patterns that govern motivation. Life goals affect motivation and hence behavior. Beliefs also affect behavior. One of the most important of these is the concept of the individual. Another important pattern is the transmission of norms. A third is the way that people are taught to interact with others. A worldview encompasses the ensemble of beliefs that shape motivations and incentives.

Shaping the Mind's Eye

What Is the Individual?

The concept of the individual is not a fixed concept. That is not to say that in every society people do not view themselves as individuals. They do. But how they differentiate themselves from others can diverge dramatically. While in European and North American culture it is positive and healthy to be seen as an individual with strong tastes and desires, these attitudes are not seen as positive in many cultures, particularly for women. This distaste of individualism is not just oppression of the masses—though it is used for oppressive purposes—but represents a deep-rooted desire for harmony in life and relationships.

In many societies, the individual is viewed within the context of key roles. The role and the individual are closely linked. The mix and balance of roles is important. When an individual dies, it is not just the person who dies but also the role of that person within the fabric of society. Consequently, funerals have such an important function as they seek to mend the hole in society's fabric by bringing people together.

As people move into the city, the role of the individual changes. Many people are forced to adopt dual roles: their city persona (the face they put on to the public) and their village persona. It is important for outsiders to understand the pressures faced by people who need to live in two or three worlds. Their psychological burden is immense, as is their creativity. People navigating between two cultures can become good *culture brokers*, for example, mediating between rural society, national-level actors, and external donors. Culture brokers are essential for the success of any activity involving interactions between different peoples or even between genders or statuses within the same culture.

In relation to conservation, it is important to know whether people see their actions as a result of individual decision making or as acting from a social role. Addressing the problems caused by certain people could differ depending on these different viewpoints. For example, is a person acting out of a desire for personal gain, or is the act a result of desire to fill a socially important goal? Is the person trying to manipulate the role for personal gain?

Take the case of a clan leader who accepts a logging contract. His justification is that the contract is in the best interests of the clan and that it is his mandate as leader. He may be hiding individual motivations behind a role. Conversely, he may be fearful and suspicious of loggers but afraid to show that fear because it would not fit with his role in society. Therefore, to dispel any notions that he is weak or fearful, he signs the contract.

Edwin Krumpe and Sam Ham from the University of Idaho have put together a slide show called "How Beliefs Can Be Used in Communication Programs to Affect Local Conservation Practices" (Krumpe and Ham, n.d.). They look at the role of environmental education, noting that it is effective when there are problem behaviors based on an information gap. Environmental education is not effective when there are malicious acts and acts motivated by revenge or greed. Krumpe and Ham have crafted a "belief-centered approach" to environmental education that shows where researchers can help both to design effective communication and to evaluate the effectiveness of the initiative.

Life Plans Are Universal

All over the world, people create life plans. A person's goals depend on his or her age, traditions, education, gender, and social status—and also chance. Some people have few goals and just live day to day, while others have elaborate life plans. Some strategies are successful, while others fail. Aspirations and goals change with contact and pressure from many sources. Studying aspirations and goals helps conservation planners understand what people value and the old and new ways people use to mobilize resources. It is an excellent idea to interview key informants (see chapter 12) in every major social category about their life goals.

There may be a basic sequence of goals within a given community: acquiring education and/or skills, gaining "experience," marrying, constructing a house, increasing status, educating children, and establishing a legacy for future generations. Attached to each goal are resources that need to be mobilized, such as cash, relationships, land, and house-building materials. Different generations are at different stages of their lives and thus have very different motivations and needs.

Following the Rules

How are people made to follow the rules of society? How are these rules transmitted? These are important questions because following rules is perhaps the most crucial aspect of a conservation initiative. Everyone may agree on the problem and what is to be done, and rules can be hammered out. But what if no one sticks to the rules?

The Role of Shame

Shame and embarrassment play a key role in keeping people in line. People do not want to be perceived as deviant or different, and they do not want to be cut off from social networks. Shaming can take place on the level of teasing or on the much more serious level of allegations of witchcraft. It can sometimes be the only way that less powerful people have of dealing with more powerful people. Shame is also used to suppress individuality and entrepreneurialism. Shaming is the way that sanctions work and as such is an essential part of the community's tool kit for conservation work. Shame can also negatively affect conservation, as when remote or marginalized communities feel ashamed of being "backward" and want to show that they are modern by signing logging or mining agreements.

Gossip as Social Control and Communication Mode

The importance of gossip and rumor in social groups cannot be overestimated. Practitioners with extensive field experience know that negative gossip can ruin any endeavor, whether or not the gossip is based in reality. Gossip reflects the fears and wishes of humans. Often gossip is founded on the desire to attribute blame. It is psychologically painful to acknowledge that we have little control over most things in life, so we wish to find a cause. Gossip also serves to control people who are difficult or subversive of the social order at both the high and the low end of the social scale.

Rules and Protocols

Many westerners are shocked at the formality of societies they may stereotype as being more "primitive." There are clear social rules, strict protocols, and even physical movements that are acceptable or objectionable. In short, social interaction is ordered. From greetings in the morning to the placement of the bed at night, there are acceptable and unacceptable ways of doing things. This ordering of life means that certain behaviors make people comfortable and that others make them uncomfortable.

Observe how local people react to tourists and other visitors. Do the outsiders seem loud, pushy, or sloppily dressed? Are they forever impatient, checking their watches or drumming their fingers on the table? Do they linger in doorways or walk over people's feet (tabu in the South Pacific and Africa)? Do they touch a person's head (a grave insult in many parts of Asia and the Pacific)? Are they handing out candies with their left hands (viewed as unclean in Muslim cultures)? Do they sit with their chins resting in their hands (an expression of deep depression and sorrow in central Africa)?

CASE STUDY

GOSSIP CAN DESTROY AN INITIATIVE

Many conservation initiatives find out too late about gossip concerning the organizations or individuals involved. Sometimes the gossip is wildly inaccurate, while at other times it can be painfully close to home. In one case, the gossip about a conservation initiative was that it was cover for the Central Intelligence Agency. In another case, the gossip centered on the fact that the organization purchased expensive cars and that personnel came from high social levels.

Learning appropriate social interaction may mean a transformation in one's own psychological makeup toward greater bodily discipline. For women from urban areas especially, this discipline can be psychologically painful because it may involve behaviors of respect toward men and restricted clothing. It may mean hiding many thoughts and feelings that might normally flow. No outsider working with local people can afford to neglect the rules of social conduct. A conservation initiative will depend on local people feeling comfortable with the outsiders involved. And discipline is always, in the end, a good thing.

Rites and Rituals

Going back to chapter 2 on human nature and biodiversity, consider the importance of rites and rituals to cooperation and institutional development. Rites and rituals are structured activities that can both indicate and change status relations and relations between humans and other species. For example, a marriage ceremony is a ritual that links two families or clans. An initiation rite can link an individual with a sacred totem, which is a spirit protector in the form of an animal. It can turn a boy into a man.

Rites and rituals can evoke powerful emotions of togetherness and "transcendency." When someone receives a certificate of successful training in a ceremony, he or she feels pride and ownership of the activity. If a ritual highlights diversity and stewardship, the emotions evoked will be channeled in that direction, while other rites and rituals (fraternity party initiations, royal weddings, or breaking ground at a new development site) can evoke division, status differences, and exploitation. Rites and rituals have been said to have a direct relation to ecology through the regulation of access to resources and timing of production and consumption in order to control overexploitation (Rappaport 1979).

Gender and Norms

Understanding beliefs about differences in genders is critical in working with local populations. Both women and men are constrained by beliefs about gender. Often we neglect the role of men and their constraints in terms of participation to focus on discrimination against women. Development and conservation projects have turned to women because they are less mobile, more tractable, and eager to learn. Yet often they have little clout, even after years of participation. So both men and women have to be involved and active in a learning partnership.

CASE STUDY

AND REMEMBER THAT BELIEFS AND NORMS ARE OFTEN CONTRADICTED

In a small isolated village in Cameroon, a woman we will call Alice lived happily with her "wife" over many years. She had a large house, a boat, and a cocoa plantation. She never wore a dress but always danced with the women. Alice had two children who prospered despite their mother's unusual behavior. As a result of her own hard work and her children's success, she became one of the richest members of the community. Yet in Cameroon people will tell you that homosexuality is strictly a European import.

Generational Dynamics

Fathers Work for Their Sons is the title of a book by Sara Berry (1985), the eminent historian of African economic history. It also expresses the state of many rural communities where less "educated" parents not only work for their children but also learn new norms from them. The parents are often not happy about this situation, but it seems beyond their control. This issue can lead to intergenerational tension that disrupts the flow of learning in a community. Generation also has profound implications for how people use land and resources, particularly as commodification proceeds with resulting changes in the social economy (Russell and Tchamou 2001).

Religion and Conservation

Faith-based conservation? Yes, it is growing, and not only as an agenda of the Republican Party. In many parts of the world, religious leaders are seeing the links between their beliefs and the need for conservation and better stewardship of the world's resources. An important element of religion is social cohesion, which means that people feel part of a larger system and so are motivated to act together. Religion also shapes norms of behavior through rules and practices (see "Spirituality, Ethics, and Values in Conservation" in the Resources section).

In chapter 2, we discussed how Christianity might have discouraged nature worship. The concept of "Christian stewardship" is attempting to reverse that course. In the remote Solomon Islands, many Christian groups have environmental programs, including an initiative of the United Church that buys timber harvested sustainably and sells it to European buyers. In the Democratic Republic of the Congo, the Baptist Church has created a program called "Peace, Justice and Stewardship of Nature," which is involved in several environmental activities. This program was created during a war period when the Congo had little contact with the outside world.

Hinduism and Buddhism have a long history of promoting environmental values, even as practices of Buddhists and Hindus do not always live up to the ideal. For example, the Hindu notion of *ahimsa* means "no harm to living beings." This includes not killing or eating animals. In Hinduism and Islam, the eating of bushmeat is frowned on. Sacred groves that are refugia for many species and that protect watersheds are still common in India, even as they sit in highly degraded landscapes. The temples in Hindu Bali are said to act as regulators for irrigation that have operated sustainably for millennia (Lansing 1991).

In general, however, many religions have been slow to incorporate environmental values. In part that is because they reflect and transmit mainstream social values. It may also be said that religions have been focused on social control or, more humanely, on the spiritual improvement of the individual and society and not on humans' relation to their material world. In fact, the material world is often portrayed as an illusion and other species as without souls. In human evolution, it was perhaps first more important that people not kill one another than that they not kill other species or destroy their habitat.

As environmental degradation proceeds, the mandate of religions may change. The material world, including other species and even the cosmos, become miracles as precious as human lives. The fate of humans is seen to be tied inextricably to the fate of the rest of the world. Environmental values become incorporated into mainstream values and practices of conservation as common as the practice of faith and charity (Kellert 1996). Conservation initiatives must build on these foundations in whatever culture and tradition they find themselves.

Our Knowledge about Knowledge Evolves

Knowledge about natural resources once was divided into two types: place specific, local, or indigenous and scientific. Now we know that indigenous knowledge involves elements of science, such as a theoretical framework, hypothesis testing, and experimentation. Scientific research is based on assumptions and "best practices" that are not always objectively verifiable. Scientific knowledge incorporates information from many different locales and does not necessarily have as its aim the improvement in the living conditions of people at specific locales. While indigenous knowledge is based on understanding natural systems at a specific locale, it also can incorporate concepts from other areas. Ethnobotanist Brent Berlin (1992; see also chapter 13) shows that botanical classification systems created by different ethnic groups bear strikingly similar characteristics, indicating that there are deep principles operating in our understanding of natural resources.

In many cultures, knowledge about natural resources is integrated with practices and beliefs about behavior. Soil fertility is degraded not just because of deforestation or poor agricultural practices but also because of disharmony in the village or the practice of sorcerers. Greed and selfishness are often seen to be causes of fertility loss or the disappearance of species—this is not at all unreasonable.

Yet there are gaps in local people's knowledge. Groups accustomed to abundance of a species may not realize that when species disappear, they are severely depleted or gone for good. For example, on Makira Island, Solomon Islands, people believed that a certain species of pigeon was "hiding somewhere" when in fact it had disappeared. They may not realize that the rates of use of a species or habitat are unsustainable. Or some people may realize but not have the ability or power to transmit this information to the wider community. Indigenous knowledge may become glorified, highly differentiated from other forms of knowledge, or promoted carelessly as a solution to all problems (Agrawal 1995).

Science and local knowledge have complementary roles to play. Scientific monitoring methods, such as transects, plots, calculation of catch per unit effort, and surveys, can provide data useful to resource users as well as scientists. With time and patience, scientists and local people can learn enough of each other's knowledge systems to be able to work collaboratively and share information (see chapter 15).

Knowledge Systems and Conservation

Particular kinds of knowledge and knowledge systems are germane to conservation research. The most obvious is knowledge of plants and animals—identification, location, use, scarcity, or abundance. The study of local knowledge of plants and animals, or ethnobiology, is taken up in chapter 13. Other important categories of knowledge include the following:

- Categories of social statuses and roles and how these have changed over time (see chapter 6)
- Technologies and ways to make a living (e.g., boat building, charcoal making, and rubber tapping)
- Histories, sagas, legends, and cosmologies (how the universe or world originated)
- Beliefs about the spirit world and how humans relate to spirits (Bennagan and Fernan 1996)
- Art, poetry, songs, and dances that represent important cultural beliefs or stories

Should conservation research concern itself with such "cultural" matters? Making a living from the land and resources requires more than extraction, processing, and selling. It is important to understand why people do things in a certain way. Answers may reside in the realm of materialism (e.g., people may cut a tree because they want to build a canoe or sell the timber for money), or they may reside in a spiritual realm (e.g., people extract the bark of a certain tree because it is used in a potion that protects against spirit poisoning). Artwork and poetry can represent ideas about nature.

Similarly, art, poetry, dance, and drama have been used successfully in conservation initiatives to compel interest. Acting out dramas about environmental problems has proved very effective in the South Pacific island of Vanuata with a group called the Wan Smolbag Theater troop.

We have touched on some aspects of belief and knowledge systems, including cultural values, that affect behavior, rules, norms, and the role of religion in conservation. The Resources section "Spirituality, Ethics, and Values in Conservation" lists some websites and other resources that are devoted to a greater understanding of these dimensions. In chapter 13, we talk about how ethnography can help researchers understand beliefs, values, and "worldviews." And remember that the "planners" of conservation projects are not without values, ethics, beliefs, and spirituality. As we discuss in chapters 8 and 9, reflecting on your own values and beliefs and those of your partners is a pathway to learning and growth.

8

Ethics, Targets, and Planning

Do the Right Thing

Ethics are moral principles that guide standards of behavior while doing social research. One common principle of research ethics is to safeguard the confidentiality of people interviewed. Another is to avoid abusing the power or authority of your position or interfering with matters that are not the business of your employment institution or job duty. Most large-scale organizations have published their institutional ethical guidelines—it is a good idea to read and understand them and to follow them in the field. Box 8.1 and the American Anthropological Association (1998a: 10) provide examples.

Research ethics often include commonsense behaviors, such as not to drink and drive. Ethical behavior also means being sensitive to the cultural rules of the local community: respect for elders, proper dress, and relations between men and women. For many conservation researchers, ethical principles stretch to include their own levels of consumption. These individuals minimize conspicuous consumption and do not drive around in brand-new luxury vehicles.

A few concrete ethical principles for field research include the following:

- Be clear about incentives and payment for participation in any initiative
- Take care about raising expectations about payoffs to any initiative
- Be humble and let local people be experts and guides
- Respect obligations and meeting times

**Box 8.1.   The Biodiversity Conservation Network's
Ethical Guidelines (Excerpt)**

Be aware of and respect the cultural, social, legal, religious, and economic
relationship of local communities to their land, marine, and natural
resource base.

Receive permission to enter and operate in the proposed project area from the
appropriate government agencies and local community groups, including
indigenous cultural communities, and observe standard natural area
conduct to minimize disturbance of the site.

Involve, provide information to, and learn from local people in all phases of
the project.

For example:

 Consult local people about special attributes and traditional uses for
  plant and animal resources.

 Employ local people for collecting, and use collecting as a basis for
  professional development through training.

 Collaborate with local people on the design and implementation of any
  management plan.

 Acknowledge the contribution of traditional knowledge to research
  efforts in reports and publications.

 Publish no traditional knowledge without informed consent from the
  people providing the information.

 Disseminate information at the national level regarding the value of local
  participation in project activities.

 Disseminate research plans, results, and specimens.

For example:

 Include host country scientists in research strategies and data analysis.

 Prepare appropriate presentations for local schools and universities
  regarding the specific work being done in the area.

 Make research results available to scientists and community
  organizations in English and an appropriate local language.

 Provide duplicates of specimens to local and national institutions, local
  education centers, and interpretive centers at reserves.

- Share personal information if you expect others to share with you (have on hand photos of family members)
- Dress appropriately
- Move into an appropriate time flow and be patient
- Do not waste people's time or call meetings at inappropriate times
- Respect anonymity

There are larger ethical issues in conservation and development work that relate to profound questions of the heart and matters of fairness and justice. Ethical questions have been raised about providing relief to refugees suspected of war crimes or aiding certain repressive regimes. Relief, development, and conservation efforts can sometimes inadvertently prolong or worsen conflicts. Another question addresses whether these initiatives really help local communities in the long term or whether they create conditions of dependency while generating career opportunities for outsiders. These issues should be widely reflected on among staff in every institution.

Accountability and the Social Impact of Conservation

No matter how remote or isolated, every community has social divisions. Old people, young people, men, and women have different status, knowledge, and tasks. Some people are leaders; others are followers. Some are role models; others are troublemakers. Even in a small village, there are different factions that fight for control over and access to resources. We discuss this aspect of social life in chapter 6. Learning the history of development efforts at a site and about different social sectors and factions is critical for working at the community level.

Decision making in indigenous societies typically involves all factions—if not actively, then at least to some degree. Yet top-down conservation initiatives may not allow this process to move at its own pace. Leadership structures change with new opportunities and challenges, often leaving less literate and more "traditional" people behind. Conflicts are common at conservation sites. Questions are raised with regard to practices, rights, and who qualifies as a "resident" or "user." These conflicts are often serious and can result in significant loss of livelihoods and/or even lives.

Given the serious nature of the challenges that face remote and rural populations, sensitivity is required. Many subsistence and cash-generating practices may be technically illegal. Very small increases (from an outsider's perspective) in resource flows can disrupt the status quo. This reality means that virtually any activity that brings cash or other resources into a community, or even looks like it might do so, is going to change the balance of power. Outsiders, no matter how well meaning, have a large impact.

Therefore, among staff implementing conservation initiatives, two central questions must be discussed:

1. How to help manage conflicts that may arise during various phases of the initiative
2. How to help develop a fair plan for the distribution of benefits

In order to begin this work, staff must answer the following:

- Who controls resources, in reality (de facto) and by law (de jure)?
- Who will benefit from the proposed initiative?

The Ethics of Choosing Sites and Partners

An initiative may be designed to work with a preselected population often identified through a rapid rural appraisal or a needs assessment (discussed in the next section; see also chapters 12 and 14). "Target groups" vary in size but usually are in close geographic proximity for ease of contact. All too often, the most remote groups' needs are unmet because it is deemed too difficult to get to them. This is unfortunate, as it leads to inequity in the initiative.

An initiative can choose to work with a group that has special needs or knowledge in relation to biodiversity, such as forest users or communities seen to have important knowledge of plants and animals. Other target groups can be entire populations of people around national parks, catchments, or watersheds.

Any conservation effort has to look at whether benefits and services are going directly to help those who are managing resources and not to the many layers of project and nongovernmental organization (NGO) management. Poor choices for target communities include the following:

- Very privileged communities (e.g., "the president's hometown")
- Those with serious internal conflicts (unless conflict management is the goal of the initiative)
- Those that have had numerous development efforts in the recent past, particularly ones that have not been successful or useful to the people

A community may approach your organization and show initiative, but before agreeing to work with them, you must delve into the motivations of the individuals speaking on behalf of the community and learn about subpopulations and factions in the community. It is also important to get a sense of the history of the community's relations with other initiatives and organizations (see chapter 9).

Taking the Pulse of the Community

Needs assessments are carried out at the level of the village. They describe the population according to indicators or specific characteristics that are identified with a certain type of need, such as improved food security, relocation, or income-generating activities. These identified needs guide planning. Too often, however, external projects do not bother to ask about needs, or because of their limited mandates, they fear delving into needs that they cannot meet.

Another form of needs assessment is a customer service survey. Customer service is a relatively new idea in development and conservation initiatives. This kind of research entails the donor and/or NGO canvassing potential beneficiaries about the kinds of services needed and ways to deliver services. This research can also be done during the life of an initiative. Focus groups and key informant interviews are used together with an institutional inventory (see chapter 12). The aim of the study is to see which groups and institutions are already providing services and how a new project can fit existing needs and institutions. Customer service research leads to customer service plans that incorporate users' ideas for how to deliver services (United States Agency for International Development, n.d.).

A customer service survey is a good way to get a handle on what people need and how they are best able to use services. Such a survey can be an eye-opener to donor-funded NGOs that do not have community-based constituency. They may be accustomed to being "in charge" of the development process. Customer service brings a focus on what local people value and how they can best use ideas, services, tools, and information. Contrast the traditional project and customer service approach in box 8.2.

Strategies, Not Projects

A long-term plan for a conservation initiative should emphasize strategies rather than activities. Keeping the primary goal of conservation in mind, there may be many pathways to achieving goals. Flexibility and choice give room to learn and adapt (Salafsky and Margoulis 1999). Some approaches will fail. New opportunities will emerge that must be seized while they are available. Strategies can proceed in a less-than-straightforward way toward the goal. Meeting perceived threats head-on may result in backlash, conflict, and damage to the initiative. Remember, for every beneficiary or winner, there are losers. Conservation is about some people not getting their way. Having a set of strategies requires understanding people and learning from them in a flexible, open way. It will also mean preparing for clashes with vested interests.

Box 8.2. Contrasting Project Approaches

Traditional	*Customer Service*
Projects are planned by outside staff and a few other "experts."	Investments of donors, NGOs, and other funders are prioritized and programmed in wide consultation process.
The donor is the key customer.	People in conservation areas are the key customers.
Project planners know what is needed.	Local people know what is needed.
Projects are best able to deliver services, tools, and information.	Local people decide what institutions and organizations are the best service deliverers.
Projects gather information for their own use.	Information is gathered for use by customers.
Projects have a fixed menu of services or tools.	Projects may expand or diversify with demand.

At the outset, the knowledge of outsiders is limited, and the appropriateness and timing of activities cannot realistically be determined. This statement goes against much of what we learn from traditional project design approaches, which encourage planners to create elaborate designs with rigid targets and preconceived measures of project success based largely on speculation or superficial research.

Yes, we know: You cannot get money if you do not submit elaborate and often prepackaged plans. But push your donors a little—challenge them to adopt the new approaches found in many private-sector organizations that encourage initiative and decentralization. You will discover allies on the inside of many hidebound institutions. If that does not work, try funding the initiative on small incremental budgets. Do not give in to the temptation to write it all out in a project plan in order to get the funds when in fact you really have done very little on-the-ground research. You may get the money but then be stuck with an unsound plan that you are contractually obligated to implement.

We observed that a significant proportion of conservation resources is put toward setting targets and developing indicators that will later be dropped as irrelevant or uncollectable because local conditions were unknown by outsiders planning the project. A great deal of energy is taken up gathering superficial information for donors and public relations (or, in the case of research institutions, articles for scientific journals) rather than carrying out the field research necessary to learn about local conditions and build partnerships. Send one or two trained local researchers into the field for several months. This approach may be less costly and disruptive and more effective than other ways of getting planning information. Drawing on the ideas and plans of existing institutions and partners also reduces wasteful planning processes.

Start with in-depth documentary research about a population and a site. The next step should be low-key participant observation within specific communities. After an appropriate time frame, a customer service inquiry can lead to the development of strategic partnerships (see chapter 9) that meet the needs of the communities as well as addressing pressures at a wider level.

If relations with local people come first, the initiative will not be sabotaged, and local knowledge will be in the forefront. Impact at the larger landscape level comes from engagement with specific communities within the context of larger institutional change and partnership with groups working at different scales. It is only by understanding social relations (social process, institutions, and groups) and knowing which institutions are effective that conservation strategies have a chance of being embedded in local social structures—in short, of being sustainable.

In chapter 15, we talk about the appreciative inquiry (AI) approach, which builds on the strengths of communities rather than centering around their problems. This approach gives a very different flavor to encounters between outsiders and locals. The outsiders are not there to provide answers and bring in prepackaged "projects" but to facilitate discussions and bring their scientific skills to provide information to the local decision makers.

CASE STUDY

HAVE YOU DONE YOUR HOMEWORK?

A major research institute planned a large-scale study of resource management systems in a francophone country. Well into the design phase of the research, which was to be very costly, the designers had not reviewed the existing literature because none of them could read French.

Phase in to community work in a series of integrated steps rather than trying to figure out from the beginning what might be appropriate or effective. Here are some simple steps to follow that are based in part on the AI approach:

Step 1: Institutional Inventory

- Inventory a wide range of local institutions
- Assess the social capital of local institutions through an approach such as AI (see chapter 14); discuss when institutions have been working at their best, what has been learned, and how to apply that knowledge
- Determine priorities and investment strategies: Where do local people invest their time and money?
- Clarify external organizations' resources and goals
- Learn local history, culture, and social structure, particularly in terms of previous projects and initiatives; study social, political, and economic ties from the site to external actors and investors

Step 2: Strategy Development

- Work with key subpopulations in the community to develop unique but complementary strategies based on their particular

CASE STUDY

CONTRASTING AI AND CONVENTIONAL APPROACHES

We tested two approaches to village meetings in three closely related villages in central Africa. In the first two meetings, we talked about problems or issues relating to conservation, while in the third we began the meeting with a discussion of strengths within the community. The third meeting revealed the presence of active community groups, which had already raised considerable funds to address community needs, while people in the first two villages had not mentioned these groups, and were focused on requesting assistance from us.

visions; discuss measures that can be taken to use an inclusive approach that will get everyone on board

- Explore partnerships between external and local organizations on a small scale to build trust and test approaches; discuss the nature of strategic partnerships
- Get and disseminate information on strategies and approaches that have been successful in other areas
- Put into place training and capacity-building systems for each group
- Discuss and refine strategies, based on new information, at regular meetings that coincide with community events

Step 3: Commitments and Follow-Up

- Develop commitments to work together over a specific time period and to raise funds or garner investment together to achieve goals
- Continue to work with subpopulations and key groups in specific projects that meet their needs
- Choose and train diverse community members to carry out community research and monitoring and provide feedback (for guidance on setting up community research programs, see Community Research Network Conference 1996, 1999)
- Pay attention to the information these people provide

  The outsiders need to verify that all sectors of the community are being consulted and provide an objective view of the impact of the actual activities on the biodiversity and the population, always working with local researchers. Outsiders can also attack wider problems of policies that create "perverse incentives" (see chapter 3) and lack of information about laws and policies. The outsiders will put in resources, but by no means all of them.

Step 4: Evaluation and Review

- Carry out collaborative review of activities in light of initial strategies and new information
- Make field visits, including cross-site visits, and write up reports or appropriate extension materials that are shared with all partners
- Bring in external information and analysis on resource use patterns, decisions, policy, investments, markets, and other factors that may not be available at the local level
- Share lessons with different audiences (for more information on communication and evaluation, see chapter 16)

Box 8.3. The Makira Conservation Initiative

The Makira initiative is a good example of how a long-term approach can bring about an effective conservation strategy. Makira Island is part of Solomon Islands, a nation in the western Pacific. This island was threatened by loggers and faced a population explosion. Conservation International (CI) and the Maruia Society of New Zealand formed a partnership with a local NGO, the Solomon Islands Development Trust, to work with communities in central Makira. This partnership received a grant from the Biodiversity Conservation Network, but the grant was enough for only three to four years of funding.

The partnership realized early on that at least ten years was necessary to build an institutional framework for conservation in Makira. This framework would be based on small enterprises to generate income, community-formed committees to manage funds, and resource planning with the clans as well as education about the real costs and benefits of logging. Decentralization of development and enterprise work from the capital in Honiara to Makira over several years has been a key element of the plan.

Understanding the dynamics of leadership has been particularly critical, and a CI researcher has been stationed on Makira to work with leaders and enterprise development. His knowledge of the local language and custom makes him an excellent culture broker. He is also a trained zoologist who can help the clans understand the impact of hunting on the bird population.

In short, planning conservation initiatives involves building relationships of trust and commitment. Research helps acquire a steady stream of information that aids decision making and documents successes and failures. Partnerships are expanded with continued assessment of community and partners' abilities and needs and the necessity to address wider threats.

Box 8.3 describes an initiative that allowed a positive process to develop between the local community and external conservation agencies.

The Carrot and the Stick

In early stages of the initiative, the local research team can assess likely incentives and sanctions. What will motivate people to conserve or manage resources differently? Will those who do the work get the rewards? Are conservation activities used to create new avenues of distribution or to reinforce old avenues? Will those who use the resources most intensively be getting benefits from the initiative? If not, how will they be motivated? Who is or will be monitoring use of the resources and is or will be capable of enforcing sanctions in the case of misuse?

In any initiative, there are always beneficiaries and those who do not benefit. Box 8.4 provides a simple typology of types of beneficiaries. There are often those who lose (or at least risk losing) time, cash, or other assets. Conservation project staff need to think through the consequences of benefit flows in relation to conflict and conservation impact.

Short-circuiting social research may result in negative consequences for communities and partners. Often, social researchers are called in after the fact to determine what went wrong—why local people did not buy in to the project or why the project did not have the expected impact. In terms of project planning, sustainability, and ethics, it is far better to use social research from the outset and throughout to

---

Box 8.4. Types of Benefit Distribution

Equal and Equitable

Benefits divided evenly and fairly (local people must define "fairness"); those who did the work are willing or able to share with others; everyone participated equally.

Equal and Inequitable

Benefits divided equally but not according to effort or participation; people who did not do work got benefits, and this is perceived as unfair.

Unequal and Equitable

Benefits divided fairly, but depending on effort or other socially acceptable criteria; those who did the work got most of the benefit, and that is okay.

Unequal and Inequitable

Benefits captured by elite or small groups who did not necessarily do the work; some groups or individuals were prevented from receiving benefits.

ensure that local partners and communities assume ownership for the project and are willing and able to maintain it.

In another project supported by the Biodiversity Conservation Network (BCN) in Solomon Islands, the project management did not follow through on social research that had been planned based on an excellent baseline study. After training local women to conduct low-key interviews concerning the impact of the project at the community level, the project did not provide any support for these women. The information they collected lay in a file and was not used by managers. That information included the fact that logging in one area was so severe that it was silting up the reef and causing soil fertility problems to the extent that the public health nurse was concerned about malnutrition. In addition, the women reported that people wanted to fish on the reef, in the conservation area, rather than in the deep sea, where the project had trained them to fish. When BCN staff was finally able to get to the site, this reef fishing was under way, and the entire conservation area was in jeopardy. The deep-sea fishing enterprise also looked to be unsustainable.

The Final Frontier: Your Hidden Assumptions

At all stages, take time to uncover assumptions about human behavior and resource management, causality, measurement, and development trajectories. Development trajectory means assumptions about the patterns, trends, and pathways in development. Do all societies tread the

---

Box 8.5.   Assumptions

Assumptions	Contrary Evidence	Strategy
Indigenous people are natural stewards of their environment.	Some indigenous people are carrying out illegal logging.	Document who is doing what, their situation, status, goals, and access to resources.
Migrants or leaseholders have a negative impact on biodiversity.	Some migrants carefully tend secondary forest areas and have a plan to reforest the watershed.	Consult with key informants and triangulate data. Correct assumptions and make recommendations.

Table 8.1. Paradigms in Conservation and Development Projects

Focus	Assumptions	Analyzes/Measures
Conservation	Biggest problem is loss of biodiversity regardless of cause: It is essential to preserve wild flora and fauna for future generations and genetic base.	Rates of change in key indicators; habitat size and quality Results = increased areas under protection; slowing rates of species and habitat loss
Community development/ empowerment	Biggest problem is lack of appropriate resource tenure/political power: Communities must manage resources, and government is not efficient or effective.	Institutions and social benefits; policies; indigenous knowledge and participation are goal and means Results = greater community control over resources
Economic growth/ poverty alleviation	Biggest problem is poverty: Without economic growth, neither communities nor governments will be able to conserve; conservation must bring economic benefits.	Economic benefits; returns to labor and investment; capacity to save and invest; increased well-being implicit Result = higher economic level for resource users
Paradigm shift	Biggest problem is social justice with respect to environmental issues: Local communities unite with workers and consumers against waste and perverse incentives.	Valuation systems and markets; energy and information flows; structural change; policies and political will Results = paradigm shift; changes in allocation of resources to promote investment in conservation

same path of ever increasing "progress?" How do people define progress or success?

Assumptions are underlying concepts and ideas about how the world works. They go so deep that they are not tested or even discussed. Most people in the world assume the existence and active presence of deities and/or spirits. Because they cannot test everything, scientists make assumptions on the basis of past research and proceed according to "generally accepted" practices. Assumptions can include ideas about the length of time needed for research or the training necessary to carry it out. For example, anthropologists (including both authors of this book) assume that long stays in a community are necessary for understanding important facets of social life. But we could be wrong. Perhaps short stays yield more "objective" data.

Are the assumptions of a conservation initiative grounded in experience, secondary information, or theoretical perspectives of conservation planners? If there are no stated assumptions, can you identify the hidden assumptions? What are other stakeholders' and partners' approaches to development? Do these approaches vary by gender and generation? Box 8.5 provides an example of assumptions that could misguide planning. The example shows that it can be a mistake to assume that a certain ethnic group is by definition the best steward of the local environment.

Table 8.1 presents common paradigms that feed assumptions about how to go about conservation work. Where does your initiative fit in this table?

9

Partnership

There are two basic approaches to the conservation of biodiversity. The most celebrated one has been the establishment of parks and protected areas: put a fence around the biodiversity, and keep people out or limit their access. In most parts of the world, the resources and political will to establish and maintain parks and protected areas are scant. Thus, many countries are experimenting with a second set of approaches to conservation: community and collaborative management. Partnership is at the heart of this endeavor. There are many different forms of community management, from total community control to temporary, experimental joint management efforts.

In addition, there is increasing pressure to make conservation pay for itself through the fostering of conservation enterprises, debt-for-nature swaps, or other such financial mechanisms. To facilitate this work, partnerships with organizations outside the conservation sphere is essential. If appropriately structured, these partnerships can set the stage for greater buy-in to conservation and thus aid the sustainability of conservation efforts.

This chapter discusses an appropriate philosophical approach to partnership that involves empowering local people and strengthening local institutions. Desirable qualities of partnerships are discussed, as are five primary goals. The experiences of the Biodiversity Conservation Network (BCN) with partnership challenges are followed by a discussion of partner selection criteria. A case study in Zambia shows how project staff used a participatory appraisal tool to explore a potential partnership alliance with community groups. The chapter ends on a brief note on how some conservation nonprofits productively work in alliance with corporations.

Conservation Is a Study in Partnership

Community management for biodiversity conservation dovetails nicely with the recent wave of partnership creation across private voluntary organizations (PVOs), nongovernmental organizations (NGOs), and communities. In 1995, the United States Agency for International Development (USAID) announced a New Partnerships Initiative (NPI) to foster collaboration and shared responsibility between government and civil society in newly emerging democracies. The NPI aims to create an enabling environment to empower NGOs, develop small businesses, and strengthen democratic local governance. Ideally, partnerships aim to strengthen local capacity so that local people and state officials can hold each other accountable for the development of the society, polity, and economy. Therefore, the NPI is a movement to strengthen grassroots capacity and the institutions that serve them.

As conservation and development practitioners, we must adopt a major shift in our approach to working in the field: from top down to collaborative. This involves learning how to be a good listener, using correct methods to elicit local knowledge, including partners early on in program planning, and building linkages between diverse institutions. In addition, a philosophical shift is needed that Jones (1993) articulates well:

> The people . . . have the unconditional right not only to *participate* in any struggle to improve their own condition but to *govern* the process. . . . Northerners should recognize that southerners, in addition to having the *right* to self-determination, are also better *qualified* to choose southern development priorities by virtue of their local knowledge and cultural understanding. . . . Northern PVOs must . . . commit themselves to learning about the history and culture of their partner's countries and communities. This helps the parties come to a shared understanding of the underlying causes of the problems they are addressing together. (7–9)

Participation is one thing, but to govern? This is indeed a major shift for conservation practitioners who tend to lag behind their development counterparts in seeing the value of community-owned initiatives. Many organizations currently struggle with these challenges, which are, in fact, learning opportunities. Chapter 15 discusses community-owned research methods that help conservation practitioners strengthen local institutions and guide local participation in conservation.

Often, employee mind-sets and the culture of conservation organizations are obstacles to building authentic partnerships. Many research and conservation groups are not accustomed to fully collaborating with local people. Staff might believe that their knowledge is superior to indigenous knowledge. The assumption is that they know the issues better, have the money, and can do the work faster. Staff may resist empowering local people if it threatens their jobs or if they have to share power and control. Managers may not be prepared to help staff transition into this type of program delivery. Often, groups fear financial transparency. Yet developing conservation programs grounded in the knowledge and ownership of local people is the only way to proceed.

The partnership approach encourages accountability among conservation professionals. Taking the time to study the history and culture of the human environment before plunging into activities seems daunting when one's desk is piled high with reports and demands from "command central." Yet it keeps the focus on the ultimate customer: the local resource users and managers. Hence, now organizations state that they want to become "learning institutions." In fact, conservation initiatives cannot succeed any other way. Authentic partnership demands multidirectional learning, information sharing, and trust.

Many institutions build strategies for partnership around needs assessments conducted in communities in a designated geographic area. In these cases, project managers first ask communities to identify their needs. This approach involves putting people first and is very different than staff designing projects and then looking for partners to bring on board. In this approach, the needs of the people guide programming, then the staff do a self-assessment to look at their own skills, motivations, goals, time frames, and budget constraints to assess what they have to offer as partners to local people.

Partnership is a two-way street. It is difficult but worthwhile to remember that while external institutions may hold the dollars to fund projects, local groups have the right and should be encouraged to screen such projects and take the time to assess whether all institutions can smoothly collaborate within a partnership. Although funding opportunities can be irresistible, there are stories in the field of local groups experiencing burnout and feelings of bitterness after formally or informally working with PVOs or other large-scale institutions.

In addition, while becoming acquainted and exploring possibilities for working together in the future, PVOs may not be transparent or even well informed about realistic chances for obtaining funding.

When funding falls through, local people may be deeply disappointed. All told, there is much evidence to convince local partners to regularly scrutinize external agencies and to review our motivations and capacity in as much detail as we review theirs.

Across many PVOs and NGOs, there is consensus on criteria for effective partnerships. Some of these are listed here:

1. Shared common vision and mission
2. Flexibility and two-way learning
3. Mutual trust
4. Time commitment
5. Clearly defined roles and responsibilities
6. Linkages with institutions, not individuals
7. Effective communication
8. Willingness to address difficult issues candidly and promptly
9. Respect for autonomy
10. Appropriate timing on contract formation

This is where the rubber meets the road: These criteria can make or break a partnership. For example, the issue of appropriate timing on contract formation can drive a wedge between groups trying to forge an alliance. Some managers prefer to let the alliance remain experimental for at least a year. This flexible approach gives participants time for roles and responsibilities to emerge based on experience, not conjecture. The time frame also gives people the opportunity to get to know each other, learn respective communication styles, and build trust. A flexible approach gives participants room to redesign the partnership or choose not to continue.

Many managers could not tolerate such an "extended time frame," which would translate for them as inefficiency and wasted time. Cultural context, personal management style, budget and donor pressures, and other factors unique to your program influence the timing on contract formation.

Set Goals in Partnership

This section presents five positive outcomes from partnership. These are lessons learned through PVOs, such as CARE and Save the Children, and NGOs, such as the World Wildlife Fund (WWF) and the Institute of Environmental Science for Social Change (ESSC) in the Philippines.

Mutual Capacity Building

Organizations devoted to conservation cannot work effectively without the help of partner institutions. The complex nature of biodiversity conservation demands different types of knowledge and an interdisciplinary approach to formulating solutions. Partnerships build a pool of resources and ideas that may be drawn on so that best practices may be identified, shared, and implemented. Linking with other institutions mutually enriches the experience of every PVO, NGO, research institute, and community-based organization (CBO) and is vital to the development of each type of institution. Save the Children USA (1996: 1) reports, "As the partnership evolves a synergistic effect is achieved. The level of program is enhanced and both organizations are strengthened institutionally through the sharing and learning process."

Local Knowledge Strengthens Project Planning

Sometimes staff at larger organizations, particularly those with technical qualifications, ask, "What do we get out of the partnership?" It is important to understand that local people have intimate knowledge of their environment, sociopolitical dynamics, cultural values, and local language (Harshbarger 1997). Local people also are knowledgeable of the needs of their households and communities. Practitioners increasingly recognize that given the appropriate tools, participants can translate these needs into solutions on their own terms. The failure of "experts" to tap these local sources of strength and knowledge has undermined the success and sustainability of many conservation and development initiatives. However, under conditions of authentic collaboration, the partnership approach facilitates local participation in program conceptualization and design as well as shared control of the development agenda and budget.

Local knowledge is especially germane to biodiversity conservation. For example, it is well known that people in forest communities have an intricate understanding of the plants and animals within their ecosystem. For years, anthropologists have been using ethnobotanical studies to engage local people to enumerate all known species in an environment and their numerous uses and market values. In Centro Maya's forestry project in Guatemala, staff relied on one local expert who was very knowledgeable about the rain forest to guide the design of their conservation project that involved harvesting from ancient trees for profit. They respectfully refer to this man as a "forest wizard" and would not want to do the work without him (Harshbarger 1998).

Sustainability

Strengthening local institutions through partnerships is a strategy to help ensure that people will be able to make productive and long-term investments, reduce risk, and increase the diversity of options open to them—all means toward creating the "enabling conditions" for conservation. In turn, this approach improves the track record of the external agency and therefore strengthens that institution's way of doing business. Examples of objectives for institutional strengthening that are linked to productive investment are the following:

- Support for problem-solving capacity in organizations that serve local people
- Understanding and building on local practices of savings and investment
- Encouraging dialogue across generations, genders, and localities
- Involving local traders, merchants, and other entrepreneurs in dialogue and planning about resource management
- Working with government to change laws, regulations, and situations that discourage productive investment (attacking "perverse incentives")
- Collaborating with more activist organizations that are pursuing reform. Sometimes this partnership has to be discreet in order to maintain presence in a country

Scaling Up

Nongovernmental organizations increase their scale by partnering in "umbrella organizations" to learn from each other and to address mutual concerns in dealing with governments, PVOs, donors, and communities. These umbrella organizations create linkages between the work of individual NGOs and these groups at regional and international levels. Working together is far more effective than working alone to further institutional and development agendas. Umbrella groups are especially important to build linkages with governments, to put pressure on officials for important policy creation and reform, and to increase levels of accountability between governments and NGOs.

CONGAD is an umbrella organization of 106 Senegalese NGOs. It has a board of directors and focuses on sharing lessons learned across NGOs. In particular, members share information on how to become registered, independent entities with tax-free status. CONGAD frequently acts as a liaison or mediator when local NGOs have problems with the government. In addition, at the regional level, an association of twenty-seven NGOs (CIONG) in Theis District meets regularly for training and to discuss issues of organizational development.

Linking partners with other partners and grassroots organizations is another way to increase program scale and impact. For example, Save the Children uses a "primary–secondary partner model" through which it provides intensive support to primary partners who replicate programs with secondary partners. Save the Children provides training but otherwise has limited contact with secondary partners. This model increases beneficiary coverage, increases collaboration between NGOs, and can increase in scale to where it is possible to engage government officials in policy discussions (Save the Children USA 1996). As stated earlier, one primary goal of partnership is to have an impact on government policy and increase state–society accountability.

Long-Term Cost Effectiveness

The cost-effectiveness of the partnership approach has been debated. Because of intense orientation and training periods, start-up costs are relatively high compared to direct delivery or other traditional institutional approaches. Ideally, in the long run, partnerships train local organizations to become self-sufficient: to develop their own human resources, programs, structures, and systems and to use their local networks to reach far into communities. Linking partners with

CASE STUDY

SCALING UP IN SOMALIA

In Somalia, NGAAD is an association of approximately thirty women's NGOs and groups who work together in partnership to acquire funding and to pool knowledge so that development can occur in the best way possible to meet the needs of communities. Under conditions of extremely scarce resources, these women reached the consensus that it is more effective to work together than to compete and fight over donor funds.

partners and partners with grassroots associations creates ripple effects that eventually increase program impact and cost-effectiveness.

Institutional development builds the skills and talent of local organizations so that they become financially self-sufficient to write proposals, engage in fund-raising and compete in every way for funds from external sources at all levels, obtain contributions from a local constituency, or start a business. This type of partnership is a good long-term investment (Alcorn and Royo 2000). Local beneficiaries are grateful for project training but continue to agonize over how their groups will support themselves over time. For this reason, cross-sectoral approaches designed to increase sustainability are being used to incorporate economic activities into health, education, or conservation programs.

Some feel that an emphasis on partnership takes too much time and effort. Indeed, we have seen some initiatives that are "networked" to death. They hold countless consultations and meetings, getting enthralled by the partnership rather than the work. Grounding partnership in the field and in concrete activities rather than at "headquarters" goes a long way toward solving this problem.

How to Be Strategic about Partnership

An institution's vision and mission statements should guide how that group works in partnership. The key to effective partnerships in conservation is to retain a focus on fighting threats to degradation and destruction of the biodiversity. The partnerships have to be strategically designed to engage institutions at different levels with each other so that they can build on each other's efforts. For example, a partnership of a local NGO with a legal rights organization can build case material for better policies on community management. Partnership of a scientific institute with local communities can lead to capacity building at the local level, long-term support for monitoring, and a higher quality of data resulting from local input.

Strategic partnerships need a strategy. At the policy level, strategy is best set by a wide consultation process, such as in a national biodiversity strategy action plan (NBSAP). These policy-level planning processes are now more open to the wider public, including NGOs, the private sector, and finance ministries. Fiji developed a multistage NBSAP combining social and biological research, policy review, and open meetings at several sites around the country. It became evident that, to succeed, the plan had to engage key members of the community, such as the Finance Ministry, the Office of Tourism, and the private sector in general. In addition, the needs and resource use patterns of marginal communities, such as poor Indians, city dwellers, and remote island dwellers, had to be considered (Fiji Government 2000).

At the level of a conservation project, partners articulate a strategy by agreeing on roles and responsibilities. It is a process that takes time. Often, in a new partnership, staff and participants are not sure how the project is going to unfold and should not be forced to rush into an agreement. As mentioned, some groups work together for a year or longer before they ever put anything down on paper. In order to build a solid partnership based on trust that supports institutional development for conservation, it is important to hold regular meetings, share information, and discuss one's comfort level with the new partnership in the presence of all partners.

Selecting appropriate partners involves identifying and understanding the target population, understanding the problems they face, and identifying common objectives, as discussed in the previous chapter. In general, there are two well-established criteria with regard to selecting partners. First, partners must have the same vision, or guiding principles. If potential partners have dissimilar visions, the partnership will be overly turbulent, resulting in a mismatch. However, a local group often will not have a formal vision statement. Key informant interviews can be used in order to grasp their approach, whether or not it is formally articulated (see chapter 12).

Second, external organizations should aim for partners with "ties to the grassroots." Often, organizations that best serve the client population are "owned" by the people being served. Therefore, where a choice exists, it is preferable to select an organization owned by the target population (Stuckey 1994). Equally important, the organization should be client focused and serve a real need. Make sure to verify claims. In some instances, groups will claim to act on the behalf of local people but in reality are not providing tangible benefits to their local partners. According to Stuckey (1994), other selection criteria may include the following:

- A track record or potential for long-term work
- Programmatic capacity and services
- Political affiliations
- Commitment to participatory development
- Willingness to share ideas and information
- Institutional and technical capabilities
- Financial viability
- Geographic focus

There may be a tendency to select partners that seem "strong" because of individuals who speak several languages, are computer literate, or are politically savvy. However, sometimes "weak" or fledgling organizations may be a better choice of partners in order to serve vulnerable groups more effectively (Stuckey 1994). Take time to consider the diverse universe of potential partners. Sometimes "strong" can be sexy but weak, and sometimes "weak" can be powerful. Think strategically for the long term.

Examine your biases with regard to selecting partners. Scientists want to work with scientifically oriented groups, and community development types seek NGOs that mirror Western models. Often, educated professionals overlook international mission groups and local church groups that have historical, reliable ties, and extensive networks with local communities, local associations, and community-based organizations. Partnering with religious organizations can be a powerful way to reach real people in a geographic area (see chapter 8). Youth groups and associations of entrepreneurs can also be effective partners.

Develop your own selection criteria to identify two or three potential partners. Then arrange for preliminary interviews with key informants from each institution or group to start the process of getting acquainted.

The BCN examples shown in box 9.1 illustrate that partnerships evolve and can include many different types of organizations. The BCN's projects were complex, including at the very least an enterprise component and three different kinds of monitoring: socioeconomic, biological, and enterprise. In many cases, the enterprise involved marketing to other countries or regions within the country. Few organizations could manage these activities alone. Some of the problems that emerged included the following:

- *Inadequate support for the local organization(s) from the international organization.* The international organization took the bulk of the funds and provided little in the way of training and capacity building for the local organizations. Local organizations can become "data slaves" as their information is siphoned off to others who write up reports and articles. People are becoming aware of these imbalances, even in very poor and remote regions, and are demanding more respect and decision-making power.
- *Communication problems.* Different organizations have different styles of communication, and there can also be status and cultural differences. For example, a local group may operate on consensus decision making, while an urban-based NGO has a hierarchical management structure that facilitates decisions by a few leaders.

Box 9.1.   The BCN's Experience in Partnership

The BCN's experience with partnership is richly documented in the 1997 BCN annual report and 1998 *Stories from the Field*. Here, the twenty BCN funded projects recount the successes and challenges after two to three years of project implementation. Partners include local communities, local and international NGOs, research institutions, government agencies, and universities. Over half the projects underwent "partnership predicaments" during 1997. Some events that illustrate the partnership process include the following:

An international organization handed over management of the project to a local NGO.

Different visions for ownership of an enterprise almost split up longtime partners.

A partnership among three local communities that manage a marine conservation area survived difficult management decisions and a hiatus in project leadership.

A partnership was forged between a local community and a drug development company, brokered by a regional university.

A government agency entered into a historic partnership with a major U.S. university and local communities for sustainable forest management.

Waiting for decisions from the consensus can be frustrating when there is a lot of pressure to get quick results, while pushing for quick decisions can damage fragile organizations and promote more aggressive persons as "decision makers."

- *Power differentials.* Status and access to political power can affect the partnership in other ways by channeling benefits to certain privileged groups (men or educated people) and leaving out others. The result may be that the most powerless folks do a lot of the work and get little or no compensation. Ultimately, this type of imbalance will sabotage the initiative (for further discussion of BCN partnerships, see Mahanty and Russell 2002; Margoluis et al. 2000).

Successful partnerships are often the result of culture brokers, as discussed in previous chapters. These are the folks who understand and can work in at least two of the institutional cultures involved. For example, these individuals may be able to live in a village because they are from the same area or spent many years there and also have the skills to work successfully in a local NGO. Someone may also be able to work in an international NGO and feel quite at home with local NGO partners. But there is a great deal of stress involved in being a broker. Traits that make one successful in village interactions—patience, respect, and willingness to listen—are not necessarily those that garner success in major institutions, where competition for resources and attention is fierce. In addition, projects or institutions that depend solely on one or two individuals are at risk.

What to Put in a Memorandum of Understanding between Partners

A memorandum of understanding (MOU) is a contract between two organizations that links them to specific actions according to a timetable and tied to specific resources. Often, the MOU is signed between a local and an international NGO or between a donor organization and an NGO. It is a good practice to write MOUs that are flexible yet detailed about what should be accomplished in the partnership. The most important component is the handling of financial resources. If the donor or NGO has auditing requirements, financial reporting formats, or restrictions on funding certain activities, these have to be spelled out in the MOU, as do any ethical guidelines that are binding to the organizations involved.

The MOU needs to discuss the responsibilities of both parties but should leave open time and space for renegotiation. In some cases, the partnership becomes difficult and has to be reviewed. If substantial funds are involved, it is unwise to proceed with financial transactions without an MOU. In one case in central Africa, an international NGO did not sign an MOU with a national group but proceeded to carry out several joint activities. When the partnership broke apart, there was no agreement about how it was supposed to have worked, and a great deal of confusion ensued. On the other hand, an MOU is not a panacea to resolve partnership problems nor should it be implemented too quickly.

A Partnership Appraisal Can Clarify Expectations

A partnership appraisal is a process where potential partners get to know each other to assess the strength of their match. The time line presented in table 9.1 later in this chapter is one of the participatory methods used in the participatory rural appraisal (see chapter 15). The partnership appraisal is a learning process where tools are guides that can be adapted to match the literacy levels of the group, adjusted to fit cultural conditions or to fit group suggestions on a case-by-case basis (Harshbarger 1996a, 1996b).

In the partnership appraisal, participatory methods allow potential local partners to stand in front and take charge of the field exercises.

While project staff facilitate, the participatory approach creates conditions for joint exploration based on multidirectional learning, information exchange, and shared leadership. As potential local partners take charge laying the groundwork for future projects through these exercises, they gain ownership of the initiative that is to come. Community ownership is critical to the sustainability of the initiative beyond the exit of the external organizations including monitoring, evaluation, and self-financing.

Before you choose a participatory approach, make sure that your work meets the criteria discussed in chapter 15. If goals of extensive time commitment and community empowerment are not present, partnership appraisals can be done instead through interviews, focus groups, and roundtable discussions with potential partners. And keep in mind that appraisals can raise issues but cannot in themselves resolve deep power differentials.

A Partnership Appraisal Using Participatory Methods

In this context, a historical time line is a chart that depicts a potential partner institution's history. In a group, participants craft historical time lines to illustrate the story of how their institution was formed and to pinpoint important events. Denoted events help staff understand the unfolding of problems or successes in particular areas, see how the organization articulates with the community and other organizations, or observe the evolution of a need over time.

These qualitative data help staff appraise a potential partnership with that organization, that is, how well they might collaborate to serve the community. In addition, time line data may also determine how the proposed project may or may not fit in with the local sociopolitical context or ecological environment. Without raising too many expectations, the exercise sets a precedent for two-way learning within the partnership. It can be quite revealing to compare historical time lines between institutions within a community or by gender within a group because they reveal differences in the perceptions of the importance of various events.

CARE International–Zambia (CI–Zambia) conducted a participatory partnership appraisal in Kalulushi, a town in the Copperbelt region, and facilitated several exercises with potential partners for a proposed water project. During one exercise, the men and women of the Resident's Development Committee (RDC) in Chibote Compound in Kalulushi created two time lines. These time lines are shown in table 9.1 (Harshbarger 1996a).

Table 9.1.   Residents' Development Committee (RDC) Historical Time Lines

Date	Event
Men	
1974	Kitwe council start to upgrade the settlement
	Settlement handed to the council
1984	Piped water cut by Kitwe Council
1992	RDC formed
	RDC starts working on roads
	Digging of wells and clearing of garbage
1994	RDC starts working on proposed market site
1996	CARE Zambia visits settlement
Women	
1978	Piped water brought to the settlement
1980	Piped water destroyed
1991	Worker trained in settlement development
	RDC repair roads
1992	RDC formed
	Cleared settlement
	Repaired toilets in the settlement
	Three workshops held
1994–95	RDC visits Nkwazi and race course settlement in Kitwe
1995	Council buys tools for the settlement
	Marketplace cleared
1996	New pit latrines constructed
	Visit by PUSH engineer
	Agreement to construct a market is reached
	Visit by CARE Zambia

Source: "Guidelines for Partnership Appraisal and Formation: The CARE-International Zambia Model," by Camilla Harshbarger, 8.23.96. Courtesy of CARE®.

The time lines provide an important historical context that all potential partners need to know about. The Chibote Compound already had a water project in the past, and that water project failed. What can we learn from that experience? Piped water had a very short life span in the community, and it was "destroyed" in 1980 because of vandalism. This finding can guide CI–Zambia to do as much as possible to ensure that the entire community has ownership of the next water project so that, instead of being vandalized, it will be protected and maintained. In addition, staff will inquire about the RDC's relationship with Kitwe Council, where the "piped water was cut." Was the water cut off for political or financial reasons? Was there a drought?

The time lines show that the RDC is a fairly new organization, formed in 1992. During the presentation of the time lines, CI–Zambia queried the group as to the type of training they received in workshops in 1992. It is hoped that this information can be used to indicate a starting point for possible training and capacity building if the proposed project takes off. The RDC's latest project (1995) is the clearing of a market site. This shows that the group is relatively organized and has initiated at least one development project. Note that the women's time line is more detailed than the men's. Why? Are women more detail oriented? Are RDC women more active than RDC men, or do they dominate the committee?

Answers to these and other questions provide an institutional profile of the RDC and their relationships with other institutions and the community and outline the history of the water project in Chibote. The time line is an effective learning tool to cue partners on what kinds of questions to ask each other and how to assess a good match for partnership (Harshbarger 1996b).

Is It Wise to "Create" Groups?

There are times when community groups are mobilized so that they can become partners in a conservation initiative. Even vulnerable or informal groups have networks that can be mobilized into active groups. Although mobilizing an association or group requires a substantial investment of time and resources, the investment can pay off if the following occur:

- There is broad agreement among different sectors of the community.
- The initiative is founded on local knowledge.
- The grassroots approach enables partners and the community to monitor and maintain the initiative.

Institutions have to start somewhere. Self-initiated conservation institutions, such as land trusts and pressure groups for the preservation of certain habitats, are quite successful in the West. What it takes is people having a stake in the outcome and having the means to organize. This is not as simple as it sounds in many countries. In the West, many people involved in local conservation efforts are landowners and thus have a long-term stake in what happens to their land, watersheds, coastal zones, and other areas they enjoy. Other stakeholders in local conservation are nature clubs, bird-watchers, recreational users, hunters, and fishing enthusiasts. They have the time and the resources to be involved in these activities.

In many countries in the developing world, local people do not have clear title to land, or, if they do, the land may be managed among many families who do not necessarily agree on use and development. (This is not to say that secure property rights lead to a conservation ethic, as has been claimed by some theorists. The structure of a local and global economy can be as important as the nature of property rights in determining conservation "ethics"; see "Spirituality, Ethics, and Values in Conservation" in the Resources section.)

The state or large landholders/concession holders may have the power to control use of the land and its resources. People in remote or marginalized communities may have very little clout in political decision making. There can be serious repercussions if powerless people try to subvert development attempts (e.g., the Ngoni in oil-rich areas of Nigeria and rubber tappers in Brazil).

Mobilization of local groups has to done by local people themselves or with the help of outsiders who have considerable long-term experience and trust. Of course, anyone who has funds or even looks like he or she may have funds in the future can mobilize some people: But what kind of people will be mobilized, and how sustainable will their efforts be?

The most successful "mobilization" by external partners thus builds on existing institutions and engages people to take action on things that matter to them. In the vast majority of cases, this will mean that there is a disconnect between what external partners want and what local people want—and we should not forget that local people are not at all uniform in their needs and goals. Conservationists may fear that this rapprochement means diluting the conservation message. In fact, it is an opportunity to learn what is important to people. Without a deep knowledge of what is important to people, conservation remains an external agenda. As an external agenda, it will encounter resistance, even sabotage, over the long term.

Knowing what is important does not mean that conservation initiatives are obliged to act on each need. People may want chainsaws, but giving them chainsaws is not necessary. Respecting why they want to have chainsaws is necessary. Local people may express needs that are conservation related but couched in language not familiar to conservationists. For example, food security problems may be the result of loss of traditional food crop varieties, loss of forest cover, soil fertility degradation, or overfishing—all conservation concerns. Economic insecurity can be due to loss of traditional skills tied to the use of particular resources that have become scarce or off limits. And concerns about tenure can mean that there is a de facto "open access" situation—no one is really controlling access to the resource, so it is being overexploited. This situation represents another key conservation issue.

If groups are disempowered, the mobilization will almost certainly have to address that situation first. For example, a conservation initiative working with indigenous groups in Palawan Island, the Philippines, had to first help the groups obtain Certificates of Ancestral Domain Claim in order to ensure that they had more secure rights to their territories. Without these rights, they could not launch rattan enterprises promoted by the conservation initiative.

A final word on creating partner organizations. Do so carefully, as it can become a self-fulfilling prophecy: If you look hard enough you will find the program "need" within the community. Sometimes funding opportunities and the desire to show quick "results" rather than community needs or preferences drive group formation. This approach can raise questions about equity and sustainability. The group may not be grounded in local institutions and so may not be effective at achieving long-term conservation goals. It may include the most vocal but not the most respected community members.

New Horizons in Private-Sector Partnerships

Conservation groups are increasingly developing partnerships with corporations. The Forest Stewardship Council in Mexico is partnering with companies and foresters around the world to agree on and implement one set of standards for forest conservation and management. Harvested lumber is certified as having met standards where wood is not taken from old-growth forests and endangered areas and participating groups use sustainable forest management practices. Home Depot and Lowe's—the top two home improvement retailers in the United States—will now buy only from well-managed forests. The Forest Stewardship Council (FSC) in the United States partners with the WWF, Greenpeace, and others. These strategic partnerships are glob-· ally important and are on the rise. As the FSC's former director Hank Cauley says, there is "going to be a domino effect" (*Atlanta Journal-Constitution* 2000).

It is worthwhile considering the possibility of building corporate partnerships and inviting corporate board members as partners in local initiatives. Increasing numbers of corporations are looking for ways to give back to local and global communities. Effective long-term conservation strategies include key players at the micro- and macro-levels, and building productive alliances with corporate players is one approach.

Local private-sector actors can be tapped as well. The director of the largest agro-industrial firm in the Congo, after being asked whether he wished to participate in an advisory group for an environmental program, said he would be pleased to do so. He remarked, "No one ever asked before if we were interested in environmental issues." Logging companies are even teaming up with conservation organizations to stem unsustainable hunting (on the partnership of Compagnie Internationale du Bois and the Wildlife Conservation Society in the Republic of Congo, see Central Africa Regional Program on the Environment 2001).

But, as in any partnership, care must be taken to anchor the corporate partnership in reality. The participation of a company or industry may stem from genuine concern (e.g., the tourism industry concerned about degradation), consumer pressure (e.g., timber certification), the threat of boycotts, the personal interest of owners or managers, or merely public relations. Do not make assumptions: carry out the partnership appraisal and take time to establish trust and mutual understanding.

10

Organizing the Research

This chapter discusses several questions common to almost all research projects. We have learned that, in order to organize the research, you have to organize your thinking first. This involves checking the validity of assumptions that guide thinking, mulling over research questions, and discussing these questions with local partners, key informants, and colleagues. The literature review also clarifies thinking. Building models and generating hypotheses gets the research agenda up and running. Researchers in conservation have to explore and choose various scales and units of analysis and decide on the appropriate mix of qualitative and quantitative approaches. Sampling procedures are selected on the basis of an understanding of the population under study, time constraints, available information, geography, the weather, and many other criteria. The chapter concludes with a discussion of how to organize your research team and create conditions for successful collaboration in the field. (See box 10.1 for definitions of some terms used in this chapter.)

Thinking It Through

Before starting up field research, review the pros and cons of different approaches, the methods involved, and types of analyses that will be useful to inform conservation planning. Assess the resources, funds, trained personnel, consultants, and time allotted for research over the life of the initiative. How much time is available for conducting preliminary interviews, locating local ethnographers, pilot testing surveys, and setting up monitoring activities? How much time will be devoted to creating conditions where partners can collaborate to the

---

Box 10.1. Some Terms Used in This Chapter

Enumerator—a person collecting data in survey research
Database—a data storage record on paper or in a computer
Hypothesis—an informed guess about causes and relationships that is
  typically posed as a "null hypothesis" that must be falsified
Unit of analysis—the items, individuals, or groups being measured for a
  specific study

---

fullest extent possible? Does the work require extended stays for government, research, and nongovernmental organization (NGO) personnel or consultants in very rugged areas? How has the community and NGO staff been prepared for this work?

By consulting key informants, find out whether the conservation activities and research approaches proposed are congruent with local values. Do not get information solely from local staff who may represent certain groups or the educated elite—verify with a wide range of local people. Will certain types of community participation endanger conservation staff or local people? Is community participation ethically justified? Are you asking local people to contribute a lot of time and information with very little hope of benefit or perhaps taking the other extreme of minimizing local participation in order to work "more efficiently"?

Think in advance about different ways of viewing the community and changes that are likely to come about in the implementation of conservation activities. Fit methods and analysis to the approach of the initiative. For example, if the initiative is supposed to build community capacity, train and position community members on the field survey and design teams.

How flexible are your methods? Are there groups or partners in the community that can monitor and maintain the technology once the outsiders exit? If not, think about adopting more appropriate technology.

Morass of Models

Many conservation practitioners adopt the approach of building models for planning research as well as action. These models could be formal or relatively informal. An example of formal modeling would be a model that tested the relationship between deforestation and population density (see, e.g., Burns et al. 1994). It would be necessary to have or to collect good-quality data about forest cover over time as well as good demographic data. But explanatory factors might also include soil quality, urban sprawl, economic activities in the region, and historical circumstance. Rates of deforestation could be associated directly with population densities or indirectly through the fact that agriculture is more productive in one area and hence will support higher population densities.

A formal model takes time to develop and test. If the parameters are wrong or key parameters are missing, it may be completely off track. In the case of ecology or conservation biology, models of the viability of species populations as well as many other parameters are tested and refined. In the context of human ecology, a controversial example of formal modeling involves models of "optimal foraging" systems in relation to human hunters and gatherers (see, e.g., Kaplan and Hill 1992). Optimal foraging is controversial because some human ecologists feel that these models have little explanatory value; they model what people do and not what some genetic survival algorithm drives them to do (Vayda 1995a, 1995b).

Flow diagrams and decision-tree models may also be developed to outline steps and processes such as in determining the "adoptability" of agroforestry systems (Franzel et al. 2001; for a method of doing so, see Gladwin 1989). Other types of models that attempt to explain decision making of multiple stakeholders in conservation and natural resource management include negotiation support models (van Noordwijk et al. 2001) and agent-based models (Galvin 2001).

Unless the research is drawing on tested models or explicitly sets out to design and test models, it may prove difficult and ultimately unrewarding to employ data-intensive formal models in areas where demographic (and other) data are poor and/or hard to come by. Informal modeling, however, can help researchers outline the elements of the systems involved and make some connections between elements in order to plan research and action. An informal model could be as simple as a map that estimates where pressures on certain species and habitats come from. It could be an institutional diagram that describes how different institutions or groups might contribute to problems and solutions at a conservation site. (Venn diagrams, described in chapter 15, are useful for this type of model.) Another informal model is related to a specific project or initiative: what it can accomplish over a given time frame under specified circumstances.

Targets might be set on the basis of a model of problems and possible solutions. For example, a project may have funds to help communities with ecotourism. The model developed collaboratively by project staff and communities shows that to have a conservation effect, the ecotourism has to reverse the degradation of a marine area. To attract people in the community, it has to compete successfully with coral reef fishing, and to be economically viable, it has to capture a certain market share of the region's tourism. These objectives will then be the subject of project activities and monitoring (see chapter 16; for guidance on informal models, see Salafsky and Margoluis 1998).

The Question Comes First

Models, observations, secondary data, and other sources are used to generate one or more research questions. We develop various hypotheses to guide us as we explore and answer the research questions, and we use field instruments in the form of interviews, surveys, or participatory field exercises to test these hypotheses. Data analysis and outcomes of hypothesis testing provide powerful explanations that give us options on how to handle the problem under study and to plan programs.

Deciding on research questions sounds easy, but it is actually a complicated process that requires much discussion as well as knowledge and understanding of the project area and the people who live there. That is why we encourage collaboration with key informants and partnerships with local institutions that have knowledgeable staff. Sometimes researchers use inappropriate field methods because they are not completely clear on the questions they are asking and on the data they need to answer those questions.

Along with scale, social context, budget, time frame, and other factors, the type of research question will determine what type of field method to use: How have forest users organized themselves? What are the ways that forest users conserve natural resources? Why do they choose these methods? These are examples of basic questions asked at the start of a project to educate researchers. They may be effectively answered with qualitative data acquired through key informant and other types of interviews (see chapter 12).

To what extent do income levels affect the conservation practices of forest users? Formal surveys and the analysis of quantitative data can help answer such a question (see chapter 14). The data will be used to test a hypothesis, such as "Income has no effect on conservation practices." If the hypothesis is validated, data from interviews would reveal that, in the target community, income level or household wealth is not correlated with conservation practice.

The data may reveal, however, a correlation between income level and certain kinds of conservation practice, in which case the hypothesis is invalidated. Further study is needed to show why such a correlation might exist. It could be the result of related variables, such as location, size of household, or gender of household head.

What are the needs of the populations found along the perimeter of a national park? How are they using biological resources? In this case, if the perimeter includes an extensive area, group interviews or rapid rural appraisals (RRAs) would provide information for a needs assessment or to start up a project. If the perimeter is not a huge area, a baseline or customer survey (see chapter 14) can be used to systematically collect information and capture change over time. Even if the area is large, you can do a survey if resources permit.

How can this community become empowered to build, finance, and maintain its own water supply? The appropriate choice of method would be a participatory rural appraisal (PRA) or appreciative inquiry (AI)— action research that is used to empower communities (see chapter 15).

How do the people of a certain clan use and classify plants and animals? This kind of question necessitates ethnographic methods: ethnobiology (see chapter 13), key informant interviews, and oral histories (see chapter 12).

Other chapters explain in more detail when to use qualitative data collection methods (interviews, RRAs, or PRAs), quantitative methods (surveys), and ethnographic field methods or a combination of approaches. The point here is that it is critically important to formulate clear and meaningful research questions and hypotheses so that you can make intelligent choices about methods (for a more comprehensive presentation on this topic, see Bernard 2001 and "Research Guides" in the Resources section).

Read Up!

Government reports, student theses, project reports, and other "gray literature" documentation are some of the most important sources of data on which to build models and formulate research questions. A true literature review means reading everything you can get your hands on, from published books to theses written by local or expatriate students. Read and learn from the reports produced by other organizations that previously worked at the site. Read donor reports. Analyze the literature with regard to gaps—see whether the information is out of date; overlooks political, cultural, or economic dimensions; or neglects major categories of actors. Your research may help fill a gap.

Use the lessons learned from the initiative to inform current planning (see chapter 8) to define or refine your research question. Examine and consider updating or expanding databases created by other institutions. Review their survey instruments and decide how to do it better. Acquire government census reports and study the data. Visit government ministries in the capital city to build networks and acquire maps of the conservation site. Study demographic and health survey reports. Study what is known about the community, the site, and similar communities and sites. Learn about the area from a regional perspective. Might there be an opportunity to work on a regional basis with cross-border programming?

If time permits, you may wish to find someone who can do the following:

- Archival research to analyze government or private archives, such as colonial records of timber concessions, private correspondence, and museum records, in order to get a picture of the structure of resource allocation and control. Who got timber concessions? How were they managed? What were the profits? How were concessions subsidized? What were attitudes about local people as workers, as resource users, or as impediments to progress?
- Records analysis to review, for example, business records to understand trends in profits and losses: salary levels, unusual losses or gains, likelihood of underreporting, and taxation levels. Records can be used for other data, such as censuses, registration records, and litigation records. They are useful if supplemented with interpretive information: Why were businesses losing money on paper? Why were disputes increasing? Were some being handled out of formal channels?
- Text analysis to search for key words and phrases that indicate themes and patterns in texts, such as oral histories, field notes, and written documents. Computer programs are available for text analysis.

Who and Where? Issues of Scale and Research Units

Many conservation initiatives start at a very large scale and then try to work down to the community level. Others start at the site level or work in one small area and never move to a wider scale. In this section, we show how more accurate and useful information can be obtained by working both ends of the scale: at the level of human territory and boundaries and at the "landscape"/regional level.

Global Scale

This scale addresses the impact of humans on nature, global ecosystem functions, and climate: global climate change, the spread and impact of synthetic hormones, desertification, and changes in weather patterns. Social research questions center on understanding large-scale patterns of resource use and institutions that govern resource use at large scales (states, treaties, conventions, corporations, and markets). But the local level is also important in understanding global trends and actions. Researching local action on logging, dams, pipelines, waste disposal, chemical use, or choice of technology is important for understanding global implications not just in the concrete sense of mitigating destruction but also in building coalitions and virtual communities that cross neighborhoods, regions, and even continents. Economic globalization and large-scale development affect local as well as global ecosystems.

Ecoregion Scale

The concept of the ecoregion is promoted by some conservation organizations to illustrate how conservation planning needs to take into account patterns of wildlife migration, key areas of biological importance, ranges of top predators, and other biological factors. The World Wildlife Fund defines ecoregions as "relatively large units of land or water containing a distinct assemblage of natural communities and species, with boundaries that approximate the original extent of natural communities prior to major land-use change." An ecoregion can cut across national boundaries. Examples include the East African montane forests and the East Cordillera Real montane forests. Social research questions focus on broad demographic and economic trends or on specific practices that represent regional threats (e.g., unsustainable logging, ranching, hunting, or pollution). Community-based conservation, policy reform, protected areas, and changes in practices might be part of a strategy for regional conservation and hence subjects of research. Generally, the territories of specific human populations are much smaller than regions or ecoregions (see the following discussion), so research must also seek to understand social networks, larger political and social structures, coalitions, and communications channels. Some conservation groups, such as Conservation International, use the "hot spot" classification to bring attention to regions that have significant biodiversity that is highly endangered (www.conservation.org). Since its inception, this concept has been criticized and refined by better tools and data (Dinerstein et al. 1995; Olson and Dinerstein 1997;

The Nature Conservancy 1996, 1998; for a discussion of regional analysis that is more informed by social science, see chapter 11).

Landscape Scale

This scale typically includes protected or endangered areas and territory or "buffer zones" around those areas. An example is a wildlife management area that might include several ethnic groups or clans (see the Wildlife Conservation Society's Living Landscapes at www.livinglandscapes.org). As in the ecoregion, social research centers on understanding wider social networks, how alliances could be created and maintained, and other social and political structures affecting the area as well as the particular dynamics of constituent groups.

Habitat Scale

Habitats are areas that contain and support specific species or mixes of species. Species such as the spotted owl or mountain gorilla are a key focus of conservation. Local people can be motivated to conserve species that have value to them. But what about species that they do not value or even recognize, that destroy their animals or crops, or that may be exploited for economic gain? Research will focus on populations in or adjacent to habitats of the species, on populations that present threats to the species (such as hunters or loggers), and on how to build advocacy groups composed of both internal and external stakeholders. Local populations can be motivated to conserve habitats that are key to their subsistence, livelihoods, or cultural pride—if they are able to devise and enact effective rules and sanctions against overexploitation. Habitat and ecosystem boundaries, however, often do not correspond with social boundaries. Many groups may use a marsh, grassland, or forest. Thus, research might identify, study, and work with owners, user groups, and other stakeholders in the habitat.

Watershed Scale

The watershed is the land drained by a water source. People cannot live without water. Water has brought together many groups across kinship, village, clan, and even national boundaries. Social research in the past has focused on water user groups, including irrigation management groups, groups managing fishing grounds, river users, water source protection groups, and watershed catchment groups. Some conservation theorists have argued that the watershed is a natural unit of conservation with respect to communities, while others see that human groups often use several watersheds or part of a watershed and there is no necessary relation between the watershed and a human group's territory. Microwatersheds, or catchments, can be differentiated from larger watersheds that drain rivers or tributaries. The former may include one or a few settlements, while the latter may comprise much more complex population dynamics. For further information on the watershed as unit of analysis, see Rhoades 1998, Lal 2000.

Common-Property Resource Scale

This includes lakes, seas, rivers, fisheries, air, water tables, and government or community forests. Both social and biological scientists who wish to understand how these resources can best be managed do research at this level or scale. Like the watershed, resources at this scale may or may not be congruent with a self-defined population. Identifying subpopulations and their roles, needs, and interests is a critical step in understanding management.

Ecoregions, landscapes, and even watersheds may have little congruence with human territories and sociopolitical boundaries, such as kin groups, villages, townships, and counties (see the following discussion). This is particularly true since political boundaries in many countries were drawn without consideration of indigenous social boundaries, which may have been more closely related to ecological boundaries, such as watersheds or biomes.

The different scales and the incompatibility of units of analysis constitute the crux of many of the difficulties in reconciling conservation planning with human-scale units. For example, most policymaking and project planning concerning biodiversity conservation and resource management occurs at the national level, while conservation planners see benefit in crossing national boundaries to promote the integrity of habitats of wide-ranging species. Villages or family-level social units typically manage territories at a smaller scale than the watershed, but it makes little sense ecologically to concentrate on saving forest downstream while it is being clear-cut upstream.

Social Research Needs Social Units

The unit of analysis is the level of the population you are studying. For example, if you interview 100 female fodder collectors about all sorts of variables that describe their livelihoods and families, then the unit of analysis is the individual. If you interview 100 female fodder collectors exclusively about their last collecting trip, the unit of analysis is the trip, not the collector. If you find out what locals call a "household," number the households from 1 to 1,000, and then interview an adult in every third household; the unit of analysis is the household.

If you want to understand infant mortality at a global level, and you select statistics from fifty countries, the unit of analysis is the country, not the infant who died or the mother or the household that incurred the loss. The same unit of analysis can be used at different scales. For example, household demographics (the household as a unit of analysis) can be studied at the village or the regional scale, depending on availability of data. But sampling procedures will naturally differ depending on scale and the aims of the research.

Most conservation research uses several units of analysis simultaneously. In this case, for ease of handling, you may want to maintain relational databases. These are databases that are organized by logical categories, by instrument, or by research episode and can be used simultaneously for analysis. For example, after conducting a few surveys, you may notice that your survey data can be organized by theme. For any given household, you may have data that describe the demography and character of the household and data that describe in detail forest collection histories and activities. In this case, you may wish to maintain two databases—one for the household data and one for the forest data—that are cross tabulated so that you can understand the relationship between household variables and forest use variables. Microsoft Access© can create these relational databases.

What are common units of analysis for social research for conservation? The following sections discuss a number of options, when they are appropriate, and how they might be linked.

Individual

Interview and track individuals who use resources, are important in decision making, and are involved in the initiative. Often it is more appropriate to use the individual as a unit of analysis than the household because households do not act uniformly. Indeed, households do not "act" at all. Households can be varied in composition, and it can be difficult or misleading to compare them. An example of using the individual as the unit of analysis would be a study of medicinal plant specialists.

Household

There are times, however, when the household is an appropriate unit of analysis. Households can be important units of labor, investment, and production within the village, and if you want to get a general measure of well-being, use of resources, skills, or economic activity, the household is the easiest unit. At the very minimum, adult men and women must be interviewed, often separately, within a household. But make sure to check out other important social units, such as clans, lineages, work groups, and associations. A study that measures reliance on marine products in a community could use the household as a unit of analysis, keeping in mind that outside stakeholders, including family members not residing in the household, may also be using the resources.

Extended Household

More than one generation can live in one household, compound, or hamlet. In addition, family members can live in cities or towns, temporarily or permanently. These family members can continue to contribute funds to the family or claim land and other benefits from the family holdings. Thus, their role must be factored into an understanding of the local economy. A study that focuses on investment into a community will need to seek out external elites who might be located in the towns or cities or even overseas.

Lineage or Clan (Landholding Unit)

In areas of the world that hold land and other resources in common, it is important to identify and study the landholding unit(s). In many cases, there will be many layers of ownership and control—from individuals' private plots to forest areas used by many different groups. As discussed in chapter 5, lineages and clans can be important landholding units because they structure inheritance of land and marriage rules (how women get access to land). Within a clan's holding, one can find different family claims that can be more or less flexible. To study land use, the landholding unit may be the best unit of analysis. Often, the household or village is used as the unit of analysis, but this may be misleading because this is not the unit that allocates land. However, clans and lineages can decline in importance as land is privatized and resources are commodified.

Resource-User Group

It is often possible and important to identify groups of users of a specific resource, such as a forest or a lake. These groups may be formally organized, informally organized, or not organized at all. If you wish to understand the pressures on a certain habitat or ecosystem, identifying and interviewing resource users is critical. Resource-user groups or individuals become a key unit of analysis. To understand common-property resource management, investigate both formal and informal user groups as well as individuals who may use the resource, including those who use the resource illegally or clandestinely.

Village

Like the household, the village is a convenient unit of analysis that is used often without questioning whether it is the appropriate unit. If the aim of the research is to get an overview of an area's population characteristics, say, for a rapid rural appraisal (see chapter 11), the village can be used. But in terms of understanding land and resource use, there is no guarantee that the village is the correct unit of analysis. Villages may straddle resources, and clans and lineages may be more important than villages in terms of allocating and managing land. Land or resource disputes may or may not be decided at the village level. Hamlets within a village are often more important in terms of resource management, as they contain extended families or occupational groups that control or use resources (see chapter 5). Remember that the identification of subpopulations is a critical step in social research for conservation. Holding village-level meetings is not adequate social research.

Stakeholders

Stakeholders in a given resource can be residents or nonresidents. The term gives certain legitimacy to the idea that all interested parties have equal claims to a resource or piece of land. Thus, loggers and remote government officials are put on the same footing as communities that may have existed in an area for millennia. Using the stakeholder as a unit of analysis may thus delegitimize local communities. On the other hand, identifying and understanding the roles of stakeholders is critical in the vast majority of cases where various groups and populations exploit a resource. A village population may be the main users of a forest, but hunters from the city can come in, traders set prices for nontimber forest products, and loggers haunt the boundaries of the village. A cross-site study of stakeholder groups participating in conservation activities revealed which types of groups tend to be most effective over time (Mahanty and Russell 2002).

Township/Province/Nation

The township (county or subprovince) or province may be an important unit for understanding general patterns of land use, such as market development, transportation, extent of cash cropping, population densities, concessions, and plantations. Analysis of the role of each administrative unit in allocating land and resources must be done because often decisions are made at the national or provincial level, and the township (or county) has little or no control over the decisions. For example, Global Forest Watch (of the World Resources Institute) carries out studies of the logging sector in selected countries (Bikié et al. 2000). These studies focus on national policies as well as on the performance of individual concessions. Decentralization is an emerging focus of conservation policy research as countries attempt to move decision making closer to actual management and use of resources. Hence, analysis of the relations among multiple and changing levels of authority is necessary.

Watershed

As discussed previously, the watershed or catchment is a unit or level that has the potential to merge social and ecological units within the context of resource management. Even though administrative boundaries may not be made according to watersheds, groups within watersheds can understand the concept and see the need for common effort. For example, in the Belgrade Lakes area of south-central Maine, landowners and local conservation groups have funded the purchase of the Kennebeck Highlands, which represents a key area of the watershed, in order to protect the water quality of the lake (Kennebeck Highlands Project, n.d.). Individuals and groups monitor the lakes to check on water quality. In terms of research, using the watershed as a unit of analysis enables comparison of different management approaches and their impact on water quality and other ecosystem variables. Chapter 11 discusses this level of analysis.

Ecoregion

In order to work at the ecoregional scale, smaller units of analysis, both biological and social, have to be identified and links made among them. Although such tools as satellite imagery and geographic information systems (GIS) may initially delineate the region and sub-units, the identification of subunits must be ground-truthed (verified through fieldwork) and the links determined empirically. Important social subunits have already been mentioned, but parameters such as soil quality, water flows, markets, and migration patterns that cut across both social and biological units can be critical in understanding land use (see chapter 11).

Project or Initiative Participants or Beneficiaries

Although it is very common for a project to focus largely or exclusively on studying project participants or beneficiaries, this focus does little to advance social research for conservation. Often, participants are self-selected and are the elites in the population and may or may not be the key users of the resources. At the very least, project-level research should study participants and beneficiaries in the context of the wider population. Interviewing nonparticipants can be tricky, but it can be done within the context of a wider survey or longer-term study. After reading this book, conservation initiatives may take a more institutional approach and thus not focus on a few individuals.

Taking the Long View

Social research in a conservation project is often a one-shot deal, even if the project is funded for three, five, or even ten years. There are several ways to get time-series data to show trends:

1. Remote sensing shows changes in vegetation and land cover. These images need to be interpreted carefully, but interpretations of present remote-sensing data can shed light on the past by defining certain patterns (see chapter 11).
2. Archaeology (expensive and time consuming) assesses past land use. Archaeology has shown, for example, that many areas formerly thought of as "wilderness" were much more heavily settled in the past (Roosevelt 1989).
3. Oral histories (see chapter 13) focus on land use changes and trends, triangulated and complemented with other methods.
4. Records and data reviews can be used.
5. Monitoring (see chapter 16) is the most systematic way to assess trends from the present to a future date.

All these methods provide a deep historical picture of how use of land and resources have changed over time (see the discussion of land history in chapter 13).

Numbers and Words Speak Well Together

Qualitative and quantitative methods are almost always used together (see box 10.2). Even while conducting a formal survey where data will be analyzed largely statistically, we literally never stop collecting qualitative data. We observe people and the environment, interview key informants, and continuously talk with (informally interview) local people. All these data collection methods are part of the learning process.

Participatory field research also produces qualitative data and can be used with formal survey methods. Your choice of method depends on several factors: scale, research question, conservation focus, time frame, and budget. How to choose an approach or a combination thereof is discussed in subsequent chapters.

Qualitative methods, such as observation and unstructured or semi-structured interviews, generate in-depth information about the population under study and descriptive information about the conservation site and wider community or region. These qualitative data allow us to build models and research hypotheses and are used to interpret research

---

Box 10.2. Quantitative and Qualitative Methods Work Together

Based on observation of forest-user groups, it looks like women have less access to cash than men do from their labor in one community. Researchers want to find out whether there is a difference between cash amounts received for women's and men's groups. The hypothesis is formulated—There is no difference between men's and women's work groups with respect to cash payments—and tested by collecting data on the numbers of workers recruited by men and women, their respective tasks, the number of hours worked, and the type of payment received.

Analysis of the quantitative data uncovers the fact that men tend to recruit workers for *harvesting resources for sale and pay cash*, while women recruit for *food crop production and fodder collection and pay in kind or rotate labor*. Further research, perhaps group interviews, might look at the timing and seasonality of the work, skills, the relationship between workers, and other factors that would explain the difference in men's and women's compensation. This analysis could lead to a reappraisal of how a project seeks to involve men and women in a reforestation enterprise.

findings from survey research (see chapter 14). Land history research, ethnobiology, and other ethnographic methods generate qualitative data for case studies and a deep understanding of the social and physical world (see chapter 13). In PRA and AI, participatory research is used to propel people into action so that they take charge of their own conservation initiatives (see chapter 15).

Data for quantitative analysis may be collected in field surveys, databases, or structured observation. Data are collected using representative samples where statistical outcomes describe the sampled population with a specified level of accuracy. To carry out proper quantitative analysis, there must be an adequate number of identical or comparable units observed. Sampling procedures determine who or what will be included in the study. Units of analysis determine at what level or category the sample will be drawn (households, individuals, villages, hunting trips, rattan bundles, and so on).

Quantitative methods are powerful because of their capacity for replication, measurement, and statistical analysis. Remember that fallible humans are behind the numbers—we create the research design. Be careful to clearly define terms and research questions and to describe the strengths and weaknesses of your methods. Quantitative approaches alone do not provide the knowledge and insight needed to address research questions in a conservation initiative, while qualitative approaches provide insight, but the research findings are not generalizable to other sites. Since each approach has strengths and weaknesses, we recommend that you use them together. We discuss how to do this in later chapters.

Getting the Sample Right

The whole purpose of survey sampling is to collect data and to be able to work with a subset of a population instead of the whole population yet be able to make statements about the whole population based on the subset, or sample. This section briefly describes criteria required for some of the sampling procedures commonly used in the field. The discussion is introductory, not comprehensive. We encourage you to get training in statistics or to partner with someone who thoroughly understands how to design samples that are realistic and suitable for complex and strenuous field conditions.

Nonprobability Sampling

Key informant interviews, group interviews, RRAs, PRAs, and certain types of surveys are based on nonprobability sampling procedures

---

Box 10.3. Nonprobability Sampling

Convenience sample: A group of individuals selected because of their accessibility and availability to the researcher. *Purposive sample:* A group selected on the basis of specified criteria pertaining to the purposes of the research. For example, for an understanding of rattan gathering, a purposive sample includes several rattan gatherers within the communities studied.

(see box 10.3). The two examples shown in box 10.3 are convenience sampling and purposive sampling. They allow you to get data quickly, but there is inherent sampling bias.

Nonprobability sampling meets the first purpose of sampling (collecting data) but not the second (generalizability). Data from these samples can be used only to describe interview respondents, not the population from which the sample was drawn. If you wish to survey a representative sample but have time and money constraints, it is better to use nonprobability sampling and just go for the information you need. In many circumstances, using nonprobability sampling is a way to work smartly (see box 10.4). For example, RRA and PRA have a long and successful field history based on nonprobability sampling. But do not decide to use RRA or PRA because they are "easier" than surveys; RRAs are used to meet specific field

---

Box 10.4. Nonprobability Sampling in the Dust

In Liberia in 1998, during a time of peace, a democracy institution based in Washington, D.C., was partnering with local institutions to organize the first multiparty democratic election. They had limited contact with the people of Liberia and wanted to assess the need for civic education in rural areas. In a short period of time, an expatriate researcher designed a short survey to ask people about the topic. The survey was dovetailed into a larger assignment and therefore did not take top priority. The field team stood on dusty town corners and administered the survey to whomever was walking by and agreed to participate.

This example of convenience sampling is biased by the chosen time, location, judgment, and appearance of the enumerators. However, the sponsoring institution got a glimpse into needs for civic education that could be used as a starting point for further research. In addition, the survey was productive in that it took advantage of a window of time of relative peace in Liberia—sometimes you have to get the data while you can.

---

criteria, and ethical considerations, strong partnerships, and long-term time commitments are all special requirements of PRA (see chapter 15).

Probability Sampling

Field surveys use probability sampling procedures. These samples include random, stratified, systematic, and cluster (and multistage combinations of these). They are representative samples, meaning the statistics that describe the sample are used to describe (or represent) the population from which the sample was drawn (see box 10.5). Probability sampling minimizes researcher bias because the sample is chosen at random and every unit of the population has a chance to be selected. Probability sampling also allows for an estimate of the level of accuracy of the sample statistics, using standard errors and, more generally, the notion of repeated sampling.

Samples are drawn from sampling frames—ideally, a list of every member of the target population. Sampling frames are important because the representativeness of the sample depends on each member of the total population being included in the sample frame. Examples of sampling frames are the names on a village census, a list of members of an indigenous rotating credit club, or all the names of members who belong to an agricultural cooperative. Sometimes the search for existing sampling frames is exhausting.

If a sampling frame is not available for the conservation area, it may be worthwhile to build one by conducting a census (see chapter

---

Box 10.5. Probability Sampling

Simple random sample: Each sample of size n has the same chance of being selected to be in the study.

Stratified sample: Divide the population into homogeneous strata, such as occupation or ethnicity, and then take a simple random sample from each stratum.

Systematic sample: Randomly select an element from the first k in the sampling frame and then select every kth subsequent element.

Cluster sample: Identify and list clusters that contain sampling units with a common property, such as city block or village. Draw a random sample of clusters from the list. Include in the sample every sampling unit within the chosen clusters (single stage), or select a sample from each cluster (two stage).

Adapted from Agresti and Finlay (1997).

SAMPLING CHOICES AND FIELD REALITIES

As I prepared to administer the farmer survey in Wum, Cameroon, I could not find an appropriate sampling frame. Annual tax rolls were spotty because people refused to pay taxes. Voter registration rolls were inadequate because people refused to vote. Schools had no reliable records of parents or students. The Ministry of Agriculture only had lists of names of economically successful "leader" farmers. The recent census materials that reportedly would have lists of household heads by village quarter had just been sent to Bamenda, the provincial capital. Should I wait for that census, or should I proceed with my own?

---

14), which can also double as a gift to the community. Otherwise, you can reassess the need for representativeness and use nonprobability sampling or a completely different method. Just be sure to describe the strengths and weaknesses of the research methods in any report or analysis. Remember also that only by using a representative sample can you generalize from your sample to the wider population.

If the population is relatively homogeneous and a reliable sampling frame is available, it makes sense to create a simple random or systematic sample. Simple random can be tedious because it requires each sampling element in the sampling frame to have a number. Systematic sampling gets around this. You randomly select an element from the first k members in the frame (e.g., the first 8) and then count off every eighth member, which is then included in the sample. The number k is called the "skip number" (Agresti and Finlay 1997). But bias can creep in if most or every eighth house is on a corner or behind other houses. Be aware of systematic bias.

If the research question involves a population residing across ecoregions or agro-ecological zones or if the population falls into ethnic or occupational groups or other logical and homogeneous strata (categories or hierarchies), then it makes sense to use a stratified sample. The population is divided on the basis of specified criteria, and then a simple random sample is drawn from each stratum. Take care, however, in making assumptions about the uniformity of groups, as even recognized ethnic groups can be very diverse. People straddle different groups as well.

Cluster samples are used when a complete sampling frame is not available and to save the time and money it would take to do a census in order to create a sampling frame or to cover a large territory. Here, criteria such as city block, village, or geography are used to divide the population into clusters. A list is compiled of these clusters, and then a random sample of the clusters is selected. In single-stage cluster sampling, everyone in each selected cluster is included in the sample. In two-stage cluster sampling, a sample is selected from each cluster, for example, one person in a household door-to-door survey. Two-stage is more common than single-stage cluster sampling (Harshbarger 2001).

Box 10.6 displays several different baseline studies carried out by social researchers at Biodiversity Conservation Network (BCN) sites. Each one chose a different sampling design based on their needs and capabilities.

Two issues that emerged from the choices are as follows:

- When researchers tried to survey 100 percent of the population, they sometimes missed households because people were away or unavailable. Hence, they could not reliably say that the analysis reflected the whole survey area.
- When the researchers tried a systematic survey counting off by every kth house, it was difficult in areas where houses do not sit along a road or path. In fact, it was necessary to know how many houses there were and their location, so a rough mapping and random choice of houses might have been preferable.

Teams Take Time and Work

Collaboration in the Field

Implementing a survey in the field is tough. We have seen field professionals compromise their sample design because of exhaustion, confusion, shrinking time, and an incomplete understanding of the importance of sampling to survey outcomes. To avoid this, talk to your key informants, partners, and other researchers who have worked in the area and let them help you plan the fieldwork. Make sure your team knows the importance of maintaining survey standards in the field so that the work can be completed successfully. Finally, if you need help with the sample design, collaborate with an expert.

Box 10.6. Fieldwork Strategies and Sample Designs at BCN Sites

Social Development Research Center (SDRC) survey of households in project sites in Palawan, the Philippines: Stratified by ethnicity (indigenous and nonindigenous) and surveyed every fifth household within the strata (Social Development Research Center 1995–1996)

Why: To compare wealth and resource use in two subpopulations

Harvard University survey of households in villages around the Gunung Palung park area, Indonesia: Stratified by geography and then random sample of households using previous Harvard census as sampling frame (Kaiser and Lisa 1998)

Why: To compare logging versus nonlogging households as well as by wealth category (determined in census)

EDA Rural Systems survey of households in Akash Kamini Valley, Garwhal, India: Random sample of households based on existing census data (Sinha and Verma 1997)

Why: To use a representative sample in order to generalize about the entire project site

Conservation International (CI) and Solomon Islands Development Trust (SIDT), Makira Island, Solomon Islands, household survey: 100 percent coverage of participating village households (Connor et al. 1998)

Why: To get 100 percent coverage, as the survey was an entrée into the community and not just a data-gathering exercise

SPACHEE and Tikina Verata survey of households in Tikina Verata, Fiji: 100 percent coverage (Sauni et al. 1999)

Why: Survey was important to village administrators to help them in their work in addition to assessing project impact

King Mahendra Trust for Nature Conservation (KMTNC) survey of resource users around the Chitwan National Park, Nepal: Cluster sample and random sample within cluster (KMTNC socioeconomic survey, Biodiversity Conservation Network 1999)

Why: Clusters represented different resource-user communities as determined by prior research

---

Building a Team

Sometimes an individual researcher can work alone, but it is often preferable to work in teams. Whenever possible, build a field research team with local instead of outside researchers. Local professionals and trained community members have a keener understanding of the local conditions and may be better able to quickly establish rapport and get

better information. Local researchers are familiar with research protocols, know the lay of the land and communities, and have valuable experience that outsiders can learn from. In some cases, however, local
(and nonlocal as well) researchers can pursue their own agendas or even
exploit community members, so a team leader must keep a watchful eye.

Team leaders rotate researchers and enumerators so that they can
learn by sharing experiences, field skills, and knowledge of the local
culture. Fieldwork is tiring, and tempers can ignite. Be prepared to mediate conflicts between team members. Discuss with the team how to
work with translators and how to manage drivers and other support
personnel. Also discuss how to respond to informants who want to be
paid for interviews.

The Challenges of a Multidisciplinary Research Team

Social research is one component of a conservation initiative. Conservation biology and ecology provide the biophysical parameters of
any conservation initiative. Formal economics may play a role in valuing a resource or habitat or assessing the financial viability of a conservation enterprise. Business expertise may be needed if an enterprise is
involved. Legal experts may examine the laws, regulations, and decrees
with respect to use, access, and ownership of resources. Community organizers or educational specialists may help with training and institution and capacity building.

Ideally, a team is made up of a mix of "outsiders" and local people,
genders, and people with different training and background. But such
heterogeneity comes with a price. Transaction costs (time and effort spent
in the activity in relation to results) of team building can be steep. Communication across cultures, genders, and disciplines takes time, patience,
and above all commitment. There have to be incentives for collaboration.
Incentives for scientists may include the joy of getting new and interesting data, the prestige of working on an important project, getting articles
published in scientific journals, advancement in the field, and tenure if
they are on a faculty. Incentives for local people may include the prestige
of participating in an important initiative, acquiring knowledge and
skills, making contacts with outsiders, financial rewards, and long-term
benefits to their community or family. In terms of interdisciplinary collaboration, researchers need to understand that data, information, and
knowledge from colleagues are necessary for their work to advance.

In order for this necessity to collaborate to be felt, it has to be built
in to the initiative. The individuals in the team have to come to the
undertaking with mutual respect and commitment to looking at issues
and knowledge from different approaches and angles. High-wattage

prima donnas may not be the best choice for multidisciplinary field re-search, even if individually they do outstanding work. Yet many ex-tremely fine scientists are also excellent collaborators with local partners as well as with researchers from other disciplines. As discussed in chap-ter 3, emotional intelligence is a key characteristic of social research.

Including Local Partners

Identify and involve local partners in the research as soon as possi-ble. Attempt to meet people from all levels of the community, not just leaders or those who speak up, before selecting research and imple-mentation partners. These efforts will be respected because they show good diplomacy and will pay off in richness of information and bal-anced perspectives. Include selected partners in planning for the field-work as soon as you get conceptually organized. For example, you will need to include partners in the design of the field instruments. Some colleagues in partnership can be interviewed as key informants, or col-lectively their knowledge of the local sociopolitical context and biologi-cal environment can inform the various steps of social research. Partners should be brought in early in order to immediately start the process of multidirectional learning and collaboration. The partnership can evolve only through trust and mutual understanding, and this takes time. Working with local partners should also promote local buy-in and in-crease chances for community ownership of the process (see box 10.7).

Getting Around: The Mud, the Broken Car, the Wrong Day . . .

Careful planning for research in the field is critical, especially in the initial stages of getting to know people and a site. The way you and the team present yourself can determine how the whole initiative fares.

Box 10.7. *Turaqa ni Koros* as Research Partners in Fiji

A conservation initiative in Fiji enlisted the aid of the village administrators, or *Turaga ni Koros*, to carry out research and monitoring. They were trained in biological monitoring and also in carrying out socioeconomic baseline surveys, which they did with minimal supervision. The data and results remained with the community and were used for planning conservation and development activities (Aalbersberg et al. 1997).

Examine existing databases created by other institutions. Use documentation about what is known about the community, the conservation site, and similar communities and sites to build field instruments. Do not collect a lot of extraneous data that will never be analyzed, such as long lists of species in local names, when, for example, you have no taxonomist to identify the species. Calculate the costs of collecting new data in relation to the utility of the information for different stakeholders, the quality of data sources, and the replicability of data collection. Do not duplicate efforts—coordinate and harmonize with others.

Plan interviews at appropriate times of the day, week, and year. Take into careful consideration seasonality, road conditions, and the migration/livelihood patterns of people. Plan heavy research for the optimal time of the year. It can be inappropriate or even hazardous to interview during ritual events, celebrations, religious days, and political campaigns. Observation at these times should be low key. Expect delays and setbacks and factor them into your research plan. Be mindful of interview fatigue within the community and work efficiently and respectfully. Do not waste their time. Coordinate research with activities and plans to visit communities and initiate research only after the community understands activities. If necessary, bring research or conservation personnel to further explain the initiative. Make sure that everyone associated with the initiative is telling the same story. You can plan interviews on market days to find groups of people, but be aware that people have tasks to accomplish on these days. Also note on these days that households may be near empty. Group meetings should have a focused agenda/output/action plan and be part of a viable tradition for airing different views within a group setting.

Factor in analysis and communication of findings as an ongoing part of the research, not as an afterthought. Based on your "feel for the data," start data analysis by discussing hunches, likely outcomes, key themes, and general trends with partners and key informants. Allow enough time and money for data entry and analysis and updating and maintaining useful databases.

Pilot Test

A critical step in field research preparation is to pilot test each field instrument. Then, on the basis of feedback from field respondents, enumerators, partners, translators, and key informants, fine-tune the questions. Do whatever is needed to hammer out an instrument that can be administered and coded with ease in the field. Make sure the interview does not last too long. During the pilot test, ask key informants how they would structure the interview and setting to make people most at ease.

Debriefing: Laughter, Tears, and Insights

Each evening, especially in the beginning of a field study, it is imperative for the field team to have group meetings to debrief: to share learnings and insights and to address questions raised during the implementation of interviews, surveys, or participatory field exercises. Although we may think our questions are transparent, local people may be confused by or not like certain questions. Using translators can further complicate the wording of questions. It is common after the second or third day to rephrase a few questions or eliminate redundant queries. Keep night meetings short. You can be sure the team wants to do good work, but at the same time they need downtime. Practice effective time

Table 10.1. Research Management as a System

Component	Process	Key Questions
Data collection	Read and catalog existing data first before collecting new data. Do not collect survey data that cannot be analyzed (e.g., long lists of species in the local language).	What are the gaps in existing data? What new data are needed? What is the most effective way to collect the data?
Storage/filing	Classify and cross-reference data, maps, slides, and other materials. Keep in mind that these materials can represent an important archive for local people.	How can different information streams and data points be integrated? Where are backup files and records to be located? Where will charts, reports, and survey data be stored? How can we retain these for use by local managers?
Reporting/ monitoring	Develop simple, clear, and concise report forms and formats in a participatory process. The reports have to be useful to those who prepare them. Turn reports into extension and communication materials immediately. Read reports or eliminate them.	Are there duplications in questions or reports? How will the data be used? Who has access to e-mail and to the Web to access reports? What language are they written in? What are the information needs of key audiences?

(continued)

Table 10.1. Research Management as a System *(continued)*

Component	Process	Key Questions
Quality control	Develop interdisciplinary quality standards for data collection and reporting that are agreed on across the partnership.	Who reviews reports and prepares questions or responses? What are accepted standards for each discipline?
Training	Do not use apprentices, interns, and students to do work that should be done by local people. Train local partners to do as much of the data collection and analysis as possible.	Who can learn my job and replace me? How long will it take? How can volunteers, interns, and assistants be used as facilitators and helpers to local people?
Analysis/ presentation	Assess technology in terms of maintenance, ease of access, and usefulness in the local context.	Who will maintain computers or GIS equipment? Who knows the software and other technologies?

management so that team members do not have to bear unnecessary burdens.

Keeping It All Together

In a conservation or any other initiative, research feeds directly into decision making if you are organized. Analysis begins with the first piece of data collected. Research management is tied to other parts of managing the initiative, such as the activity plan and budget. Maintaining good financial and other records is essential. Keep record keeping simple and transparent. For administrative purposes, make simple charts that show trends in participation and use of financial resources in the initiative. Benchmark the contributions and participation of different partners in the initiative with a target of full or substantial local ownership.

Components of research management are considered as a whole system within and for a conservation initiative, working toward a goal of institutionalizing the initiative over a given span of time. Table 10.1 lays out the different components of research management and how they work together as a system.

11

Regional Studies

Findings from a study which focused its attention on a community and which simply regarded its environment as boundary conditions, are only valid at the scale of that community. Not only can these findings not be extrapolated to other communities in a different context, but they also cannot be simply integrated within a larger homogeneous region.

—Lambin and Guyer (1994: 5)

Conservation strategies require both regional and local information. This chapter discusses regional-level data collection, while local-level research is covered in the following chapters. Doing some research at the regional level before going to the local level has the following advantages:

- If you start to collect information systematically at the regional level, you can develop a database that can be used to put local-level research into a wider perspective.
- You can outline wider pressures on the resource base and networks, such as transport, markets, and the shape of common-property areas, such as lakes and rivers.
- You can craft conservation strategies that are linked not necessarily to specific sites but to forging wider constituencies for conservation.

Regional studies are only part of the equation: It is necessary to get to the field quickly to ground truth, verify, and enrich regional-level data and to understand local management systems and trends. Spatial data and surveys will tell us what is happening but not why.

169

The chapter combines methods from geography, economic anthropology, and development/rural sociology. First, it discusses how regions are defined and then looks at spatial methods for characterizing and describing regional systems. The next section focuses on rapid rural appraisals that can get you into the field to examine specific areas within a region. The final section looks at regional analysis from economic anthropology, specifically the study of regional market systems, and makes some suggestions about the study of regional social and political systems.

"Region" Is a Slippery Concept

Many social researchers collect in-depth information about a site and generalize from that to a wider region. Perhaps they have visited other communities and done some interviews or even surveys to look at variation among the localities. But without a representative sample, the information they collect at different sites cannot be generalized to a wider region.

Let's be clear: Generating a representative sample for a region is not at all easy, particularly in countries with poor census data. In the first place, we have to define what is meant by "region." A region can be defined politically, economically, ecologically, and socially. French geographers use the term *terroir* to denote an area that is appropriated by a group for their livelihood and is thus both a geographic and a cultural space. Conservationists are interested in ecoregions and landscapes that encompass key habitats or ecosystems and land uses surrounding these areas. Local conservation activists may be focused on watersheds or rivers in order to deal with issues of water quality, while community organizers may be oriented toward an area controlled by a specific ethnic group, a county, or a parish.

A conservation initiative can define a region according to its objectives and strategies. An ecoregion is not likely to be isomorphic with political or social boundaries, even the boundaries of protected areas. Indeed, transboundary conservation is increasing in importance as a conservation strategy (e.g., Cumming 1999; Van der Linde et al. 2001). If an organization is taking an ecoregional or landscape approach, multiple sampling strategies are needed. The larger region is broken down into subregions that are characterized and compared in terms of ecological and population variables. A subregion can become the focus of in-depth study when there is understanding of how it relates to the wider region. But as we have said, regions can be defined along many different parameters, such as agro-ecology, population clusters, watersheds, infrastructure, political administration, ethnicity, and market systems.

We will divide regional analysis into two types: "natural" regions and "heuristic" regions. Natural regions could be market towns and their hinterlands, distinct territories of ethnic groups, provinces or counties, biomes, or watersheds. Natural regions are uncovered by research in the course of understanding the local economy, ecology, and social structure. The researcher draws heuristic regions with regard to specific questions or concerns to compare and contrast features of different sites or different land uses. For example, a "landscape" around a protected area (PA) may be drawn that does not reflect agro-ecosystem or population boundaries but encompasses proximate users of the resources of the PA. (This delineation may or may not be useful to understand direct pressures on the PA, depending on the importance of distant users and decision makers.)

Regional analysis is iterative, moving from the identification of "natural regions" to questions or action issues and then back to a definition of region. The point of regional analysis is not to get the definition and boundaries exactly right but to recognize and include in your research an understanding of networks, connections, and flows from a wider area. It means, for example, that you have to work in more than one village and understand flows and connections among villages and towns.

Let's take a look at the subregion of Tshopo around the city of Kisangani in northeastern Democratic Republic of Congo, where Diane Russell carried out fieldwork for her dissertation in 1986–87 (Russell 1991) (see map 11.1).

The subregion is divided into what were then called "zones" and in turn into "collectivités," many of which are relatively isomorphic with the territories of ethnic groups, such as the Topoke or the Turumbu. We need to take into account the fact that ethnic groups may have been relocated or redefined to fit specific territories during the colonial era. There are two major biomes: riverbank and forest. Thus, natural regions could be defined as follows:

1. The whole subregion, the zones, or the collectivités in that these are units of political decision making—the "tribal-linguistic" groups and clans—that control access to land for farming and house building
2. Market towns, including the regional capital of Kisangani, and their hinterlands in that these are the units of bulking and distribution of key commodities (rice, coffee, game, gold, and diamonds)
3. The watersheds of the major rivers—the Congo, the Tshopo, the Lomami, and the Aruwimi—in that these are the units affected by change in water flow and composition
4. Rivers and adjacent riverbanks inhabited by riverine peoples

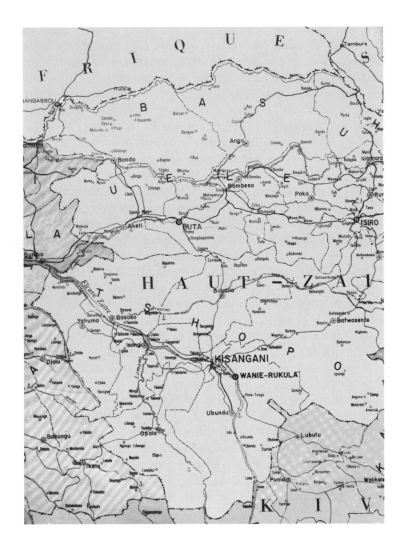

Map 11.1.   Tshopo subregion within the Democratic Republic of Congo.

5. Forests managed by the units in item 1 in this list, "open" forest
(all land theoretically belongs to the state), concession areas, different types of forest (e.g., forest dominated by *Gilbertiodendron*
dewevreii or mixed forest), and forests within protected areas

If the aim of a conservation program is to decrease the trade in
"bushmeat" (refer to box 4.2) in this region, it will be important to identify the following:

- Logging and mining camps
- Roads and river transportation networks, including river-based markets
- Military installations
- Plantations
- Markets (both formal and informal; see chapter 5)

The region is defined by the network of bushmeat marketing locations (bushmeat killing locations would be too diffuse). The points in the previous list have to be located and entered into a Geographic Information System (GIS) or a map, along with other characteristics, such as population, any data on fauna, forest cover, and river network. Data on species, number, weight, type of weapon, and identity of hunter would then be entered with the aim of measuring critical locations in relation to other features, types of people involved, and species hunted.

If the conservation effort were geared toward protecting freshwater biodiversity, you would map human populations along the river as well as any economic activities that could pollute the river (tanning, logging near riverbank, or plantations near riverbank). The region is defined by a stretch of river designated as threatened, or it might extend to the watershed of the river(s) if it is determined that activities in the watershed affect fish populations.

The conservation effort might focus on cataloging and reinforcing indigenous knowledge and management systems. In this case, the territories of ethnic groups are likely to be most significant, and the region would comprise several ethnic groups living in the forest or even one ethnic group. Within that "region," however, it might be critical to know the territories of landholding clans if the clans or lineages specialize in certain types of forest exploitation such as canoe making, iron working, or charcoal making (trees used to make charcoal) or hunting.

Protected areas are embedded in regions defined by market systems, political and cultural boundaries, and ecological systems. To understand the regional relationships affecting a PA, one would again focus on markets and transportation networks, concession areas, military installations, and ethnic and political boundaries. It is a mistake to concentrate all research on local populations and conservation sites when the most serious pressures come from afar.

What if you take the approach of focusing first on the threats to biodiversity or ecosystem function at a particular location or site as advocated by some conservation guides? Perhaps the greatest threat to biodiversity in Tshopo would be bushmeat hunting. If this threat is traced out, you may define a "bushmeat marketing region" with different nodes. But if this is all you do, you may miss important boundaries and natural regions that bear over the long term on the health of biodiversity and ecosystem function: political boundaries, watersheds, and clan territories. What if bushmeat marketing depends on the location of logging camps, which in turn depend on political decisions made at the provincial level? What if certain ethnic or military groups specialize in hunting, perhaps forming organized cartels and marketing networks?

Delimiting the range and territory of all actors and influences is critical. Different strategies and approaches must be crafted for regional-level threats as opposed to local problems. For example, if military or national-level political actors are involved, this may pose a danger to local people and conservation staff (Hart and Hart 1997; Hart et al. 1996). At this point, activists outside the country or based in the capital may have to take the lead in uncovering and addressing threats. But they should do so working closely with local groups.

Bigger Than a Site but Smaller Than a Region: What Is It?

As discussed earlier, landscapes have been adopted as units of conservation by many organizations because it is recognized that territories around protected areas or endangered habitats have to be included in a conservation strategy. It is not enough to demarcate or restrict work to a PA because actions from "outside" can significantly affect species and habitats within a PA. In some countries, there are few if any PAs, and so landscapes may be wider units of conservation that are negotiated with villages, clans, or even diverse ethnic groups. For example, Lakekamu Basin in Papua New Guinea, the site of a Conservation International project funded by the Biodiversity Conservation Network (BCN), is an area inhabited by three distinct ethnic groups.

The watershed is an important unit of analysis for ecosystem studies. It may be small enough to encompass one social group or large enough to hold many. In some cases, a group may range over several watersheds, using streams as boundaries for family or clan agricultural, collection, or hunting areas (Rhoades 1998).

Landscapes and watersheds are scales between regions and sites. In other words, they are often too large for intensive field research but may be too small for regional analysis. Hence, both the smaller units and the wider region have to be delineated. The smaller units could be villages, hamlets, or other settlements, while the larger region could be defined by political units (e.g., a county) or an ecoregion. To learn about the socio-economic links between a landscape or watershed and both the smaller and the larger scales means that a combination of regional and site-based research methods must be used. These could be centered in a GIS or physical map, but remember that the spatial dimension does not always capture important relations between local actors and wider phenomena. For instance, the links between consumers of products (e.g., wood, non-timber forest products [NTFPs], or bushmeat) and hunters may not be georefcrenceable, that is, amenable to being located on a map.

Threats to watershed integrity often emerge in distant capitals. For instance, in New York State, the decision to build a water treatment plant in New York City will have enormous ramifications for the upstate watershed, as subsidies to maintain that watershed diminish because of declining incentive of New Yorkers to work with watershed residents.

Spacing Out

Geomatics

Geomatics comprises remote sensing, global positioning systems (GPS), and GIS. Poole (1995: 13) notes, "Geomatic technologies are now being used locally for applications that were once assumed to be the reserve of research institutions and centralized agencies." Human ecologists are also using geomatics to understand regional patterns of land use.

Remote sensing uses satellite images or aerial photos to create maps of terrain that are used in GIS. A good resource on remote sensing is a book by Wilkie and Finn (1996). This book explains the science behind the different types of images available, how to choose among them, and what to do with them. Some images are readily available from public agencies, while others are proprietary or very costly. Satellite maps can be used as base maps for community mapping (see chapter 15) or as reference maps for tracking long-term changes. Satellite maps can capture hidden activities, for example, illegal or "unofficial" logging or mining. Social scientists are increasingly learning the skills of interpreting remotely sensed images (Brondizio 1994, 1996; McCracken 1999a, 1999b).

There are two basic forms of images used in a GIS: polygon/vector and raster-based images. For conservation research, raster-based systems are highly important because they can use remotely sensed images, which, when sequenced over time, can help in the analysis of vegetation changes. Polygon/vector systems can be used to digitize community maps to delineate political boundaries, networks such as roads or river transportation, habitat patches, or sitings that have been precisely located by a GPS.

Getting the data into raster GIS involves coding each pixel (unit of image representation). A pixel represents the various wavelength reflections of the remotely sensed image, but then the wavelength reflection must be coded to depict significant categories on the ground: dense forest, secondary forest, savanna, plantations, and so on (for an excellent resource on this topic, see Liverman et al. 1998).

It is beyond the scope of this book to teach the use of GIS, but we can offer the following pointers:

- A GIS is only as good as the data that go into it, and data need to be updated periodically. Thus, a good GIS is labor intensive. This point needs to be up front when considering whether to invest in GIS. If the goal of a conservation initiative is local ownership, who will maintain the GIS? On the other hand, GIS is a powerful tool, and many indigenous groups are using it to demarcate territory, map resources, and negotiate with government.

- If the coding is not reflective of real categories of land use or is very general, the GIS is not going to be very useful. Just knowing what is "forest" and "not forest," for example, can provide gross estimates of deforestation but will not say much about trends in land use. Types of forest and succession have to be differentiated. Good data require both fine-tuning the satellite imagery and ground truthing (verification by surveys, observation, and other data collection exercises in the field).

- A GIS can be used to demarcate both "natural" regions and heuristic regions. Ecosystem and social boundaries can be defined. But one issue that has emerged is the tendency for these tools to solidify boundaries that may in fact be quite fluid. Ecologists have a hard time agreeing on boundaries of ecosystems or even what a boundary might entail. Similarly, social groups often have overlapping rights, claims, and territories. One conservation project in Melanesia recognized early on that they would have to use in-depth genealogical research to untangle the history of land use and claims. In Palawan, the Philippines, an initial mapping exercise using GIS did not demarcate important family or clan forest areas and as such had little use for local management, though it was useful for negotiations with the government on ancestral domain claim.

- There is a danger of GIS becoming an end in itself and not a means to solve specific research and development problems. Thus, there has to be good communication between GIS experts and research or development managers. An example of this collaboration is determining the appropriate scales and fineness of data necessary to answer questions. In some countries, getting data at the appropriate level is very difficult because databases do not exist or the scale of existing data is too large for use by local researchers.

Human ecologist Emilio Moran and colleagues at the Anthropological Center for Training in Global Environmental Change (see "Human and Political Ecology" in the Resources section) use geomatics extensively in their work in the Amazon, where they aim to link regional-level spatial information with local land use choices of farmers and ranchers. They include an understanding of policy as well because it is clear that individuals' choices have been shaped by subsidies and other incentives to use land in a certain way. Ethnicity also plays a role in land use patterns. Moran et al. (1994: 332) describe the interplay of satellite imagery and collection of data in the field:

> Analysis of satellite data allow us to ask questions about dimensions of the region's ecology that are harder to address by ground-level surveys, limited as they must be in total area covered. Unlike site-specific studies, satellite data permits a regionally broad analysis rarely possible with field methods alone. Field studies can verify the accuracy of satellite image analysis and assure the accuracy of the regional assessment.

Peter Poole reviewed various case studies of use of mapping and GIS by indigenous people in their quest for control over their territories. He describes a sophisticated use of GIS by Canadian indigenous communities:

> Combining the resources of 23 Cree communities, Manitoba Keewatinowi Okimalanak has developed a GIS database which covers a third of the province of Manitoba. . . . Seasonal patterns of traditional practice and wildlife movements can be readily retrieved. This system has proven effective in responding to proposals for industrial resource development. (Poole 1995: 44)

We discuss further types and uses of community mapping that may or may not use GIS and remote sensing in chapter 15.

Maps Are Not Dead Yet

Old-fashioned mapmaking, cartography, still has great utility. Maps are portable and easily readable. Overlays with acetate can be made that serve the same function as GIS overlays, albeit with much less analytic capability (but more portability in areas with no electricity). Using satellite maps as base maps is a good idea, but these must be enhanced with data on political and social units in order to link social and biological data. Topographic maps can also be used as base maps.

Maps can also be deceiving. Some conservation-oriented mapping neglects important human activities and as such is unrealistic. For example, one map of potential corridors between protected areas neglected to display the extent and character of agricultural activities, such as plantations and rice paddies. Another map of "global hot spots" displayed a huge swath of the Democratic Republic of Congo as the "Congo Basin Wilderness Area." This depiction would come as a surprise to the 30 million people living in this "wilderness." And frequently there are errors, such as towns missing or located on maps in the wrong place. An analysis of colonial-era maps of the northeastern Congo revealed many more towns than depicted in maps found in ethnographies written after the colonial era. These ethnographies downplayed commercial relations of "remote" peoples and depicted them in "pristine" environments (Russell 1983).

Satellite maps can reveal hidden or clandestine activities such as logging and mining. In Cameroon, one project manager displayed a map that clearly revealed logging roads that were unreported by the government. Global Forest Watch, an initiative of the World Resources Institute, had been mapping logging concessions in Cameroon but did not have this information. What to do with the new data? This question was not easy to answer given the sometimes precarious position of environmentalists in the country.

Chapter 15 presents a more detailed discussion of mapping in community-based conservation. There we see how on-the-ground mapping builds capacity and can empower local people to take up the challenge of logging, incursion, and weak property rights.

Is There Still a Place for RRA?

Rapid rural appraisal (RRA) is a method used to conduct interviews over a large territory to find out what you need to know in a relatively short time, compared to other field methods. Multidisciplinary teams of researchers, which include as many local partners as possible, conduct the interviews. These people from research institutes, nongovernmental organizations (NGOs), community groups, and government agencies are knowledgeable about research topics and local conditions. They are able to formulate questions that allow key themes and indicators to be identified and explain how data fit into the big picture.

Working with nationals can also boost the confidence of local people to be interviewed. Training in appropriate techniques and protocol is still warranted, however, even if the team is all local.

Rapid rural appraisal interviews are semistructured to foster probing, open-ended questioning and mutual discussion. The goal is to learn from local people. Therefore, researchers must use good listening skills. The RRA team meets at the end of the day to discuss what they have learned and to prepare questions for the next day. Rapid rural appraisal uses an evolving interview guide. Observations by the team are as important as interviews in the case of RRA.

Rapid rural appraisals began to be used in the late 1970s in Southeast Asia. Field experts reported that conducting surveys took too much time and effort and drained resources. Enumerators often overcollected data—they were wasteful. Researchers determined the statistical precision of survey work was not required for many of the objectives of program planning. Survey design methods assumed that field people knew what to ask when often they did not. Rapid rural appraisal was developed as a way to increase learning between researchers and local people and to speed up the delivery of useful data. Rapid rural appraisals

WOMEN FARMERS IN BANDUNDU

To understand the farming practices of women in Bandundu, Zaire (now Democratic Republic of the Congo), a two-phase RRA was implemented. This RRA was meant to help the design of an extension project for women. The team consisted of an anthropologist (nonlocal but with experience in the country), a Zairian geographer, and later a Zairian extension specialist and a Zairian agronomist. All researchers were women. The RRA looked first at possible target villages and women's groups in the region selected and then interviewed individual women farmers in selected villages. The RRA uncovered that women were under severe pressure because of the loss of forestland and had little or no control over assets, even their own labor. This finding led to an "empowerment" strategy for the project that focused on woman-to-woman extension (Russell 1989b).

were a major, creative breakthrough in fieldwork based on the premise that research methods build knowledge and should serve all people involved—we are not enslaved to them. The RRA is the forerunner to the participatory rural appraisal (PRA), which stretches our thinking even more to build learning and knowledge to benefit and empower local people, partners, and researchers (see chapter 15). Some of the principles of RRA, which are often forgotten today, are spelled out by pioneer Robert Chambers (1999):

- Optimal ignorance and appropriate imprecision: finding out only what is needed, measuring only as accurately as needed, not measuring what is not needed
- Rapid progressive learning that is flexible, exploratory, and interactive
- Triangulation: using different methods, sources and disciplines and a range of informants in a range of places and cross-checking to get accurate data
- Face-to-face interaction and multiple dialogues
- Seeking diversity and differences

RRA Design

Rapid rural appraisals usually employ purposive sampling. Thus, they produce rich information, but the results cannot be generalized to wider populations since they are based on a nonprobability sampling procedure. But scientific generalizations are not typically a goal of RRA. Rather, it is a diagnostic and planning tool. Box 11.1 describes a range of methods that can be used in conjunction with RRA.

Delineate natural regional features such as biomes, market systems, and political and cultural boundaries before creating the RRA interviewing framework. Each subregion should be depicted as part of wider regional processes and landscape features. Include a diversity of segments of the population in the study. Interview several individuals within subregions: ethnic groups, castes, migrants, and specialists. Interview people who differ in class, race, age, gender, and economic, social, and political status. Include decision makers or economic actors outside the subregion or region if they have significant activities or influence on land and resource use. For example, in the second phase of RRA in Zaire described in box 11.1, 100 women farmers were interviewed using a questionnaire, and dozens of other people were also informally interviewed, including local authorities, teachers, extension workers, church leaders, traditional chiefs, and

---

Box 11.1. Methods Used in Conjunction with RRA

As with any field endeavor, RRA requires a review of the literature, government reports, previous studies, databases compiled by other private voluntary organizations or local NGOs, and any available censuses. Review secondary data with a critical eye. It may be possible to significantly reduce the fieldwork if there is good recent literature available. The RRA must build on what has been done and be aware especially of any recent studies carried out in target communities. Research fatigue is a real issue even in seemingly remote areas.

Direct observation is used to increase learning. Try to see the interaction and activities from a local perspective and work on decreasing your own cultural biases. Discuss observations with key informants.

After RRA data yield information relating to research hypotheses, it is always possible to conduct a formal survey or baseline to test the hypotheses. If resources permit this type of follow-up, you gain the benefits of both informal and formal approaches. Often, however, it is not possible to conduct a follow-up survey. This is acceptable as long as you acknowledge the limitations of your data. Do not assume that your RRA has discovered the "truth." Make sure to verify results with an array of local experts and partners.

Various participatory exercises can be conducted to supplement core data collection. Some of these exercises include seasonal calendars, Venn diagrams, and transects (see chapter 15). Although these methods are commonly associated with PRA, they are also used in RRA. They are great icebreakers in the community and provide rich information. When properly facilitated, they give insight into how local people perceive the world around them.

---

clinic staff. Regional authorities and large-scale traders were interviewed as well.

Capture variation in the environment by interviewing groups near to and far from roads and markets or inhabitants of different micro-ecozones (e.g., riverbanks or slopes). A map or, more likely, a series of maps is essential for RRA. If there are no maps available, then find knowledgeable experts or staff to create one. A finished map always makes a nice gift in return to local communities.

The Good, the Bad, and the Ugly Faces of RRA

Use RRA when you need to characterize populations within a conservation area that encompasses several ethnic groups and resource management systems. Rapid rural appraisals are frequently used as needs assessments to understand viewpoints of different actors—local government officials, villagers, extension agents, or large and small traders—and to look quickly at several different communities in a region to assess potential, variability, and vulnerability. Data gleaned from RRAs are then used to inform baselines or other formal surveys, to strengthen proposal writing, or to start conservation planning. Rapid rural appraisals can be used throughout the life of a conservation initiative, during preliminary research for planning, for topical research when probing a specific topic, and even for monitoring exercises.

Rapid rural appraisals can be highly useful to inventory possible collaborating local institutions, to build a regional social-institutional map to plan future research and activities, to situate a small study or activity in a regional context, and to characterize large areas in terms of key indicators. But results of one RRA should never be interpreted as a blueprint for action.

The RRA may be a useful tool under certain conditions and with certain modifications but tends to be overused because the alternatives are not thought through. For example, funding a master's thesis student to carry out an in-depth study of an area might yield better data and be cheaper. In addition, the student will develop a sense of community dynamics and be able to identify local partner institutions and individuals. Planning for this research approach takes time and patience, however.

Rapid rural appraisals run ethical risks if the results are not shared with the communities that provide the data. One RRA carried out in the South Pacific by a major international organization, for example, gathered enormous amounts of data on marine management from twenty communities but did not budget any way to return the results to these communities. The budget did cover high-priced consultants to advise on and carry out the research, data analysis in the United States (which is very expensive relative to other countries), and workshops in the capital cities to review the results with national-level authorities. With some adjustment, the study could have budgeted to carry out mini-workshops in each of the communities. In addition to the point on ethics, study results need to be returned because it is the communities managing natural resources that need the information. Moreover, feedback from the community can help explain the findings and point out errors or modifications.

In addition, RRAs will not answer the "why" questions. They will describe features of a community, some issues and background information, and viewpoints of major actors, but there is not time for ethnography and other methods that identify underlying patterns of behavior. We cannot stress enough the importance of understanding that what people say is not necessarily what they do, and it is only through an understanding of behavior and practice—social reality—that effective initiatives can be designed. One way of doing some ground truthing is to use documentation to verify claims. For example, if people talk about the strength of their local institutions, ask to see rosters, minutes of meetings, or concrete outcomes of work, such as buildings and agricultural fields.

Perhaps the most important caveat of RRAs is that they can raise expectations. Imagine that you are living in a poor village and a team of professionals sweep in with a large vehicle and ask you all about your problems and needs. You are going to assume that some benefits will soon be coming, and you will wonder who is going to get these benefits. If you are like most people, you will try to position yourself and your activities so that outsiders see you as a future collaborator. You may be quite irritated to spend hours providing information to the team to discover that there will be no benefit for you or your family.

Networks in Space and Thought

Why Should Conservationists Study Markets and Trade?

Conservation researchers have multiple objectives in conducting market surveys and studies of trading networks. Market structures and patterns of trade are important data in understanding pressures on the resource base and ways that local people make a living (see chapter 4). In addition, conservationists often wish to understand markets for products or goods that use threatened species or habitats in order to stop or reduce the trade. In other cases, they wish to understand and invigorate markets for "sustainable use" or low-impact products or services in the hopes of changing incentive structures in local communities (e.g., in the case of BCN projects).

Goods Go Abroad

Let us look first at studies of markets for and trade in commodities. In the 1970s and 1980s, anthropologists adopted central place theory from economic geography to study the structure of regional markets. They were interested, for example, in how different regional market structures with distinct shapes and compositions affected the size and composition of local markets. In central place theory, markets for different sorts of goods are nested and spaced in relation to size of population centers according to consumer demand. But anthropologists found that in developing countries, many market structures did not fit a consumer demand model but were driven by commodity extraction

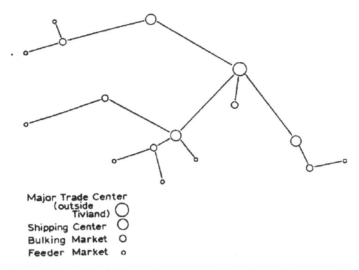

Major Trade Center
(outside
Tivland) ◯
Shipping Center ○
Bulking Market ○
Feeder Market ○

Figure 11.1. Dendritic market structure. Note how disconnected the centers are from one another. (From Smith 1976: 43, reprinted by permission of Academic Press; original from Bohannon and Bohannon 1968)

(Smith 1976). Thus, their shapes were "distorted" from what central place theory would predict (see figure 11.1).

Some theorists went further to examine the nature of trade in specific commodities: who was doing the trading and how the trade was structured. For example, Appleby (1976) studied the structure of the wool trade in Puno, Peru, and found that ethnicity and the nature of the global market for wool were important factors in determining the structure of the trade. Thus, the social and ethnic identity of traders and producers may influence relations and benefits from different types of trade, indeed, the structure of the trade.

Understanding the structure of trade in key commodities in an area is essential to obtaining an accurate picture of the local economy, including land and labor use. Price trends have implications for the livelihoods of local people and for the exploitation of resources. For instance, the drastic decline in world cocoa prices and the collapse of the cocoa agency in Cameroon led to significant deforestation in the early 1990s (Sunderlin et al. 1999.) The cocoa economy shaped trade in other commodities, household economics, marriage choices, regional infrastructure patterns, generational relations, and even spiritual matters (Russell and Tchamou 2001).

Often, existing studies and records can be used as a baseline. However, existing data may comprise only one enterprise or producer area. Government statistics on commodities can be useful, but take care because they can be outdated and incomplete. To complement these data, field research on key commodities should include the following:

- *Consulting with key informants in order to create a rough map of the market chain.* Market chains are the social and financial networks involved in the production, processing, bulking, refinement, and sale of products from commodities from producer to final consumer. They can be very simple (e.g., farmer A goes to the market to sell her tomatoes to those who will eat them) to highly complex, involving formal commodity markets and complex transformations of the product. Chart the margins, or price differentials, at different levels of the chain. These margins may depend on secondary processing, transport cost, social identities, global price trends, or lack of power of the producer or small trader.
- *Inventorying and studying bulking or secondary processing centers for the commodity.* It is much easier to trace patterns of supply and depict the overall structure of the trade from these centers than from areas of production or final sale. Often, these centers have rosters of suppliers (producers) that can be used to create a sample frame for later interviews.
- *Interviewing major traders in the raw commodity.* These may or may not control or be involved in the bulking and processing. Major traders can often have satellite operations operating in the same or different regions. Head offices may be located in the capital city with affiliates in regions. Find out about pricing structures, quantities, qualities, and varieties of product transport systems. While it may not be necessary or possible to trace out the whole market chain from a given location, it is good to have a rough picture. Are margins very small at different levels? Are there many levels in the chain? These questions can help you understand the structure of pricing to the producer.
- *Interviewing petty traders in the commodity.* This is a good idea if such traders fill an important niche, for example, serving marginalized areas or trading in lower-quality goods.
- *Interviewing producers in target areas about trends in commodity prices and production and relations with traders.* Assess implications of the market trends for land use by combining with farm-level research (see the discussion of the natural resource management survey in chapter 14). Probe also about bargaining and collective action for better prices, as this indicates strengths and weaknesses of community institutions in terms of external actors.

Trade and Markets of Interest to Conservation

Research on markets and trade can also hone in on specific products or subsectors (*filière* is an evocative French term for "subsector"): the production, processing, and market chains involved in transforming and selling the product, service, or commodity. For example, studies might measure the magnitude of trade or trends in trade in items such as NTFPs, ivory, marine organisms, bushmeat, or timber. But remember from chapter 5 that some key trading networks and markets may be hidden and that some may not be spatially identifiable as they are mobile. For example, ambulant traders may go directly to the producer or hunter to buy the product or sell consumer items; there is no physical market space.

Regional market studies may inventory all the large markets in the region and a random or stratified random sample of smaller markets. Surveys collect data on "arrays," or hierarchies, of goods available (what goods are the most common to the least common), prices, market timing (markets can be weekly, seasonal, or otherwise spaced), and sometimes identity of market vendors (see Ndoye 1997). They may also trace trading patterns through these markets by interviewing petty traders who deal directly with producers.

If marketplaces are very large, such as found in capital cities, they are divided into sections. Not all the sections will be of interest to a researcher for conservation. For example, a large urban market could include a huge number of stalls selling used clothing. What the conservation researcher will be looking for is the section that sells bushmeat, NTFPs (including medicinal plant concoctions), carvings or other artifacts (to examine what wood or fiber is being used), fish, or marine organisms. These sections may not be in the central market area. For example, there may be a special artifacts market, or bushmeat might be sold along the road from the interior or near the airport.

Stores and shops should not be neglected in market surveys, as they sell different items than markets, sell on a daily basis, and perform other functions (provide credit or serve as an investment for families). But it is often impossible to inventory all shops and stalls, and typically they sell consumer items from outside the area rather than locally produced or harvested goods. It is a sad fact that many rural people trade nutritious and valuable food items for less nutritious and expensive imported foods that are pushed in these stalls, which seem to be ubiquitous in the developing world. In Fiji, for example, one researcher found that women were selling local clams with high protein value and low fat and buying fatty imported tinned corned beef from local stores. These sales led to overharvesting of the resource.

Enterprises and Markets as Incentives

Conservation programs are increasingly studying how markets for specific products, especially those that are "sustainably harvested" or "eco-friendly," can bring benefits to local people. These studies require an understanding of particular subsectors. Inadequate information about markets significantly hampers a project that has chosen to produce and sell a commodity or service.

If a product or service is not already being marketed, it is important to wonder why and not just assume that it is because of unsatisfied demand. Subsector analysis should enable a project, community, or NGO to evaluate the demand for and market structure of a given product or service. But it is just a first step. The comparative advantage of the producers, their skills in production and business, social organization, social identities, infrastructure, and many other matters have to be taken into consideration. For this reason, BCN required all projects to produce a business plan that included an analysis of existing local, regional, and international markets. Many of the plans produced were unrealistic because they wanted to show that they could be profitable in three years, which was the time BCN was willing to fund with the requirement that the business should be viable in that time. Take a look at the BCN publications for further information on how conservation businesses employ market studies. Check out organizations such as Technoserve and EnterpriseWorks International (see "Market Analysis and Conservation Enterprises" in the Resources section), which are dedicated to small-enterprise development. They have tools for subsector analysis and for developing business plans for conservation-based enterprises.

Networks Are Not Just Economic

Like markets and trade, understanding regional social and political networks is essential to crafting ecoregional and landscape-level conservation strategies. They are difficult to trace, and proxies may need to be used. For instance, patterns of investment in particular localities (new schools or roads) may reflect political patronage networks to garner votes and/or the investment of external elites (people from the locality living abroad or in large cities who have access to cash).

Migration patterns have been extensively studied in relation to conservation, for instance, the impact of migration into and around protected areas or fragile habitats. Migrants can be motivated by government policies, as in the case of the "opening up" of the Amazon, or by networks of friends and relatives who are already in an area providing assistance. Distinguishing migrants and indigenous people in an area can be fraught with contradictions, particularly when indigenous people are granted privileges and migrants seen to be greater "threats." Ethnographic research is essential here in disentangling competing claims and histories (Giles-Vernick 2001; Hardin 2000).

Other social networks include kinship networks that in many societies may structure marriage alliances and investments and social associations, such as alumni groups and religious institutions. People draw on these networks for credit, housing, marriage partners, food, land, and other resources. Household members do not act alone in making decisions but are part of complex networks of social relations. A man or woman may have closer ties to his or her family of origin than to the marriage partner. Patronage networks can be vast and highly complex (see Schensul et al. 1999).

Conservation practitioners are now looking at the key role of coalitions of local people, activists, and other stakeholders in conservation (Associates in Rural Development 2001; Brown 2000; Khotari et al. 1995). Coalitions may draw on existing social networks or be a process of creating new networks to effect specific social changes. Landcare in Australia and the Philippines is an example of a grassroots movement that spawned coalitions of similar groups working on improved natural resource management (see Campbell 1994; Catacutan 2001; see also "Community-Based Natural Resource Management/Collective Action" in the Resources section).

Observation and familiarity gained through ethnographic methods are necessary in the study of social and political networks (see chapter 13). Good data are not likely to be obtained from surveys or focus groups except to identify the most visible networks and associations. To get an understanding of power relations, communication systems, and strategies that shape the effectiveness and reach of networks and coalitions, the researcher has to live within these structures. He or she has to attend meetings, trace out connections, and observe interactions. For instance, it may be hard to determine whether participation in collective action is voluntary or coerced, as it may be a combination of the two where people maneuver to get some advantage in constricted situations. The nature of participation has profound implications for conservation initiatives (Mahanty and Russell 2002).

12

Interviewing

With interviews, we move beyond analysis of remote data and quick assessments to systematic data collection. We ask people about their community, social relations, environment, and resource management categories and practices. Information from each interview leads to the formulation of more new questions. We increase our understanding of social context and local culture by incorporating these new questions into subsequent interviews. Acquiring a deep understanding of local communities ensures that we ask the right questions in the right way. This knowledge strengthens our research strategies. Discussing, analyzing, and thinking about interview data fuels the design of each phase of field research.

Interviews are a vehicle to learn how things work in the local community. While honoring the confidentiality of informants, discuss facts and concepts from interviews with trusted local people to get a reality check on how you listen to and understand them. This type of interaction shows interest and respect for the local culture and thus helps integrate researchers into the local community.

In this chapter, we first give some tips on how to conduct interviews in general and then discuss more specific types of interviews with key informants and groups.

Taking the First Steps

In order to set up interviews and other research activities in a community, you must first find out the proper protocol and what has worked well in the past. When setting up the research activities, consult local authorities, key informants, your local field team, experienced translators, and local and expatriate conservation colleagues. Find out who is who in the community. Some leaders may wish only to be informed of project activity, while others may be motivated to probe for details on purpose, results, and what is in it for them. Occasionally, leaders wish to block the start-up of a project because of long-standing conflicts if the project benefits the "opposing side."

It goes without saying that field research requires permission from local authorities to work in the area. This is not always so simple, as there are often many levels of authority. Take the opportunity to visit ministry offices and build a support network of local authorities (see box 12.1). If you fail to do so, at best the initiative will not run smoothly; at worst, the initiative can be sabotaged. In addition, at some point you may be working with some of these officials as partners.

Building Rapport

Take time to get comfortable around local people and to win their confidence. This process is called building rapport. Distrust of local people and mutual lack of understanding will yield unreliable data and lack of success in the initiative. Create conditions where the work is fun but still taken seriously. On the other hand, do not expect full acceptance or understanding even if you are a "native." Any educated person who has been away for some time will be the subject of suspicion. This natural caution cannot be erased or glossed over, nor can conflict that comes about when an outsider enters in with ideas and promises.

Conservation project managers must align themselves with local leaders who will support their work and must win the approval of those who do not (or at least "neutralize" them). Sometimes local people are burned out on projects that were mismanaged, that failed to

---

Box 12.1.   Introduction Protocol

Always meet with local leaders first—find out protocol in terms of who is to be met first. There may be several layers of leadership.
Have a local person take you to the village for introductions.
Meet and greet as many people as possible within the boundaries of local courtesy and protocol.
Ask about local traditions and history respectfully.
Ask permission to take notes or take pictures—always return copies of pictures.

produce results, or that left them with a string of broken promises. In this context, the coordinators are reminded to have integrity of word and to be very careful to take time to follow local protocol in order to build rapport in the community. This may mean attending or hosting dinners, hanging out, and drinking local brew. It will certainly mean having serious discussions about how the project is going to work for all people involved.

The Right Way to Interview Involves Attitude Adjustment

When conducting interviews, remember that it is a privilege to walk into a community and to have people trust you enough to give you their time, share knowledge, and often get nothing in return. One pitfall in conservation and development work is that some professionals assume that local people are obligated to talk to them because project planners know more, have project money, and are there to "help." These assumptions were discussed in more detail in chapter 8. It is crucial to the success of any initiative to let go of this way of thinking. Local people can pick up on these attitudes even if they are not articulated. It cannot be said too often: build, maintain, and practice respect for local people. Not only is this good field practice, but it produces better data and long-term relationships with communities.

Invite local leaders to participate by making available facilities to expedite the research. When appropriate, give them an opportunity to advise on the scheduling, timing, and location of research activities. Consult a wide range of local leaders on the implications of who is interviewed and when and where they will be interviewed. Will interviews be scheduled in advance? How far in advance? Will group meetings be held first to introduce the research? If so, which officials should be present, and who should speak? In what order should they speak? Maybe certain officials would like to participate in the first couple of days in order to personally introduce you to villagers.

Some of these local leaders will become key informants (discussed in this chapter). Ask them how to set up the interviews. In this culture, what is the best way to approach people for an interview? When is the best time? Does your interview really justify keeping a farmer off the farm for hours in planting season? Are certain roads impassible because of the rainy season? How long should you wait until after a funeral to begin interviewing family members? Can you conduct interviews at a celebration or at the market?

After you get permission to start work, what is next? How about introducing the interviews. Start the introduction by thanking the respondents for their valuable time and information. You may wish to make small talk to increase the comfort level. However, some people are very busy and want to hurry up and get started with the questions. Be sensitive and try to meet the needs of the interviewee. Remind the informant that the interview is confidential. Names will not be used, even in the computer data bank. (Note that people might not necessarily believe this.) Acknowledge and thank the informant for the trust that is being given.

Introduce the translator and any assistants and report that they too will honor the promise of confidentiality. Inform the respondent of the amount of time they can expect to spend talking to you. Before you get started, you can ask whether they have any questions.

Talk about how the interview will be conducted: how long it will take, the general themes involved, and how you will record the interview. Release forms are rarely used in the field. Ask permission before turning on a tape recorder or video camera and before taking any pictures. We recommend waiting a few days before carrying around cameras because in some ways they represent yet another artifact that subtly emphasizes inequities. (Some journalists argue, however, that it is best to make peo-

CASE STUDY

TRANSLATE YOUR NEEDS TO TRANSLATORS

If you are working with a translator for the first time, it is extremely important that you have trained the translator and reached a clear understanding of how to work together. An inexperienced translator can subtly take charge of the interview by editing answers in order to make it "easier for you." In that case, the time and interview are lost, and the respondent is confused. But a good translator can also take care to make words and phrases culturally appropriate so as not to offend people. Translating from English, for example, may mean that the sense of the question changes significantly and becomes less direct and more polite.

ple feel comfortable with the camera as soon as possible.) Make an effort to return copies of photos of individuals or groups. During a prolonged period of fieldwork, you may wish to create a community bulletin board of photos and other documentation of your work together.

Start the interview with topics of interest to respondents. People respond best to concrete issues that are critical to their survival: food, water, health care, and housing. Continue with questions germane to the heart of your research. In order to establish a rhythm, start with the easy questions first and then sequence in questions that require probing. Some people are more comfortable with silences (this varies by culture), so give respondents plenty of time to respond. They may wish to return to difficult questions later. Be patient.

In some cultures, respondents will offer food and expect you to eat. But sharing meals takes a lot of time. Be careful how you handle the first few interviews because you set a precedent for your behavior, and word gets around quickly. Perhaps you can politely take a rain check or suggest a gathering at a later date when both you and the respondents can contribute food. Use common sense and the guidance of your key informants to plan for these potentially awkward moments.

Listen, learn, and record notes quickly and carefully. Notes can be recorded by hand, computer, or tape recorder. We recommend the good old-fashioned notebook. It is less intrusive, it does not require batteries, and it is not as likely to be stolen.

There are times during an interview when it is appropriate to stop taking notes, as when a respondent talks about the death of a loved one, an accident, an illegal action, or an incident of heartbreak. When a respondent becomes extremely emotional or shares a confidence, show empathy by giving him or her your full attention and stop taking notes.

While approaching the close of the interview, you can give respondents notice by saying, "Two more questions to go." That keeps them informed on the timing issue. At the close, we recommend asking informants whether there is anything they want to ask you. Be sure to give them time to ask. We often ask for a little feedback and say, "How did it go?" This lets the respondents know that their perception of the experience is important as well as the data they provided. Also invite respondents to share information with you or other staff at a future time in case they think of something important. Offer this only if you are actually interested, open to a dialogue, and establishing a relationship.

Finally, thank the respondents sincerely, more than once, and emphasize the importance of their contribution. As a phase of your conservation program, remind informants that you look forward to sharing research results with them.

Your departure will be guided by the rules of the culture that you learned earlier from your preparation interviews with key informants. Shifting the conversation to something other than the interview can be a good way to start your exit. Sometimes small talk or telling a joke is a good way to go. Or put the focus on something that shows interest in them and acknowledges that they have important things to do. Their time is valuable. Ask what they plan to do on their farm or at the market that day. Say a final thank you and then leave.

In order to interview nonparticipants and nonbeneficiaries both within and outside of target communities, determine sensitive ways to approach nonparticipants. This may mean informal interviewing at the market or other large social gathering.

In virtually all cultures, men and women have different kinds of expertise and viewpoints and different levels of knowledge on various topics. Therefore, it is almost always desirable to interview adult men and women in each household. Depending on the culture, you may wish to interview men and women separately on specific topics, such as income and savings or consumption patterns.

Depending on the topic, it may be necessary to include widows and female-headed households in the study. Often these households are different in terms of resource management strategies.

Initial research for planning, whether it is as part of a rapid rural appraisal (RRA), survey, or ethnographic research, starts with a set of structured interviews that involve several questions. Eventually, we may notice that we keep getting the same answers to the same questions, even phrased in different ways. This is an indication that there is consensus on the answers to those questions and that planning can tentatively proceed.

CASE STUDY

PREPARATION SAVES FACE

During an informal interview in Cameroon, a local research assistant revealed that a woman who is not a mother might be embarrassed by usual survey questions on numbers of children. Therefore, the field team avoided the predicament by discreetly finding out in advance who had children and who did not.

We need to emphasize, however, that it is important to be alert to the fact that responses could be normative answers or reflect views that are not held by significant minorities of the population. Results need to be verified with observations and informal interviews (see chapter 13).

Building the Instrument

Types of Instruments

The research questions will determine the type of data needed, and this in turn determines the type of instrument that should be administered in the field.

There are two basic types of interview instruments:

- Formal interviews involve presenting respondents with the same set of queries.
- Semistructured interviews are based on topical guides—a list of topics that need to be covered during the interview (see box 12.2).

In a semistructured interview, the interviewer can probe (ask questions that prompt the narrator to continue the story or talk about a particular aspect of their story) for more detailed information on various points of interest. The instrument evolves as researchers learn more about the communities and the issues under study, as the following chapters will illustrate.

Survey questionnaires are based on a "formal" approach aimed at capturing quantifiable data. They allow us to engage in measurement and hypothesis testing. Survey instruments ask respondents the same set of questions. The advantage to this is that the data can be coded and

---

Box 12.2.   Topical Guides

A topical guide is a list of questions organized by theme or topic to prompt the person conducting the interview. Sample themes include the following:

History of the village
Hunting techniques used
Animals hunted (list of species)
What happens to the animals
Changes in abundance of species
Changes in hunting techniques

Box 12.3. Ranking

Westerners are accustomed to ranking and prioritizing. It is part of the culture where there are many choices and voicing preferences is normal. Ranking may not be understood, or it is understood in very different ways, in different cultures. Agreeing on criteria for ranking often reveals that researchers and informants are not on the same wavelength with regard to ranking. Thus, ranking should be seen as a heuristic rather than a formal exercise that sets choices in stone.

---

statistically analyzed, assuming that the data are derived from a representative sample. This topic is discussed in more detail in chapter 14.

Field instruments can have open-ended or closed-choice responses. Open-ended questions allow for an interactive approach and dynamic, two-way conversations. Researchers use questions with open-ended responses to learn about people or a topic. Open-ended questions take time to answer, and the enumerator must be prepared to listen and learn. Closed-choice questions have a fixed list of answers into which the respondent's answer must fit. These types of queries in the field are important if comparisons are being made but allow for little new learning. Ranking questions can be misinterpreted as well (see box 12.3).

Good Questions

Structure the content of questions based on local categories. You need to understand how society is organized in order to develop a good interview guide.

It is often useful to focus interviews around one commodity, even if there are other topics you want to probe: "I want to learn about the harvesting, processing, and sale of rattan." Talking about concrete topics hits on few sensitive points, while key questions or probes about local economics and politics can be woven into the interview as the discussion progresses (see box 12.4).

Order questions in such a way that they follow in logical sequence. For example, it is not necessarily logical to ask about assets found in the home and then move on to ask about domestic animals because they are considered assets. It may be more understandable to talk about life goals and then move to a discussion of household assets within the context of those goals.

The wording of questions is critical. For example, avoid leading questions such as, "How do you like the BCN project?" A better ques-

CASE STUDY

PUT LOCAL KNOWLEDGE INTO YOUR QUESTIONS

In a survey of women farmers carried out in central Africa, it was important to determine not just whether women were married but what "level" of marriage they had attained (informal, civil, religious, multiple wives, and so on). The type of marriage was thought to determine access to key resources. Hence, it would not have been sufficient to simply ask, "Are you married?"

tion to start off with might be, "Tell me what you know about the BCN project." Ask about what people have done before asking why they hold a certain point of view. Avoid questions with yes and no answers that have no follow-up question to explain why the person said yes or no.

The number of questions will be determined by assessing a reasonable time frame for administering the interview or survey. This is another good reason to pilot test instruments. No one likes to be held hostage by an interviewer.

Box 12.4. Good Topics for Discussion

The community's previous experience with development efforts and perceived outcomes

History of the settlement or village (founding families, incorporation of different commodities into livelihood patterns, roads, and so on)

Beliefs about outsiders and different social groups

History of the introduction and disappearance of crop varieties, plants, tree and bird species, and revenue-generating options

Priority investments and life goals

Differing viewpoints of generations

Changing food, clothing, marriage, and housing preferences

Patterns of illness and death (may be sensitive, but in general people are interested in talking about health issues)

Beliefs about human behavior in relation to use of natural resources

Table 12.1 illustrates that certain kinds of questions are appropriate to certain types of instruments. General questions about resources, people, and the site are appropriate for group interviews and community meetings, while specific questions are appropriate for surveys where it is important to measure specific variables and also the diversity of response in a population. Cluttering up a survey instrument with a lot of general questions or long lists of species names that are better left to key informant interviews is a serious mistake. Our experience is that it can lead to long delays in data analysis, especially if the species names are not accompanied by botanical samples that can be identified.

Table 12.1.   Questions for Different Instruments

Questions for Key Informant/Focus Group or PRA before Survey	Questions for Household or Individual Surveys
What is the seasonal agricultural and resource availability calendar?	Can your household survive without buying food? In which seasons is this more or less difficult? How often do you go to the forest to gather forest products?
What are the important groups and institutions in this locality?	What groups do you belong to, and what is your role in these groups?
What are the most important plants harvested?	What specific plants do you harvest? Which ones are sold or bartered?
How are decisions about land use made in the village?	How much land does the household own for agricultural purposes? How do you get access to forest resources?
What are the major commodities sold by people in the area?	What are the major sources of cash income of members of the household?
How are technologies introduced into the area? What new technologies have been introduced in the past ten years?	What methods do you use for hunting birds? Why do you choose these methods?
Who are the major traders and merchants in the area? Where and when are the markets?	How much rattan was collected and sold on your last harvesting trip?
What development activities have occurred in your village over the past ten years?	What solutions do you propose for depletion of the resources on the reefs?

Interview Improvement Tips: Getting the Most from Your Fieldwork

Go for quality in interviewing: try to understand a few things well in a concentrated interview rather than many things superficially in a rambling interview. Look for the underlying patterns of thought as well as the "answers." Why do people hesitate to answer certain questions while others are easy for them?

When in doubt about the appropriate units of analysis, talk to people, not households. You can always aggregate up from the individual: do not assume that the "household, "clan," "village," or "community" is an appropriate unit for looking at resource management, production, consumption, or benefit distribution. Take care not to interpret oral responses as an accurate reflection of actual behavior. Find out what people really do, not what they think they should be doing or what they think you want to hear. Unless you specifically want to learn about norms and values, adjust questions accordingly by making sure to ask what people did in a precise instance, not what they "typically" or "usually" do.

Hands on! When appropriate, do not be afraid to be playful with children. Children are a source of pride for the parents, and interacting with them can lighten things up during the period of introduction. In addition, do not just sit around the house or yard. Take the opportunity to work in people's fields or at other tasks. You can gain a lot of respect by showing that you are willing to get your hands dirty. Put down your notebook and chat at intervals, but write up the notes immediately after the interview. Do not rely on your memory because it will very likely let you down.

Consider whether and how you want to pay local research assistants. What will pay mean in terms of ownership of the information, conflict within the community, and quality of the information? Get advice from respected elders on this decision. Finally, keep an open mind: check and recheck assumptions and insights with team members and key informants.

Key Informants Keep Your Mind Alive

Key informants are local experts who are articulate and have keen knowledge about special topics of interest. They are kind and generous people because they invest their time and knowledge in the success of your project. Long-term relationships between researchers and key informants are life changing because their shared understanding allows you to enter a different world and see another culture through new eyes. Relationships with key informants based on mutual trust are critical to understanding local conditions that will affect the quality and success of conservation projects.

If an activity focuses on conserving medicinal plants, then key informants can include healers and their customers, health care workers, and forest users. Key informants help anchor the initiative in the reality of local culture. Ongoing research involves checking in on a regular basis with key informants with regard to research assumptions, questions and hypotheses, the formulation of interview and survey questions, and the interpretation of research outcomes. Key informants are not necessarily the most educated individuals in the community. They are people who are knowledgeable on specific topics. This knowledge often comes from life experience as opposed to educational training (see box 12.5).

Good rapport with a few key informants can yield qualitative information that quickly increases staff understanding of local conditions. Interviews with trusted and knowledgeable key informants throughout the life of the conservation activity ultimately enrich the experience of all involved. Once rapport is established with key informants, there can be a ripple effect of goodwill generated throughout the community. Yet there can be jealousy as well, particularly if the key informant is not a noted or high-ranking person, who would normally be consulted. Take care to choose key informants who are well regarded and who stay out of trouble.

Social researchers increasingly realize that successful conservation projects focus on serving local people. Motivation is important. We do not build relationships with key informants only to fortify our projects and careers; we do it also to root the initiative in local culture. Widespread community support for an initiative comes more easily with the endorsement of key informants. With local support come buy-in, ownership, and the sustainability of a project over time. Project leaders who understand the role of local people in project success are motivated to empower local people to participate in the effective management of their own resources.

Box 12.5.   Expertise Provided by Key Informants

Local language and storytelling
Plant and animal identification and behavior
Natural resource use and technology
Historical and current conflicts and conflict mediation
Family genealogies
Protocol and social appropriateness
Friendship

You can see from the preceding discussion that key informant interviews can take many forms. They may follow structured formats or more informal topical guides. Anthropologists have learned, however, that the most productive interviews come in informal settings, particularly when working together. The reason is that you see how your informant and others do things as well as hear what he or she and others say. Hence, key informant interviews merge with participant observation (see chapter 13).

Small favors and gifts are in order when a relationship has been established. For instance, in Cameroon we routinely bought medicine for the chief with whom we lived in the village and shared a bottle of whisky with another chief on a regular basis. He in turn invited us as honored guests to his wedding. For a couple who provided significant amounts of data about the running of their farm and business, we helped procure some new pineapple and manioc varieties, and for a women's group we contributed to buying cloth that was made into outfits for the group. Poignantly, the leader of the group, who had become very close to our research team, was buried in the cloth. These villagers did not forget us even though our contribution to their development was extremely modest.

Oral History Gives Voice to People's Stories

Oral histories are a special kind of interview process that involves the recounting of stories of people's lives, families, or settlements. They focus on what happened and how things changed from a particular person's point of view. These histories can range from a few minutes' recounting of key events to hours, days, and even weeks of linked stories. The content and length depend on the purpose of the research. Is it to understand how several people in a village view changes in resource management practices over a period of time, or is it to record the apprenticeship of a medicinal plant specialist and healer? The former might require several interviews of people from different social sectors, while the latter might entail long sessions with one individual and perhaps a few associates of that person. Oral histories might be collected from the following:

- Healers and medicinal plant specialists
- Conservation activists
- Poachers, loggers, and chainsaw operators
- Entrepreneurs
- Government officials
- Local leaders

- Harvesters and other resource users
- Craftspeople

Most oral histories are tape-recorded; some today may even be videotaped. It takes ten hours to transcribe one hour of tape, not including translation. This fact makes oral history a labor-intensive method. But the aim of collecting oral histories is not to be "efficient" but to preserve the richness of individual experience.

Bits of oral history woven through texts make the text come alive. People can relate to the common themes of life: childhood and heritage, education and skill building, struggles to attain maturity and reach adult goals, and successes and calamities. There is also profound human reality in the cyclical and forward motion of generational change. The process of conservation works within this reality. People must be able to reflect on their lives—their heritage and the future of their families—in order to think about conservation.

Oral histories can help younger people understand what older people value and why they value these things. Oral histories preserve values. Narratives of the lives of ancestors—real or imagined—play a critical role in all cultural belief systems. Role models are extremely important to human development. Many indigenous groups are now incorporating oral histories into "modern" educational materials.

Oral histories can also center on organizational or institutional history—the founding, purpose, struggles, leadership, and evolution of a conservation organization or community group.

The invention of tradition is a warning not to take one oral history as "truth." Triangulate information from other sources and use other methods to complement oral histories.

What Is Needed for Oral Histories?

Constructing oral histories requires the following:

- Practice in interviewing and keeping the flow
- Good language skills
- Probes prepared and tested with key informants
- A time line to trace the history against events that can help people recall when things happened and put them in order
- Patience and respect
- A clear plan for how to transcribe and use the histories
- Help with audio or video as needed so that the interviewer is free to concentrate on listening rather than dealing with technology
- Permission of individuals to use tapes or videos

CASE STUDY

INVENTION OF TRADITION

Social anthropologists have long noted that "tradition" is constantly being imagined in the service of particular interests and pressures. For example, it has been shown that certain "tribes" never existed as discrete entities before colonialism. They were created in the interests of the colonial state to divide and conquer or simply to classify subject populations. Today, tradition is invented when local lifeways that were formerly fluid and informal are codified and bureaucratized. Some aspects of "tradition" are emphasized, while others are left out, but the whole endeavor may be represented as being in the service of tradition. The lesson is that tradition evolves (Kuper 1988).

Getting Together for Group Talk

Identifying and working with subpopulations, sectors of society, and stakeholder groups is critical to conservation success. These groups may be seen as threats or as potential allies. They may be heavy users of the resource or investors in sustainable development. Learning about the needs, capacities, and knowledge of key groups as well as sharing information with them can be done in group interviews. But first it is important to identify these groups within the larger population using RRAs and/or ethnographic methods. Participatory methods can sometimes be used, but it is our experience that exercises in participatory rural appraisal often do not reveal minority groups and subpopulations without probing on the part of facilitators and further research.

Depending on the type of information needed, group interviews can involve targeted (focus group) or larger group or village meetings. Where focus groups are used to probe a specific topic, general groups can be used to introduce concepts; to get feedback on field research, staff performance, or service delivery; or to form work groups.

Approach key informants and leaders first before scheduling group interviews. Poorly structured or ill-timed group interviews can turn off the whole community to the research or the conservation initiative. Too much talk with only a small group of people is bound to raise suspicion. Thus, one purpose of key informant interviews should be to find suitable venues and approaches for group interviews. In many cultural contexts, it is appropriate to interview men and women separately and most productive to schedule interviews with subcategories of people, such as youths, minorities, or migrants, who might be constrained to speak up in group interviews. Group interviews are often necessary for introduction into a community but not sufficient to know the community as a whole. They should never be relied on for project planning or evaluation.

It cannot be assumed that information will flow from people attending a group meeting or workshop to the rest of the community, even to people within the same household. Information is power. As such, it can be guarded jealously or misinterpreted.

Focus Groups: A Marketing Tool for Conservation

In marketing research, facilitators elicit preferences and opinions from panels of potential consumers in order to improve a product. In con-

CASE STUDY

VILLAGE MEETINGS IN FIJI

Village meetings are a way of life in Fiji, be they to greet a chief or to discuss a contribution to be made to the church. Conservation messages can be integrated into these meetings. As such, a conservation initiative held many village meetings and workshops, and staff spoke at regular village councils. After two years of the project, however, a survey uncovered that a significant number of the people in the villages had never heard of the conservation initiative, and many others were confused about its goals and purpose. The people who had heard about the initiative, some said, were the older men who go to meetings and drink *yaqona* (extract of the roots of Piper methysticum) together afterward.

servation initiatives, focus groups can be used for ecotourism market research or to interview potential partners (see chapter 9). Focus groups allow researchers to orchestrate in-depth open discussions that can inform the researcher on specific topics of interest. For example, focus groups use the insights of a particular category of resource user (e.g., rattan collectors or elders) to zero in on issues of importance; to get clarification on important categories, strategies, and practices; or to test hypotheses about resource use. As such, these can be considered group key informant interviews.

Focus groups are conducted with a moderator who uses a topical guide (refer to box 12.2). The aim of the focus group is to get the entire spectrum of opinions on a topic. The same questions are used with each focus group in different locations or can be modified to fit subpopulations, gender, and other variables. Questions on the guide are often formed in collaboration with project colleagues and can be pilot tested. Use a moderator who has rapport with participants and is sensitive to group dynamics. Often, observers will listen carefully to the focus group and coach the moderator or add or adjust questions.

CASE STUDY

FOCUS GROUPS IN LIBERIA

In Liberia, during a time of peace, a democracy institution sponsored focus groups to gauge needs for civic education. The team leader consulted with key informants from local nongovernmental organizations on appropriate groups to include in the study. Together, they designed the study to include several groups interested in civic education: entrepreneurs, ex-combatants, high school students, handicapped and blind people, and women refugees. Next, the team leader trained the key informants to conduct focus groups. It was agreed that local people would respond more freely to Liberian moderators than to consultants from another country. Participants wrote moderator's guides, conducted several focus groups, and produced final reports. This collaborative effort generated data useful to the sponsoring agency and launched a partnership between all participating institutions.

Focus groups can be used to compare responses on a controversial topic in a controlled setting. For example, a focus group can discuss the social impact of a conservation initiative, and the scientists can listen to several "takes" on the topic within a relatively short period of time. Focus groups are an effective way to bring key players together in order to get a preview of how the initiative may or may not be suited to the local context and whether there will be buy-in.

Interviews are at the heart of social research. Because proper interview methodology and procedure are often neglected in applied research, we devoted a whole chapter to interviews. We match types of interviews to research questions and social situations. But most important, we talk about attitude: patience, humility, and respect. Interviews present the face of your initiative to the world. Enhance mutual learning and increase your chances for getting reliable and useful information by using the guidance in this chapter.

13

Ethnographic Approaches

Regional frameworks are essential for understanding patterns of resource use and change in ecosystems, but without knowing how people think, what motivates them, and how their lives are changing, the information is inadequate. You can study the forest through remote sensing, but eventually you have to visit the trees (and people).

This chapter discusses ethnographic and related methods relevant to the cultural aspects of conservation. It starts with the concept that ethnographic methods are particularly good for understanding local perceptions, categories, and worldviews. Ethnographic work is used to introduce a project into a community and should precede survey research.

Ethnographic research requires careful planning: doing a literature review, thinking through research design, learning the concepts presented in earlier chapters, and scoping out logistics. Be sure to review the steps fundamental to any type of research project described in chapter 10. Center your fieldwork within a regional framework and sample that provides opportunities for comparison, generalization, and replication. Note that many of the suggestions on interviewing in the previous chapter come from ethnographic practice.

Ethnographic research methods place emphasis on respecting the integrity and value of local beliefs and ways of thinking. They often do not "convert" local concepts into Western themes and categories. Rather, ethnographic methods try to understand local ideas and categories as they relate to one another in their own right. Later these categories can be translated across cultural boundaries and compared through "ethnology" or cross-cultural analysis. We recommend that every conservation initiative learn and use these methods: that conservation professionals become ethnographers, or experts on the people and culture of their field sites.

Ethnographic methods use the concept of culture (see chapter 2). Culture is shorthand for the fact that human groups use common language—not just spoken language but also symbols and behaviors—in order to survive. Culture can be thought of as the "glue" that links humans with one another. It shapes categories, behavior, and beliefs across all forms of human activity, what we term "economic," "political," and "social" behavior. While society is the physical shape taken by human organization (social groups, kinship, and institutions), culture is the behavioral, mental, and spiritual form: beliefs, values, norms, and ways of ordering the world. Society and culture are closely related concepts.

Some people do not believe that the concept of culture is a useful analytic tool because it is vague and subject to multiple meanings. Many feel that economics or genetics underpin human behavior. Others find that culture is the essence of the human experience—the way that learning literally shapes our brains to deal with the complexity of life. Let's get down to a more practical question. How can ethnographic methods, using this concept of culture, assist conservation initiatives? The most obvious answer to this question is that ethnographic methods are ideal for describing how people think about and use resources and how they organize themselves to use resources. Ethnographic methods can be less intrusive and costly than large-scale surveys. But ethnography is time consuming and is thought to have a limited range. It is labor intensive. The problem of scale raises its ugly head (Fox 1992).

For these reasons, ethnography is often neglected in development and conservation initiatives—with the growing exception of ethnobiology. Ethnobiology, described more fully in this chapter, is the study of the classification and use by local people of biological resources. Many practitioners are concerned that ethnobiology is being divorced from its cultural roots and is being used too often to collect data on plants or traditional medicine rather than to understand local systems of use and belief. Thus, we feel that culture needs to remain at the heart of the inquiry.

Participant Observation: Oxymoron or Way of Life?

Can one be a good observer and participant at the same time? Participant observation is one of the fundamental tools used by ethnographers to understand behavior in a new cultural setting. The method consists of participating, as unobtrusively as possible, in the daily activities of a community. It sounds simple, but in reality it is complex. First, one must be willing to take risks, such as living in remote areas as the locals do, or risking damage to self-esteem by making cultural errors. Second, one must be willing to be in cultural "limbo" for a period of time. Finally, one must be able to be inside and outside one or more cultures at the same time, constantly assessing what is acceptable and what is off limits: being a researcher but also a friend and neighbor (Powdermaker 1966).

Participant observation involves interviewing key informants or groups (discussed in the previous chapter) and collecting information using various other methods. It does not mean sitting passively in the village watching the folks go by. But the spirit is one of learning rather than "collecting data." Interview opportunities arise as the day unfolds, along with the washing, the housework, the farm chores, or the day at the market. An outsider will never be seen as a local. One professor of anthropology remarked that when leaving after several months of fieldwork, her friends told her that she was the nicest CIA agent they ever met. But the attempt to learn and the humility of the student can earn the respect of local people.

Some concrete examples of participant observation include the following:

- Attending ceremonies in the village and important life events involving host families
- Doing garden or harvesting work with the family
- Attending cultural and religious gatherings
- Tutoring local children or helping people write letters
- Shopping in the local markets
- Recreation research in national parks (Burch 1964)

Box 13.1 details participant observation opportunities specific to conservation.

Box 13.1.   Participant Observation in Conservation

Fishing, hunting, or harvesting trips—count/measure catch
Gardening—discuss fallow time, changes in crops, weeds
Village meetings—discussions about rules and responsibilities in the community
Market—observe displays, note prices for forest products, discuss traders' supply chains
Land tenure—observe demarcation and dispute settlement
Local economy—participation in commodity production and sale

Participation can create problems as well as open doors—for example, if you take the side of one family (even the host family) over another or get involved in political disputes or causes. Problems can arise from lending or borrowing large sums of cash or getting romantically involved in a small village (unless, of course, you are serious). You may learn things that are dangerous for yourself and others to know (Brosius 2001).

What can be gained from weeks or months of participant observation? It will enable much better use of any other methodology. It gives a "feel" for the data that cannot be obtained any other way. Often, people can do surveys or rapid appraisals and come up with completely erroneous data because they simply cannot discern whether people are telling the truth or hiding their real views.

We suggest that every conservation initiative employ one person, a local ethnographer, to carry out participant observation during initial and ongoing phases. The local ethnographer will be able to spot potential partners and particularly knowledgeable and talented people. Training of local facilitators and helpers adds immense value to the ongoing research and learning. The local ethnographer does not have to be a professional anthropologist; he or she could be a local student working on a master's thesis or a member of a local nongovernmental organization that has good relations with the community. The key is to build this option in to the work plan from the outset rather than planning only quick "data-gathering exercises."

Tools

To be a good participant-observer, you need the following:

- Local language skills
- Knowledge of protocol and acceptable behavior
- Willingness to devote time, from weeks to years
- Good note-taking and organizational skills
- Patience and humility (not a valued quality in much professional work in the West)

Host families and other key informants are critical to participant observation. Key informants allow us to have relations of trust and confidence yet maintain free access to others. In some cases, staying with the chief/village head is a good idea; in other cases, it is not. Much depends on the character of the individual and village protocol. One thing is clear, however: If there are bickering factions, it is not a good idea to stay with the leader of one faction.

Thus, before settling into a village, you need to learn about the area, get advice from authorities and local leaders, and interview potential host families. Talk about what you need and what they need. Often, customs of hospitality will make it difficult for people to ask for what they need. You need to probe as well as offer small gifts that are culturally appropriate. In one very remote area, soap was highly appreciated, while in another a bag of rice helped the family a great deal. It is best to avoid substantial money transactions. Be simple: do not bring a lot of equipment or fancy clothing.

The most important tool in participant observation is a notebook, now supplemented with a computer. We recommend handwriting notes whenever possible, though an electronic organizer with a keyboard might be small and discreet enough in some cases. Depending on the social context, taking notes is sometimes a discreet act and at other times a more deliberate and visible act. There are many times when notes should not be taken at all, and your powers of recall will be tested. Every evening, transcribe and organize notes, conversations, and observations on the computer.

Organizing and studying field notes must be a daily discipline in order to keep up with the abundant flow of data. Organize notes by theme, event, person or household, or other category. Computers add a great deal of value now beyond simply word processing because programs are available to sort and analyze qualitative data (see "Research Guides" in the Resources section).

Typically, researchers are forming mini-hypotheses during participant observation that they test through triangulation. This means observing or discussing events and behaviors with different kinds of people—those of different genders, roles, generations, and statuses. Triangulation may be used to verify or to explore. For example, I may be trying to understand how the community views its leadership. To formulate a hypothesis, direct and indirect questions are posed of different sectors of society—elders, young men, unmarried and married women, and local elites. I first need to understand relations between my informants and the local leadership. Informants' responses may have to do with patron–client ties between individuals and outsiders or differences in assets, such as landholdings. Triangulating the different viewpoints will give me a much more nuanced picture of perceptions of local leadership than simply asking one key informant or even surveying people in a formal way. There is art here!

During participant observation, other data gathering is going on at the same time: census, key informant interviews, oral histories, and tracing genealogies. The methods are mutually reinforcing—there is a high learning curve. Researchers have discovered that the highest-quality information often comes from informal discussions and observations. Most people simply do not feel comfortable with formal surveys and data gathering but like to chat while gardening, cleaning the house, fishing, or drinking beer in the evening.

Men and Women Can Participate Differently

Years ago, a woman anthropologist bemoaned the fact that although she went to her field site in Nigeria to study local politics, most of the important councils were closed to women (Bowen 1964). Her hosts wanted her to take interest in the local plants and animals. A male researcher similarly complained that women were too shy to talk to him. Gender is a fact of life—you cannot change it. But you can adopt strategies to acquire information across genders. The best one is partnership between a man and a woman in carrying out research. One partner can be local, one nonlocal. However, you might create gossip through your pairing, so prepare to deal with it. Another strategy is to cultivate key informants who are socially able to communicate across genders. These individuals may be older (in respected categories) or may be more educated (village teachers or religious leaders).

The Elegance of Local Knowledge

All rural people have a way to classify biological resources that they use and that are in their environment. These classifications, or taxonomies, are created for plants, animals, and habitats and can be based on use, location, color, texture, or social considerations. Taxonomies are part of a culture but, according to ethnobotanist Brent Berlin (1992) and others, may also have resonance with the natural order. As such, learning how people classify the natural world may tell you not only a lot about local people's worldview but also about how nature works.

Creating an ethnotaxonomy means more than just generating lists of plants or animals; it is an understanding of the different levels, or taxa, employed to classify species (see figure 13.1). How are different species distinguished? How are they lumped together? How many levels are found? In some cases, a system may be simplified when people rely less on natural resources for subsistence. This process of simplification can happen in one generation.

The ethnotaxonomy is only one step. You need to ask about the history and use of species and varieties. Specialists may have different

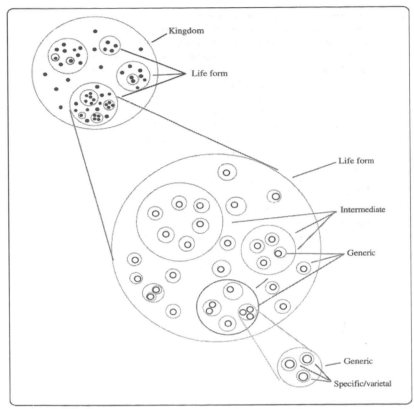

Figure 13.1. *The five primary ethnobiological ranks and their respective taxa. Biological species are indicated by small black circles. Ethnobiological taxa are indicated by faint gray circles. Relative position is meant to convey degree of affinity. (From Berlin 1992: 23; reprinted with permission of Princeton University Press)*

names for species than nonspecialists. There may be significant variation in knowledge, depending on gender, occupation, education, and age. In addition to naming species and varieties, it is also interesting to see how local people distinguish different parts of a plant or animal. What parts do they name? What parts are not named? Do names of species or varieties change depending on the season, the location, or the part of the plant harvested? What associations among species are identified, and what is the rationale for association?

Ethnobiologists working in the field of traditional medicine collect information about the uses of plants and animals to cure specific diseases. They must learn not only about the natural resources used but also about concepts of disease and healing. Alternative medical systems, such as found in India, China, and Africa, are highly complex and involve totally different views of illness and health than found in Western medicine. The use of medicinal plants is seen as an incentive for conservation, but they also may be a focus for conservation because under circumstances of open access (see chapter 4) and commercialization, medicinals are overused and depleted.

Ethnobiologists often collect specimens to place in botanical collections. They work closely with local biologists and parataxonomists, who are trained to identify species using local as well as scientific classifications. They may create transects, or plots, to measure and monitor species abundance. This monitoring can be done in a participatory manner (see chapter 15).

For conservation, it is essential to understand both the protection and the exploitation of important plants and animals. As such, the cultural systems of processing, harvesting, and otherwise transforming plants and animals must be studied. The views of farmers, hunters, or other resource managers on specific technologies can be gleaned from a study of their classification systems as well.

Botanist Charles Peters notes that ethnobiological information is embedded in a resource management system that affects the abundance of the species involved. "Destructive harvesting and overexploitation . . . can gradually eliminate plant species from the local environment. Deliberate planning, controlled harvesting, and forest management, on the other hand, can greatly increase the distribution of and abundance of lo-

CASE STUDY

THIS USEFUL TREE IS A WEED

During fieldwork in Cameroon, farmers were asked about a "multipurpose" tree (Cassia spectibilis) found in their forests and fallow lands. Researchers at the agroforestry institute wanted farmers to plant this tree to restore soil fertility. Farmers remarked, "We do not have a name for this tree because it is a weed. It destroys our fallows." Their response indicated that they did not see the tree as useful.

cal resources" (Peters 1996: 242). These dynamics have to be understood because species populations can change rapidly, and this information cannot be gleaned simply by generating lists.

Ethnobiologists study markets for plants and plant products because these locations and trades can quickly give an indication of how intensively a species is being used and by whom. In markets, medicinals may be sold that mix different plants. The mixtures may be adulterated or changed when species become rare or extinct. Martin (1995) discusses market research in ethnobotany (see also Sunderlin 1999).

In chapter 15, we discuss ways to use action research to study resource use, the classification of land and resources, intensification, and the introduction of new technologies.

Intellectual Property Rights

Although ethnobiological knowledge is disappearing fast all over the world, we cannot just hurry in and collect data. There are now in place conventions, protocols, and guidelines for working in the field of ethnobiological knowledge. Intellectual property rights have to be respected in collecting, using, or publishing local ethnobiological information (refer to the ethical guidelines discussed in chapter 8).

The matter extends not just to ethnobiology but also to plant collection in general and has become a significant bone of contention in discussions about biodiversity conservation. Some botanists and field biologists feel that it has become so difficult to collect specimens that their work has suffered. On the other hand, representatives of governments and nongovernmental organizations in areas of high biodiversity feel that they are not getting sufficient remuneration for their valuable species, particularly those used in drug development. While nations may reap more benefits, these rarely trickle down to local resource-user or -owner communities.

One remedy proposed in India is the community biodiversity register, pioneered by Madhav Gadgil and colleagues (Gadgil, n.d.). These registers are created by communities with the help of students from many technical colleges in India. They include not just species but medicinal remedies, even stories and legends relating to nature. Sacred groves are also delineated and documented.

The point is that you must familiarize yourself with laws and regulations as well as recognized ethical standards concerning the collection of ethnobiological data (see Convention on Biodiversity under "Sustainable Use of Natural Resources" in the Resources section).

Tracing the Family Tree on the Land

While oral history is concerned with an individual, genealogy looks at several generations of a family. Kinship maps are derived from the merger of several family histories or genealogies. There can be several reasons for collecting detailed family histories, including the following:

- *To get an idea of kinship relations and hence relations of power, influence, authority, and obligation in a community.* Who is the head of the clan? Who is the senior wife in a large family? What nephew will inherit the chiefly title?
- *To trace patterns of inheritance and land rights.* Who lived and farmed where? When did others marry in and get rights to land? What are the patterns of migration?
- *To determine demographic trends, such as population growth/decline, mortality, and morbidity.* These trends help explain patterns of land use, although distribution of resources and technology as well as qualities of the land play very large roles as well.
- *To understand underlying patterns of alliance and factionalism.* Which group moved away from the main clan and why? Were there land disputes involved? How do these disputes translate into changes in use or management?
- *To get insight into concepts of kinship and relationship.* What are the different rights and obligations of maternal and paternal uncles to their nephews?

CASE STUDY

GENEALOGIES ASSIST IN BRINGING TENURE SECURITY AND SETTLING CONFLICTS

Drawing genealogies has been important in ancestral domain claims in the Philippines and in mapping clan and family ownership of land in Solomon Islands, where clans have complex and interlocking oral agreements about land dating back for generations.

Genealogical information can be obtained through direct interviews or review of records found in government offices, in parishes, and with families. Direct interviews mean asking about all births, marriages, and adoptions. Difficulties emerge with the direct method because often people do not recall or do not want to recall the deaths of children, infidelities, and other "abnormal" situations. People's names can change or differ according to the status of the listener, and in some cultures it is not possible to speak the names of dead people. Records, however, may be incomplete as well. Therefore, a good genealogist consults and cross-checks every available source to get the most detailed accounting possible.

Conservation initiatives are now using genealogies to trace land use and history and to help local groups map and claim land. Often, claims must be backed up with histories of occupation of the land. It is a daunting process, but in the long run it yields rich and culturally appropriate information.

A kinship diagram is the simplest form of genealogy. It can be drawn during participant observation and recording of oral histories. Figure 13.2 gives an example of a kinship diagram going back four generations. Merging such a diagram with a history of migration and settlement will give some idea of land claims and ownership. But often these histories are very tangled and have to be triangulated, as different families have different histories.

Learning about Our Time on the Land

Ethnography, human ecology, and human geography come together in the study of land history—the story of changes brought about by humans that affect plants, animals, soils, water, and natural features in an area. Of particular interest are changes in technology (adoption of more intensive methods or the use of new substances such as fertilizers or poisons) and changes in areas devoted to specific resources (new commodities being developed or the collapse of a harvesting area). Chapter 15 reviews ways to study these changes with local people.

Recent archaeological research highlights the tremendous impact of humans on ecosystems. Many ecosystems or habitats deemed "natural" are now known to be anthropogenic, meaning that humans have shaped them through various practices, such as encouraging certain useful species, destroying others through the use of fire or cutting, or selective hunting and gathering. The oak forests of northern California are a good example. Native Americans managed them through pruning, fire, and selection before European settlers came in, as acorns were an important

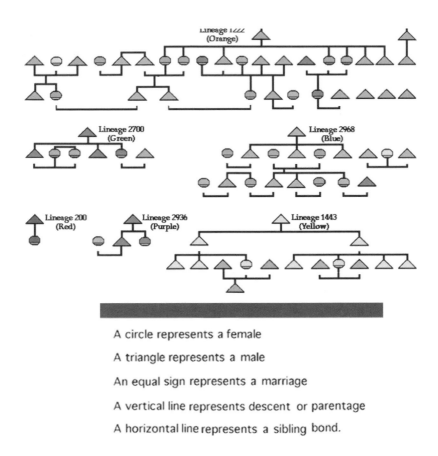

A circle represents a female

A triangle represents a male

An equal sign represents a marriage

A vertical line represents descent or parentage

A horizontal line represents a sibling bond.

Figure 13.2. *Example of kinship diagram indicating four generations, with key to symbols.*

source of food. Settlers converted these managed forests to "wild" forests by stopping planned fires to allow the vegetation to return to its "natural" state (Williams 1994). The resulting wildfires destroyed many forests.

Archaeologists help us understand how ancient peoples conserved biodiversity (both habitats and species) and how they destroyed it. For example, they determine how a variety of plants were used at a settlement and even what kinds of people used certain plants. They study extinct human settlements to determine whether collapse was caused by ecological stress, such as failure of the food or water supply or decline in soil fertility. They have shown how many large mammals disappeared from the face of the earth because of hunting pressures. But can we learn anything from this study of past humans that could shed light on today's predicaments?

Archaeology Can Inform Conservation

Site History

What other settlements existed at the site? How long have people inhabited the area? Were there more people in the past or fewer? In what ways did their practices affect plants or animal habitats?

This work is difficult where there is little in the way of material culture (artifacts) that is made out of nonorganic materials, such as stone and metal (often the case in small, mobile groups living in forest zones).

Technology History

Has hunting, fishing, or gathering technology become more intensive, allowing people to catch more with less effort? How quickly did the change come about? What happened to the population after the technology shift?

Political History

Did social stratification increase? Were some people beginning to be able to command the labor and resources of others? What happened to the biological resources as a result of this change in society?

CASE STUDY

MAYAN GARBAGE PROMOTES BIODIVERSITY

Excavations indicate that a range of cultural practices—such as the management of waste, the discard of local industry by-products, construction practices, the burial of the dead, the reuse of construction debris, and the practice of building abandonment—contributed to the soil formation process in such a way as to improve the soil quality over the long term and, by way of this improvement, to affect vegetational succession and thereby foster biodiversity (Graham 1998).

Agrarian Change: The Politics of Agricultural Production

The study of agrarian change, or how people's use of land and resources for agricultural production has changed over time, has a long and illustrious past (see "Land History" in the Resources section). Historical perspectives reveal that land use is complex, shifting, and not linear. Societies can move from more intensive to less intensive land use systems, depending on social and economic forces. Different households can use very different land and resource management strategies over time.

Agrarian studies research looks not just at changing technology or land use but also at the social formations of people who work the land. Ownership of land and resources within the wider political economy is a central question of agrarian studies. For instance, a study might describe the transformation of a society from one centered on the labor of serfs who are subject to large landowners to one where small- and medium-scale farmers own their own land.

Political change is another key theme of agrarian studies. The struggles against slave labor, serfdom, large-scale landgrabbing and landholding, contract labor, and underpaid agricultural labor have led to wide movements and social change. New technologies, such as those disseminated in the Green Revolution or in the more recent move toward genetically modified organisms, also generate struggle and social change that has been documented by activists, journalists, and social scientists.

The point is that land and agrarian history can inform conservation initiatives by revealing the relations between land use and social formations. In addition, agrarian studies show how complex systems can build up, often defying quick categorization. Patterns of land and resource use that may seem ancient can be quite recent, while others are deeply embedded in social systems.

In the Beginning Was the Word

Language is more than sound (or gesture, as sign language is a true language). In language, sounds become phonemes (significant sounds), and phonemes put together become morphemes (building blocks of words). Words are strung into sentences with grammar. Linguists have taught us that learning language is wired in to the growth of the brain. Learning language is what makes us human. Learning a particular language has a lot to do with learning a culture—its rules, categories, classifications, and its resources.

So what does that have to do with conservation? Two key points can be made: (1) If it has a name, it has a meaning and a history, and (2) names and concepts indicate attitudes through relationships and associations.

Berlin (1992: 26) says that "in Western scientific biology, nomenclatural [naming] concerns have become essentially legalistic, pedantic, and tedious. . . . The study of *ethno*biological nomenclature, however, is quite a different story . . . [it] represents a natural system of naming that reveals much about the way people *conceptualize* the living things in their environment."

When a species is useful to a population, it is given a name. That name might reflect its use, location, color, or relation to other species or other characteristic. When the species is no longer useful or it disappears, the name is lost as well.

Names of species can indicate the relations among different groups, as when one group adopts the name and use for a species from another group. Comparing names across groups can give an indication of how long the species has been known. For example, if many related language groups have the same or similar name for a species, it has been known and used for a long time. The organization Terralingua (see its website under "Language and Biodiversity" in the Resources section) links the loss of biodiversity with loss of languages, showing that when a culture loses its language, the knowledge of species and their uses and associations can be lost. A language is an encoding system that represents millennia of coexistence between humans and other species.

But there is more: Linguistics teaches us that language reflects social values. It expresses social hierarchies, protocols, and concepts of time and space. Are there terms that indicate protection or care of biological resources? How are these terms related? Is the language of the people being lost or degraded through contact and education and with it knowledge of species and habitats? Creating new terms for forest guards, conservation officers, or other new functions within a community-based conservation effort can build on the linguistic heritage.

This is the critical point: Researchers need a deep knowledge of the languages of the people at any conservation site in order to understand their behavior and society as well the foundations of their knowledge.

Ethnography Thinks Fast and Big

A program officer for a conservation initiative once asked an anthropologist whether he could help the project out in getting insight into a site near where he had worked. The anthropologist replied, "Give me a couple of years, and I might be able to say something useful about the people in that area." The conservation officer replied, "We don't have a couple of years. The loggers are coming!"

Multisite Ethnography

Ethnography does take time, and it is often limited in geographic scope. There are some notable exceptions: Multisite ethnography (Marcus and Fischer 1986) is an emerging form that focuses on the study of systems and processes. It involves the tracing out of systems and intensive interviewing and observation at a number of strategically chosen sites within the system.

As an example, multisite ethnography can be used to study a market system, say, markets for nontimber forest products or bushmeat. It differs from economic or survey-based analysis because the focus is on understanding relationships at different sites and levels of the systems. Multisite ethnography could also be used to study conservation projects, studying the multiple levels from the site to the headquarters of international organizations (Gezon 1997). Another promising focus for multisite ethnography is to examine urban–rural flows and the impact of urban consumption on land use and social organization for production (Trefon and Defo 1999).

Ethnology

Ethnology is the comparison of ethnographic research across time and space. Ethnology, together with archaeology and other methods, has been used to show how human social organization evolved from small, mobile groups to highly structured societies. These changes are linked to changes in land use, technology of exploitation, migration, warfare, and other factors. They show how groups are related to one another. The ethnologies, land histories, and ethnographies that deal with the populations in your region are fundamental documents in the literature review.

"Quick Ethnography" Means Deep Collaboration with Field Ethnographers

If research is planned as part of an initiative that is to last several years, long-term ethnography should be given a place. Other methods may be rapid and wide ranging but more expensive if large teams are used. Using existing ethnographic research and collaborating with anthropologists on the ground is the best course of action. Misunderstandings are common, however, between ethnographers in the field and conservation projects (West 2001). Ethnographers see their responsibility as mainly to "their" people, while conservationists see theirs as mainly to "their" biodiversity. Ethnographers have problems sharing their nuanced and deep understanding of people and their habitat with conservationists who are searching for quick answers to problems. We suggest the following steps to produce fruitful collaboration:

- Start collaboration between conservation projects and field ethnographers by learning about the land and resource management systems of local people
- Request short histories of the people and ask how different groups relate to one another
- Ask the ethnographer to help the project understand how local people view conservation problems and solutions in their own contexts
- Learn with the local ethnographer about divisions, factions, and subpopulations that may have differing views, management systems, and goals

If there is collaboration on these short and specific tasks, mutual respect can build and lead to wider collaboration.

Mini-ethnographies can also be part of the tool kit, with an understanding that any quickly gathered information needs to be cross-checked and verified. Mini-ethnographies are case studies of groups, situations, or categories of individuals that provide important insight into their roles, knowledge systems, and social characteristics. Examples might include the study of a resource-user group that would involve participant observation, land use mapping, ethnobotanical research, and oral histories of individuals. Such a study could be done in two or three months if the researcher is prepared with language skills and background reading. Case studies can be done in an even shorter time if there is knowledge of the people and a level of trust in the researcher. These case studies can complement cross-site or regional analyses by describing history, processes, and interrelationships that cannot be captured in larger-scale studies. Build these forms of research into the program, and it will be much richer, especially when local ethnographers are used.

14

Surveys

Surveys take many forms and have many uses. Here we focus on census surveys as well as surveys that use representative sampling so that the statistics that describe the sample population can be used to describe the whole population in the study area. Surveys have an important niche in conservation research. They allow us to quantify critical parameters that describe and explain how things work and the relationship between actors and variables in human and physical environments. Surveys allow us to establish a baseline so that with follow-up we can measure change over time. Surveys complement other data-gathering methods that might produce more profound insight and learning but are limited in other ways. For example, rapid rural appraisals (RRAs), action research, and informal interviews do not get systematic and generalizable data. These methods may not tease out important subpopulations and may fail to explore causal relationships.

This chapter focuses on census surveys and the importance of baseline surveys to conservation research, monitoring, and evaluation. This chapter follows the discussion in chapter 10 on many of the questions you need to consider before deciding to do a survey, including questions on sampling and scale, preliminary research, and how to organize a strategy to conduct survey research in the field under complex conditions.

Before we review survey types useful to conservation, let's take a look at the big picture. Surveys are powerful instruments for measurement and understanding relationships between variables important to the research. Surveys force us to carefully think through our research questions and build and test explanatory hypotheses. Surveys have scientific credibility that other methods do not have, being based on representative sampling procedures (for a discussion of sampling procedures, see chapter 10).

But we suggest there is more to consider here. We suggest that surveys are often overused in the field, perhaps as an easy solution to situations that seem overwhelmingly complicated. Or sometimes we do surveys because that is what we were trained to do.

Think of all the surveys that have been conducted over the years by nongovernmental organizations and other institutions. Most of these data are not available to other institutions, and so data are being collected over and over. If you decide to do a survey, we suggest that you design a survey and database that can be shared not only among branches of your organization but across institutions as well. Find out what data are already out there on the population of interest, and this will help you more efficiently design future surveys.

Keep in mind that conducting a field survey is a huge undertaking. You must coordinate the design with your partners and key informants and be clear about the survey's objectives and information needed to meet those objectives. Only then can you start formulating questions to obtain the needed information. Next, you must field test the initial survey and eliminate foggy language and confusing questions. You must build rapport, get permission, work with translators, build a team, and include and train local people on the team—review the steps we described in chapter 10. What about the weather? Another point to consider is scheduling time to share the results of the analysis with the community (see chapter 16). All these activities require a substantial investment of time and resources.

Then there is data entry, data cleaning, and analysis; a write-up; and proofreading, editing, and rewriting. A common shortcoming of surveys is to allocate insufficient time for analysis and write-up; these tasks, not data collection, are usually the main bottlenecks. Will the donors like it? Yes, it is all a required part of doing a survey. Sounded so simple in the beginning, but it really is not. We are not saying, "Don't do surveys!" We are saying just be sure that is what is needed and that you can run the full race. We have seen esteemed professionals take "shortcuts" to meet sampling criteria and generally peter out at the end of a field survey. It is exciting but exhausting work. The problem is that it is not desirable to tamper with the integrity of a sample after starting data collection.

We encourage you to think it over before you decide to reach for the old "tried and true" survey approach. Consider some of the other approaches presented in other chapters. Look closely at your reason for being in the field. What are the results needed? Do they require numbers? Are you looking to measure something or to create conditions for action and social change (see chapter 15)? Sometimes it is possible to get most information through key informant interviews or through

RRAs. In fact, RRAs came about as a viable alternative to surveys as researchers argued that surveys not only require too many resources but also provide too many data that are never used and are too precise for planning needs (see chapter 11).

One last note. Once we observed local people in the Philippines literally run the other way when they saw a team of survey enumerators heading their direction. Perhaps there is a message there.

Taking the Measure of the Community

Censuses query each household in the target area, and therefore a sample is not needed. Keep the census simple. Just because conducting a census can be a huge undertaking does not mean that you should ask lots of questions in order to "make it worthwhile." On the other hand, a few questions can be added to the census to help you later sort or stratify the households or villages into categories for future surveys. The amount of time it takes to do a census depends on many factors, including the size of the geographic area, the size of target population, the length of the questionnaire, and the number of enumerators available for the work.

Always refer to any censuses that exist for the study area. Accessing census data is part of the homework that needs to be done in every field study. Government censuses can be a rich source of information on the composition of households. They include such variables as education, source of water, type of housing structure, age, gender, occupation, and number of children. But they also may be flawed or very outdated. Even if the data are somewhat unreliable or outdated, however, they can still help orient staff to the study area. Formulas can be devised to update population statistics. In countries where the government is weak, there may be no census.

At the village level, a census allows for sociopolitical and physical mapping of the community and provides an opportunity to create a sampling frame for other types of research. Often it can reveal hidden sectors of the population that do not emerge with community-level or group meetings. A complete census is an invaluable introduction to all sectors of the community, including people who may be passed over even in "participatory" exercises.

Staff become intimately familiar with the study area. For field research, censuses are a wonderful starting point for becoming familiar with a community. It shows respect to take the time to visit each household. Staff are seen on the streets and in the fields. This visibility creates good public relations, builds rapport, and allows staff to get to

THE CENSUS LAYS THE GROUNDWORK

Before undertaking a survey on resource management strategies of households in selected villages in Cameroon, a census of all the households was carried out. The census was needed because government records were outdated. In addition, it was important to map the location of each house for the village map, as later the location of fields, fallow lands, and forests would be added and population densities calculated.

The census gathered basic demographic data, such as number of people living in the house, relationships, level of education, skills, and membership in groups. It also asked about the types of fields cultivated that year. This question enabled the researchers to stratify the survey sample into two groups: those who cultivated a long-fallow (forest) field and those who did not cultivate one. The difference was important, as the researchers wanted to explain why people were cutting forest to cultivate long-fallow fields.

know the community. However, keep in mind that as you gather information on the target population, you can bet they are also gathering information on you. It might be necessary and appropriate to hold several group meetings, key informant interviews, and perhaps focus groups of selected people before doing a census.

This is an opportunity to draw a map of the area. The map and the census data can be used to guide the field team, to draw samples (the census automatically creates a sampling frame from which to derive your sample for a later survey), and as a gift of reciprocity to the community, who can point to it with pride if they have participated in its design and implementation.

If the initiative is committed to participatory research and if the population is small enough, it can be a good opportunity to do a participatory exercise or paper census with full community participation in mapping and describing households (see chapter 15). A census is a valuable tool for analysis of population densities and extrapolates from these to create scenarios of changing pressures. Data can be entered into a geographic information systems unit together with other data to show resource use patterns. Use common sense to determine whether a census is needed for the study. If it is not feasible to conduct a census, use other secondary data and methods to become familiar with the population and find other sources that can be used as a sampling frame for your survey.

The following are needed for a census:

- Permissions at all levels
- Assurance that the census will not be used for purposes such as taxation or tracking illegal migrants
- Trained local enumerators
- Map of the area and a means to locate each household on the map
- A survey instrument that collects basic demographic information and may add a few questions to further research
- Data analysis capacity and resources (including time)

The Household Is One among Many Possible Survey Units

Many surveys for development and conservation purposes use the household as a unit of analysis—a house after all visible measure. The residents of the house may or may not conform to researchers' notions of family—they may include lodgers, several generations, adopted children, or more than one wife. In some cases, it is important to determine who is not in the house, in other words, who is at school, living in the city, contributing income, or claiming land. Hence, questions have to be included about nonresident family members.

The key people to interview in a house or household are the owners and users of resources, usually the senior men and women. Sometimes the very senior men and women can be functionally "retired." Interview them only on questions of history and change in practice. They can get tired easily.

Always interview both senior men and women. If necessary and appropriate, interview them separately. Do not let men speak for women and vice versa. To get younger people's points of view, interview them separately in focus groups. If people are anxious about individual interviews, do your "household survey" in a group rather than in individual houses.

Count on spending at least three weeks in the field. The time needed to conduct a household survey varies by geographic size of the area, the sample size, and the number of enumerators available to do the work. Make sure to schedule time to obtain permission from local authorities, including heads or families or clans.

Household surveys, like all research discussed in this book, can be a way to build local capacity, expand knowledge, and forge closer partnerships, as box 14.1 illustrates.

But we reiterate that households are often not an appropriate unit of analysis for a research question and certainly not the only one. Understanding patterns of investment, lines of power and authority, and resource management requires looking beyond the household at networks, kinship units, neighborhoods, and beyond.

Starting out with a Survey

The baseline survey is a snapshot of a site before or during the initial stages of an initiative. Projects use this baseline as a jumping-off point and a means to gain knowledge about the population, economy, and resource management. This knowledge feeds directly into the initial activities in the form of the following:

- Providing an initial measure for certain indicators of social change
- Mapping households and social sectors in relation to lands and other resources
- Understanding differences among households and social sectors

A baseline survey of a population establishes a base of information with a specified degree of accuracy against which change can be measured. The changes or impacts are measured by comparing monitoring data to baseline data (see chapter 16). Therefore, both types of surveys use the same indicators to measure change.

Baselines aim to capture the "before and after" picture with regard to conservation impact. The baseline characterizes groups, institutions, and processes at the site and also facilitates essential sociopolitical mapping that allows initiatives to direct interventions appropriately. However, the with–without comparison is needed in impact assessment, so you have to be careful that your before–after comparison accounts for that. That is why a good baseline survey includes a sample of resource users/farmers/local residents who will not be affected by the project intervention. Showing how they changed over the life of the project helps us demonstrate improvements to the investment resulting from the conservation initiative.

Box 14.1. Teaching Survey Principles in a Fijian Community

World Wide Fund for Nature–South Pacific Program and the Biodiversity Conservation Network developed a workshop to teach survey principles to community members involved in conservation and development initiatives. The workshop consisted of six steps:

    Step 1: What is action research?
    Step 2: Different types of research
    Step 3: Survey concepts
    Step 4: Outline/design questionnaire
    Step 5: Implementation
    Step 6: Analysis

The purpose was to expose people to survey concepts such as sample frame, unit of analysis, and bias. Many participants had participated in informal data-gathering exercises, but few had any experience in carrying out surveys. Surveys were usually implemented by outsiders. More important, however, was to discuss notions of objectivity and scientific method. In Fiji, information is gathered in group meetings, and the leadership makes a decision on what to do. Often it is the higher-status people who speak up. There was not a tradition of testing assumptions about the root causes of problems—people assumed that they knew the causes. Surveys force people to get out and talk to people as individuals and to think about assumptions to be tested. For example, during the workshop discussion of social issues to be researched, there was concern about the high rate of divorce. Several people said that they were certain that divorce was the result of women becoming too financially independent. A few people were prepared to give advice and guidance already based on that assumption. But the workshop facilitators asked, "How about testing that assumption by surveying people and seeing if there really is a connection between financial independence of the wife and divorce?" Participants saw clearly, however, that surveys are not always appropriate to get certain kinds of information. One question that was developed on the sample survey instrument concerned ranking of important fish species. Many respondents could not make sense of the question. After much discussion, it turned out that most local fishers do not go out looking for specific fish but go out to fish and pick up what they find. The ranking did not make sense to them. Participants decided that a focus group of fishers was a better method to learn about the way that fishers make decisions about what and where to fish. This method would lead the researcher to understand which species end up being most used.

Source: World Wildlife Fund–South Pacific Programme (1998).

Funding agencies often require a baseline survey followed by monitoring surveys or exercises to measure impact on the population (see chapter 16). Use a baseline to systematically survey a sample of the population of interest in the target study area. Or conduct the baseline after sites have already been selected, usually through diagnostic field methods such as RRA. Baselines among local populations are often neglected or done poorly. This makes it hard to measure program impact. Many field initiatives just hit the ground running—and keep on running.

Beyond the Baseline Survey

Short-term "projects" may begin their research with baseline surveys of the target population or area. These are limited in their usefulness for social research in conservation if they do not use scientific sampling and are not nested within a regional framework. Design your baseline surveys so that they will produce scientifically useful data. Is the baseline survey only the first step in a series of research efforts, a sufficient effort, or overkill? What do we need to know about basic practices or the extent of variation in the conservation area? Will conducting a survey put us on the right track?

The Instrument

The content of the baseline instrument is informed by the data derived from the previously described diagnostic surveys or by analysis of qualitative data derived from preliminary site visits, interviews with key informants, and analysis of secondary data. Fixed-response questions are used in a baseline so that it can be efficiently administered, analyzed, and then used as a tool to inform planning and monitoring activities and to articulate resource needs to donors and other constituencies.

Apart from general descriptive information on the household or individual, questions included in the instrument are determined by the information needs of the partners on specific topics. The baseline contains indicators to measure household characteristics and various activities. Many of the same indicators will be used in the monitoring survey.

Develop baseline instruments with monitoring elements built in. For example, when designing the baseline instrument, choose indicators for monitoring at the same time (for further discussion of monitoring, see chapter 16). While in the field collecting data, use the opportunity to put monitoring systems in place, such as planned revisits, diaries or logbooks, and focus group discussions.

KEEP THE SURVEY SHORT

Key informants and focus groups can actually answer many baseline questions before any survey takes place. Informants will help refine questions. Survey questions should be limited to those that measure impact indicators and assess significant differences in households or areas and patterns of distribution of resources and skills.

Sampling Procedure

Decide whether to use random, stratified, or cluster sampling procedures. Baselines are used for statistical analysis and comparison of data at different points in time, so probability-sampling procedures must be used (see chapter 10).

Systematically Capturing Resource Management

Natural resource management (NRM) surveys are designed to reveal patterns in the major resource use practices of people in a given region. First, a basic understanding of NRM practices in the region is acquired through a review of the literature, key informants, RRA, focus group or participatory rural appraisal mapping, transects, and seasonal calendars. Interview questions address topics such as crops, organisms, and commodities collected and sold; harvesting methods, or NRM problems; the location of gardens and hunting territory; hunting-and-gathering trips; and marketing data. How are gardens managed? How are forestlands allocated? What is the division of labor in key tasks? How much is earned from the sale of gathered products?

Then a survey instrument is developed on the basis of indicators that delineate NRM zones or agro-ecosystems. Examples of these indicators are crop or commodity dominance, percentage of food crops or wild products sold, amount of revenue from gathering and harvesting, fallow times, and use of technology. If complemented by satellite pictures or maps, NRM zones can show patterns of deforestation and intensification.

NRM baselines are best used in conjunction with an analysis of soils, microclimates, and biological inventories.

Be Prepared

While collecting data in the field, prepare for speedy data input and analysis. Enumerators are too exhausted to perform data entry at night. However, if the organization involved is using portable software, other staff can start data entry on site to ensure that the systems for coding, data entry, data cleaning, and statistical analysis are really going to work. If not, the instrument should be modified immediately. Data not analyzed are not used—this is a waste for all concerned.

If the field instrument is relatively simple (featuring fixed responses) and if enumerators are experienced, it is possible to skip the tedious and expensive data entry step. Bubble sheets are used where enumerators blacken in dots during the interviews. The sheets are then fed into a scanner, and data are electronically entered into a computer system. The bubble sheet scenario is possible only where the technology is available, but it has an additional benefit of avoiding the possibility of human error during data entry because a machine does it. The savings in time, expense, and aggravation may make it worth prearranging and sending the data sheets to the nearest university or research facility.

The following are needed before conducting a survey:

- Definition of objectives, information needed to address objectives, and methods to get information (survey is only one of many methods)
- Sampling frame
- Units of analysis
- Rationale for sampling procedure
- Good knowledge of community movements, seasons, and events
- Clarity of what type of survey is needed
- Clarity on how survey will inform monitoring and other subsequent research
- Experienced and trained enumerators
- Map
- Clear understanding of cultural categories, such as marriage, residence, and other kinship relations
- Adequate trust of informants to provide information
- Clear hypotheses to test, developed through other means, such as key informant and group interviews

- Well-developed and field-tested instrument, logistical plan, and analysis plan

Remember that surveys do not necessarily get at essential units of production, consumption, or distribution. You need to look at other social formations, such as kinship, credit, and mutual aid groups through institutional, livelihood, and class analyses (see chapters 5 and 6). Often too much information is collected that does not relate to conservation focus. Databases may not be updated or maintained, so valuable insights into trends and changes are lost. Data may not be shared across institutions or even partnerships and results of analysis not shared with the community. This hoarding of data and analysis (even if unintentional) does not bode well for the ultimate usefulness of the research.

Surveys have been criticized as being a top-down and extractive approach to research as opposed to participatory methods, but we have seen how surveys can be a learning and capacity-building tool (box 14.1). To do it right takes time, however. Short-term activities, including one-off surveys, may take precedence over the big picture that includes good survey design, monitoring, regional perspectives, and ethnography. To carry out good surveys with local participation in remote locations may mean that it is hard to have timely results to inform conservation designers and donors. It may involve a large field undertaking. Finally, the organizations involved may not have standard approaches for data collection so that it is difficult to build databases or replicate studies. Participation and learning can be combined with good science—this is the wave of the future.

Let's say it again: prune your survey instruments. Take out confusing questions, questions that involve very long and detailed responses, and sensitive questions (unless carefully tested)—in short, all questions that can be better answered in informal interviews, group interviews, key informant interviews, by observation or in reading existing sources. A half an hour is more than enough time to spend with each respondent. More than one hour is too much. Too much data means too little analysis.

15

Action Research

A seasoned development worker once commented matter-of-factly, "Most people do not want to empower other people." This comment raises the theme of this chapter: Community-owned research empowers local people. If you are not ready or committed to empowering other people, stick with the more traditional research methods described in previous chapters. Additionally, we cannot assume that "community members" are ready to empower others in their communities; often the opposite is the case.

Action, or community-owned, research (we will use the terms interchangeably) is field research designed and conducted by local people. Since they have done the thinking and implementation, they "own" it. Community-owned research can be funded by local people, nongovernmental organizations (NGOs), governments, or external donors. Development aims to teach people to catch their own fish rather than provide them with fish. Action research promotes this principle. People who are stewards of natural resources are trained to collect data; design, evaluate, and monitor projects and resources; and learn how to systematically garner financial resources to keep projects and people moving.

Community-owned research is ingenious because it provides a venue where outsiders can learn from the wisdom of local people. To ask local people to write research questions is a powerful growth experience because of the insight it yields into how other people think. As conservation researchers, we gain enormously from learning the multiplicity of visions within a landscape or community.

Sharing thoughts, discussing research questions, asking questions, sparking the imagination and intellect, collaborating, building partnerships, taking action, and getting the desired results is what action research is all about. In chapter 9, we discussed the importance of donors and project managers forming partnerships with diverse stakeholders. In community-owned research, the power shifts toward the locals who have the knowledge, the social networks, the experience, and the savvy to put the research to use.

Action and Science Work Together

Surveys, literature reviews, and ethnographic research help us understand the whole population, including subgroups and hidden power structures. Hence, these methods are used to complement participatory activities. Too often village meetings that attract only local elites are passed off as action research. Action research should provide a venue for both local and "outsider" knowledge and as such must be thorough and grounded in good social science. Action research can lead into the use of other methods. As community exercises generate research questions and hypotheses, staff may wish to conduct a short survey of a stratified or cluster sample of the population to further understand specific phenomenon.

Although teaching people to do participatory research is effective, people may get stuck over time. Help from outsiders is useful. This is why long-term partnerships and collaboration are mutually beneficial. Project or NGO staff act as researchers but also as trainers and facilitators. A project manager or NGO leader becomes more of an adviser and less of an authority figure and expert. There are many lessons to be learned from changing hats when you shift roles from speaker to listener. Another advantage of action research is that it provides a structure for local people to learn from each other and to rally around specific issues.

Social Realities of Community-Based Research

Conservation ethnographers and researchers need to be aware that their participatory research will be translated into a community of people with a history and power structure. As is the case with traditional research, community-based research can get pulled off track by the influence of elites and other power brokers.

For example, we discussed earlier a community-based project in Fiji that was created to care for the traditional marine area. After two years of participatory exercises at the community level, one of the project managers asked that they conduct a household survey to assess the total population's perception of the project. The survey results indicated that a majority of respondents had not even heard of the "community" project. Several respondents familiar with the project indicated that it was designed for elites and males. The project was indeed a successful one in the sense that there was a positive impact on conservation, but how much broader could it have been if these perceptions were charted from the outset?

In contrast, in another project in northern India, a survey was implemented at the beginning of the project to identify important institutions and subgroups within the population of a watershed. The survey identified the women's forest management institution as being most respected, above the more formal institution controlled by men. It also noted that high castes dominated the leadership and decision making. Thus, the project was able to formulate a strategy to work with the women's groups and address the needs of the lower castes (Sinha and Verma 1997).

Community-owned research projects can replicate existing power relations within the society at large. Elders are key players in conservation planning that involves land and other natural resources. However, women are often important actors in projects for agricultural production and entrepreneurial development. Conservation efforts often involve women in implementation but not in the decision making that is the domain of men. This is analogous to the gender dynamics of agriculture in many cultures, where men exercise the power and administrative control over lands while women do the "implementation," or work.

This inequity raises the question of definition of community. The community-based conservation paradigm has been weakened not by the faults of local communities but by flawed social analysis and by the fact that too little attention has been paid to wider socioeconomic forces, intracommunity variation, and power differentials that significantly affect access to and control over resources (Brosius et al. 1998). Within the community of development and conservation professionals, increased communication and collaboration is needed. Many of the lessons learned in the past decades of development work are translatable to and can benefit those working in conservation arenas. Academics with nuanced understandings of local communities need to work hand in hand with practitioners designing and implementing projects.

A collaborative approach will help heal the rift between practitioners who champion community-based research and academics who look down on it as not being "scientific." The story of the marine project in Fiji is an example of how both research paradigms can be used together effectively. A rigorous survey and an ethnographer's understanding of the social situation will identify subpopulations that may be left out of community research. Having a long-term relationship with communities increases the chances of finding ways to include relatively powerless groups in participatory initiatives. Another reality is that community-owned research involves an extensive time commitment because it is at once a planning, research, and implementation tool.

Two types of participatory action research, appreciative inquiry (AI) and participatory rural appraisal (PRA), are discussed in this chapter. Their major commonalities are that they combine some form of research with the creation of a plan or plans of action. They differ in that AI is more reflective and even more grounded in community values than PRA.

Appreciative Inquiry

Appreciative inquiry is a form of community research used to strengthen institutions and create social change. Created in the late 1980s by David Cooperrider of Case Western Reserve University, AI started as a paradigm to strengthen business organizations and is now used by corporations, nonprofit organizations, and community groups in the United States and globally. The Global Excellence in Management (GEM) initiative brought the approach to development institutions (see box 15.1).

Appreciative inquiry is based on the principle of social constructionism—that we create our worlds with language and conversations. Political and socioeconomic structures are human made and can be changed. Therefore, there is hope for social change and

---

Box 15.1.   Global Excellence in Management

Global Excellence in Management (GEM) is a university-based program of learning and education that works in partnership with U.S. private voluntary organizations (PVOs) and international NGOs to conduct capacity-building programs that support new models of institutional excellence.

GEM is known for programs that are original and intellectually alive; for its signature themes of appreciative inquiry, global partnership, and knowledge generation; for its human-centered approach responsive to the advanced learning agendas of PVO and NGO leadership teams; and for capacity-building work that is collaboratively constructed for enduring consequence. Participation in GEM programs enables organizations to discover and heighten their capacities to continuously learn, change, and innovate (see www.geminitiative.org).

social justice across families, villages, cultures, and countries. Appreciative inquiry uncovers forces that give life to these organizations and communities when they are functioning at their best. The ensuing images, conversations, and activities guide participants into optimizing the best of their organizations in a sustainable fashion.

Another tenet involves a shift in mind-set from analyzing problems to creating positive possibilities. The belief is that people are not problems to be fixed but rather that they are capable of imagining, embracing, and building positive futures. If you can imagine it, you can do it. Poor people are not flawed; they are not waiting to be saved or fixed by outsiders. Instead, with the right tools, local people will create rewarding and satisfying lives. This philosophy supports earlier discussions on how the mind-set of social researchers affects the effectiveness of our work (see chapter 3).

Appreciative inquiry recognizes that research is not objective and that the nature of the questions we ask determines the nature of our research findings. Therefore, the emphasis is on asking questions to build on what works right, to open up our way of thinking so that we are able to create the social change desired by so many.

Learning AI: The Four Ds

As with all research initiatives, key decision makers in the community must be included early on in the design of the project. In keeping with the collaborative nature of AI, the design/steering committee is best composed of a group of people that represents the diversity of the community. This group will design the questions for the inquiry. As stated earlier, local experts can write questions for their peers that are quite powerful and may raise points overlooked by outsiders. Facilitators coach the group on the importance of framing the questions in a positive way in order to create desirable and powerful outcomes. Some practitioners call this the "definition phase."

The Four-D model is widely used by AI practitioners, especially by those working in international development. The four Ds are discover, dream, design, and deliver. In this process, participants build a homegrown model for change and innovation. Appreciative inquiry builds on past successes, and this gives people confidence that they can reach their goals since they have done it before. This empowering approach increases ownership and buy-in for changes to come.

The Four-D model has several iterations and is used as a guide—it is not a formula, fixed model, or linear protocol. Appreciative inquiry requires flexible and creative thinking, so as learning occurs, practitioners can adapt AI to fit the needs of the group. In this way, the discovery process never stops.

- *Discover: Valuing what gives life.* In the discovery phase, participants interview each other about what they value about their work and their communities. Most people have never been asked. Doing so honors participants and provides the experience of being a valued contributor to the community. Other questions ask about what gives life—what fuels the group when they are at their best, as when working in a productive partnership or as stewards. Responding to these questions, each participant tells stories about peak experiences and inspirational moments from their own lives.
- *Dream: Imagining possibilities.* The telling of stories from discovery interviews sparks the collective imagination. Participants dream about what their community or organization would look like if they re-created these past successful moments on a regular basis. In the dream phase, participants explore who they want to be and how they can contribute to the world.
- *Design: Co-constructing the future.* In the design phase, participants design how to integrate desired behaviors reflective of the dream into the systems and structures of their organization or community. Design is the nuts and bolts of how to make the innovation work. Participants write possibility statements to guide this activity. For example, participants may choose to strengthen partnerships through better communication systems or improve forest stewardship with accountability partners.
- *Delivery: Sustainable innovation.* In the delivery phase, participants commit to and begin actions that will make the desired future real and sustainable. Delivery entails responsibility and action—it is about who does what, when, and with whom. Participants work out agreements for accountability and follow-up.

When to Use AI

Use AI when people are willing to let go of the power that their problems have over them. Appreciative inquiry is designed to shake up the status quo, and sometimes people are comfortable with how problems are used to enforce the status quo, territories, and power structures. In other words, AI will be successful only when participants are ready to change how they do business.

Appreciative inquiry's true application is organizational culture change, which is necessary to create conditions for conservation and sustainability. Appreciative inquiry requires start-up education and collaboration with leaders throughout the process. The best way to ensure continuity of practice is to train local people to use the appreciative approach so that it becomes part of the organization or community culture. Appreciative inquiry honors local skill, knowledge, and experience. Believing in and acting from the philosophy of AI is empowering, so use AI where local leaders endorse empowerment, even for formerly invisible subgroups.

Take Time to Do PRAs Right

Participatory rural appraisal "passes the stick" to local people; they take charge of the research. Like AI, PRA is geared toward empowering local people, and practitioners need to ascribe to that belief in order to effectively use the approach.

Participatory rural appraisal uses "a growing family of approaches, methods and behaviors to enable local people to share, enhance and analyze their knowledge of life and conditions, and to plan, act, monitor and evaluate" (Chambers 1999: 1). It is ever adaptive and changing and has generated several exciting offshoots, including appreciative planning and action (APA), participatory action research (PAR), participatory monitoring and evaluation (PM&E), and participatory learning and action (PLA). One key to successful PRA is the flexibility and willingness of the practitioner to adapt methods on the spot to get the best results, hence the slogan "Use your own best judgment at all times." Other key behaviors are humility and a willingness to learn from local people.

Examples of PRA methods are listed in box 15.2. Note that many of these methods are visually oriented and therefore used by nonliterate groups. Participatory rural appraisal began in the late 1980s in Kenya and India, being an offshoot of rapid rural appraisal (RRA), which began in the late 1970s in Southeast Asia (see chapter 11). The distinction between the two is that PRA is an empowerment process where local people do the appraisal, analysis, and action, whereas RRA is a research process conducted by outsiders to gather data for program design.

Participatory rural appraisal requires a mind-set and behaviors different from conventional research. It is based on the philosophy that "outsiders" need to learn about field situations from "insiders." This evens out the balance of power between local people and conservation "experts." The participatory methods make up the vehicle that enables people to design and ask the right questions of each other in order to solve their own problems.

Box 15.2.   Examples of PRA Methods

Key probes. Questions that can lead directly to key issues, again based on the assumption that local people are doing something; for example, "What new practices have you or other people in this village experimented with in recent years?" "What happens when someone's house burns down?"

Mapping and modeling. People's mapping, drawing ,and coloring on the ground with sticks, seeds, powders, and so on to make social, health, or demographic maps (for water, soil, or trees), service or opportunity maps, three-dimensional models of watersheds, and so on. These methods have been some of the most widely used and can be combined with or lead into household listing and well-being ranking, transects, and linkage diagrams.

Local analysis of secondary sources. Participatory analysis of aerial photographs (often best at 1:5000) to identify soil types, land conditions, land tenure, and so on; also satellite imagery.

Transect walks. Systematically walking with key informants through an area, observing, asking, listening, and discussing; learning about different zones, local technologies, and introduced technologies; seeking problems, solutions, and opportunities; and mapping and/or diagramming resources and findings. Transects take many forms: vertical, loops, along a watercourse, and sometimes at the sea bottom.

Time-line and trend and change analysis. Chronologies of events; listing major local events with approximate dates; people's accounts of the past and of how customs, practices, and things close to them have changed; ethnobiographies (local history of a crop, an animal, a tree, a pest, or a weed); and diagrams and maps showing ecological histories, change in land use and cropping patterns, population, migration, fuel uses, education, health, credit, and the causes of changes and trends, often with estimation of relative magnitude.

Seasonal calendars. Distribution of days of rain, amount of rain, or soil moisture; crops; women's, children's, and men's work, including agricultural and nonagricultural labor; diet food consumption; sickness; prices; migration; income; and expenditure.

Institutional or Venn diagramming. Identifying individuals and institutions important in and for a community or group or within an organization and their relationships.

Linkage diagrams. Diagrams of flows, connections, and causality. This has been used for marketing, nutrient flows on farms, migration, social contacts, and impacts of interventions and trends.

Well-being grouping (or wealth ranking). Grouping or ranking household according to criteria, including those considered poorest and worst off. A good lead-in to discussions of the livelihoods of the poor and how they cope.

Matrix scoring and ranking. Especially using matrices and seeds to compare through scoring (e.g., different trees or soils, methods of water or soil

(continued)

Box 15.2.   Examples of PRA Methods *(continued)*

conservation, varieties of a crop or animal, fields on a farm, fish, weeds, and conditions at different times) and to express preferences.
Shared presentations and analysis. Maps, models, diagrams, and findings presented by local people and/or outsiders, especially at community meetings, and checked, corrected, and discussed; brainstorming, especially joint sessions with local people. Who talks? And how much? Who dominates? And who interrupts whom? Whose ideas dominate? Who lectures?

Source: Adapted from *Forest, Trees and People Newsletter,* no. 26/27, 9.

Researchers must learn to listen, take the time to build rapport with communities, and let participatory methods unfold in an experimental fashion. Participatory rural appraisal builds on indigenous knowledge. Staff work as facilitators and often stand in the background to listen, observe, and take notes. Their role "is to enable local people to do their own investigations, analysis, presentations, planning and action, to own the outcome, and to teach us, sharing their knowledge. A PRA is . . . a process which empowers local people" (Chambers 1999: 2). Staying power is part of the process—empowerment takes time.

Local NGOs and PVOs increasingly want to learn PRA. In response, where appropriate, partners can be trained to use participatory methods in the field. The IDS website publishes many examples of recent PRA applications (Chambers 1994a, 1994b, 1994c). Examples relevant to conservation include the following (Chambers 1996: 3):

- *Forest policy in the United Kingdom.* Participatory rural appraisal demonstrated how villagers in Scotland are interested in purchasing and managing forests as a means of generating local livelihoods. Policy changes are now under way to allow this to happen.
- *Indigenous land rights in Honduras and Panama.* Participatory rural appraisal analysis with participatory mapping showed how the area where indigenous people's land rights were threatened coincided with those with greatest biological diversity. This analysis strengthened their claims to the land and to the right to manage and conserve its resources.
- *Management of parks in India and Pakistan.* Using PRA, local people were able to define sustainable management and conservation practices for themselves and challenge existing legislation and practices that both harmed the parks and denied them a livelihood.

Methods of PRA are diffusing rapidly and are now used in more than 100 countries, thirty of which have active PRA networks.

PRA Is Sometimes but Not Always the Best Method

Use PRA to enable local people to undertake their own appraisal, analysis, activity design, monitoring, and evaluation. Only use PRA if staff have appropriate attitudes that allow them to learn from local people, have facilitation and other skills required for a participatory approach, and believe in empowering local people. Use PRA when the initiative has a long-term commitment to follow up appraisal methods, to sustain long-term dialogue and interaction, and to support community efforts at development.

Participatory rural appraisal blends research and community organizing. However, if you do not work at the community level, you may use participatory methods with local partners when working on institutional development or other types of initiatives, as discussed in chapter 9.

Table 15.1 shows the benefits and risks of using PRA at the community level compared to surveys. You will note that PRA is not always appropriate. Participatory rural appraisal involves an extended time frame. This means that staff must have a long-term commitment to working with the community or institution in a participatory fashion through all conservation stages, including sufficient monitoring and evaluation. There has to be time for participatory fieldwork and community organizing. In addition, staff need training in PRA as well as in mediation and conflict management. Beyond that, staff and management have to be willing to allow for experimentation and be capable of adapting tools.

Box 15.3.   Factors to Consider in PRA

Determine the level of awareness, cooperation, and participation of different segments of the community in the initiative. Which segments of the community have the greatest access to the initiative? Which have least access? How was this participation determined or ascertained? Has it been verified recently? Adjust interviewing and other research activities accordingly.

Assess carefully the capacity of local communities to absorb researchers/outsiders, even for "participatory" exercises. What kinds of decision-making processes are used? What is the time frame involved?

In addition to PRA workshops, informally interview identified decision makers and as many other ordinary folks as possible from different stakeholder communities. Sometimes there are segments of the community or individuals that are left out of workshops.

Table 15.1. Benefits and Risks of PRA versus Surveys

PRA	Surveys
	Benefits
Research and action time frame is speeded up	Researchers not unduly influenced or stressed by other objectives
Better insight into community dynamics	Reduce risks to researchers/ community because not "in the open"
Better access to information/ records/decisions	Information more objective—all sectors and factions can be surveyed or interviewed
Uses local knowledge and decision structures	Lowered expectations for results because of lower visibility of research
Skills developed in community organizing	Skills developed in scientific research techniques
	Risks
Hard to involve distant or disinterested stakeholders	Researchers may not be seen as caring or concerned, especially if data and analysis are not returned to community
Action oriented; no time for longer-term research and analysis	Functionally impossible to separate research and action in small communities with ongoing initiative
High level of people skills needed	Barriers to information arise because people are not used to surveys
Risky in societies where hierarchy and respect behavior is strong	Less knowledge of indigenous decision-making processes
Often there is no follow-up to check on data or action	Labor intensive to analyze data and requires skill
Bias toward participants; less knowledge of nonparticipants	Risk of data or analysis not returned to community

The Instrument

Participatory rural appraisal has several tools, as seen in box 15.2, but the main premise of the approach is that these tools are not fixed: PRA is a process, not a procedure. It is not a set of tools that allow staff to control respondents and elicit "answers." Instead, PRA tools are flexible; they are adapted to fit local culture and conservation needs. Participatory rural appraisal is fun because everyone learns from the experimentation and innovation.

Beyond PRA: New Tools for Community Management

The development of a community management plan is a multifaceted process that addresses environmental problems and finds solutions in a community. Here we discuss the process in general and then look at two important components: community mapping and community monitoring.

Steps in the process include identification of environmental problems and mobilization of community institutions to solve problems. Problems could include overharvesting resulting in shortages, dumping of garbage, pollution, declining soil fertility, or water quality problems. Social issues, such as land conflicts, contradictory rules, perverse incentives, and market inequalities, may also be addressed. The process may involve an inventory of the community's resources and an analysis of development options. Appreciative inquiry is useful in identifying community strengths and mobilizing ideas and actions.

Mapping Provides a Base for Community-Based Conservation

Mapping a community's lands is not just a data collection exercise but part of an empowerment strategy as well. Community mapping has been used in many areas of the world to map the territories of indigenous people and to help them lay claim to ancestral lands (see example of Honduras and Panama mentioned earlier in this chapter). Often, local people want to go beyond creating sketch maps. They wish or need to create a technical map to harmonize with official maps. This is a matter of pride, and it is also gives them added clout in bargaining with authorities.

Mapping involves a series of group meetings to identify key areas, resources, sites, villages, and other features that the community wishes to identify. The features to be identified can vary from site to site. The method of mapping also varies. Community mapping at some sites is built around a sketch map; maps at other sites are built around satellite images, such as was carried out by the Mount Cameroon Project (1998), or government maps.

Scale is an important element. Community mapping is one way to carry out land use planning and management with communities at a landscape scale, involving several settlements and subpopulations, but it also can be done at a village scale. Transect walks (see box 15.2) radiating from the village into the surrounding landscape can help get the process in motion. Note that features of the landscape make mapping easier (rivers) or more difficult (steep slopes). Different groups and informants need to be consulted about names and qualities of landscapes. People have different ways of describing and classifying the land that they use and know about. Often these descriptions have to do with use of the land or with key characteristics that bear on use (altitude, soil quality, vegetation, and so on). Men and women may differ in their characterization of land, depending on their use and mobility.

Specialists may also have much finer characterizations of different habitats where they obtain plants or animals. Indigenous or long-term residents of an area may have a much more varied classification than recent migrants. Thus, when creating a map, it is important to involve all subpopulations.

Mapping has two important auxiliary benefits. The training of local cartographers to create the maps gives them valuable skills. These skills bring prestige to the individuals and to the community. The process itself literally puts the community on the map where it may have been invisible or marginal in the past. That is why this process is called "countermapping." Countermapping fights the denial of land rights that is often the heritage of a colonial or authoritarian past (for more on community mapping, see "Community-Based Natural Resource Management/Collective Action" in the Resources section).

However, it must be noted that community mapping is not a substitute for obtaining legitimate land rights, and it cannot resolve all disputes and conflicts connected to land and resources. In fact, it may exacerbate conflicts if care is not taken to work with the process as long as it takes. Mapping is a tool—and just one step—toward better management. Like all tools and research methods, it needs to be embedded in a wider reform strategy and long-term research agenda (for a cross-site analysis of mapping, see Alcorn 2000; for case studies and methodologies, see Chapin and Threlkeld 2001). The Mount Cameroon Project, in collaboration with Innovative Resources Management, has a good step-by-step guide to training that was led by Mac Chapin of Center for the Support of Native Lands (Mount Cameroon Project 1998; see the Innovative Resources Management website at www.irmgt.com).

Beyond Mapping

Using the Global Positioning System to demarcate boundaries and to locate specific sites within a map means that these data can be entered into environmental databases. From defining and mapping the local landscape, one can get a good sense of microclimatic variation. Landscape characterization can be linked to resource abundance maps that show where people find species of interest to them. A time line could then show what has happened to these species (see box 15.2). We must emphasize that this type of information is typically proprietary, so that sharing it with colleagues or local officials may not be advised.

Carrying capacity is difficult to define and measure, but getting a rough idea of how a given piece of land or a forest area could support a population can be critical. In the case of community forestry, the forest areas allocated may not be sufficient for community needs in forest products and agriculture. A calculation of projected needs could avert mismanagement: The community may be blamed if community forestry fails to achieve conservation or sustainability when in fact the forest is too small to be a production forest and the land allocated to agriculture is too small to support the population.

To assess carrying capacity, you need the community map; census data; an estimate of average holdings per family, including plantations and other land uses; an estimate of fallow times for each type of field (that would indicate total area needed for cultivation); and estimates of birth, death, and immigration rates. These data will provide a rough estimate of land needed to support agricultural production but are only a rough estimate because other factors can intervene, such as crop disease, a decline in soil fertility, an increase in exploitation, or a change in technology. Nevertheless, mapping out future land pressures can indicate whether a community forest or other planned intervention has a likelihood of working.

Mapping Land Use Zones

As part of the mapping process, you can work with communities to classify and map local land use zones, such as garden areas and different types of farming plots; plantations; different types of forest; fallow, marshy, and mangrove areas; and conservation zones set aside by locals or authorities. Use local classifications of the land. Find out the names used for particular places, such as names for nontimber-forest-product gathering areas or sacred sites, and learn how boundaries are marked (streams or rivers, stones, trees, or shrubs) and how these boundaries have changed. This exercise can be matched with the creation of a kinship map or genealogy as discussed in chapter 13. In or near a protected area, find out how people actually view and use the land and resources in that area, not what they say is appropriate usage.

INCURSION INTO PROTECTED AREAS AND PERCEPTIONS OF LOCAL COMMUNITIES

In a "reserved forest" in Cameroon, newly arrived researchers discovered that many families had cleared forest and planted gardens. Although in the past a few people had received compensation for this land, few if any of the surviving families had benefited from alienation of their lands to the state. They felt it was perfectly in their right to plant gardens, but they knew that they had to do it undercover. The scope of this "incursion" illustrates the need for new strategies of conservation. In most societies in Africa, there is no notion of permanent alienation of the land. Concessions for logging or other products are temporary and have to be renewed, even if over long time periods. New agreements may need to be negotiated for each generation.

Resource Use Characterization

After mapping land use zones, a natural next step is to characterize the use of resources on the land or marine area by the following:

- Crop or crops planted—note names of varieties and where and when these are used
- Seasonality of planting and harvesting
- Technology used to plant or harvest—who has access to which technologies?
- Social status or identity of users (e.g., if different groups are using the same land)
- Area devoted to particular resource use (size of fields, plantations, grazing areas, and protected areas)

In terms of the study of nontimber forest products, resource use characterization should focus on commodification of the resource (how it is traded and sold in markets):

- Is it used for subsistence, barter, or cash (or combinations of these purposes)?
- How has that changed?
- Is the use or sale regulated by government? This is often the case with forest products in a formal reserve or conservation area or with products that are perceived to be harmful (involved with alcohol, drugs, or poisons).
- How has regulation changed perceptions and the use of the resource? Does it enhance or diminish value?

Remember that when you learn about resource use that is controlled or prohibited, it is unethical to publish or discuss these findings without permission from informants.

Tracking Change with the Community

Community monitoring merges PRA action research techniques with scientific measurement. As such, it is the cutting edge of social research for conservation. It can work closely with community mapping. Community monitoring enables us to do the following:

- Learn and work with local categories and classifications
- Train men and women in scientific terms and methods
- Understand the links between local concepts, practices, and beliefs
- Teach data analysis as well as data gathering so that information can be used immediately by local people

This process uses PRA exercises that delineate the major habitats and landscapes in the community. This can be done on a map or as a list. Naming each place is important, as the names will be used in the monitoring and reporting. Important species and their names are then listed for each habitat. The next step is selection of keystone species to be monitored. This selection comes from community members but should include species from habitats that are under threat and that are important socially or economically (see box 15.4).

A form of community monitoring initiated by marine anthropologist John Parks was used in Biodiversity Conservation Network sites in Fiji and Solomon Islands (Parks 1997; see also Biodiversity Support Program 1998a). In Fiji, the monitoring focused on two species within the traditional marine collecting and fishing area, or *qoliqoli*, of the Verata people. These two species were called *mana*, or mud lobster, and *kaikoso*, a clam. *Mana* is found in mangrove swamps, while *kaikoso* is

---

Box 15.4.   Community Biological Monitoring in Fiji

Community members involved in the BCN project in Fiji learned to use transects to monitor species found in their *qoliqoli* (traditional fishing grounds). They chose the species to monitor based on the criteria:

- Easy to collect
- Easy to count
- Important to the community

Source: Parks 1997, BSP/Baron 1998.

found in coral reef habitat. Both were being overharvested. With the authority of the high chief, the people set up two tabu sites where harvesting was forbidden. Two nontabu sites were chosen as controls. Parks taught teams of local people how to set up transects, count the species, and record their data. He also taught them how to analyze the data and communicate the findings to the community. Monitoring after only six months revealed that there was significant increase of the species in the tabu sites.

In Solomon Islands, Parks trained the local people to monitor *ngali* nut trees (*Canarium indicum*). Transects were set out along existing forest trails, a placement that somewhat bothered scientists because the transects were not set randomly. In addition, the transects had to be explained to landowners who were wondering why people were crossing their land and measuring their trees. Trees were measured at *dbh* (diameter at breast height) so that a diagram could be created showing different size classes. Size class diagrams indicate whether regeneration is or is not taking place (see figure 15.1). Trees were remeasured annually for changes in girth. At the same time, production of trees was measured by *offtake* (harvest) of nuts to the *ngali* nut oil enterprise and for subsistence. Project managers were skeptical that people would find real value in this monitoring, for in fact it takes years to determine whether offtake is affecting reproduction, but surprisingly the teams gathered together at the appointed time a year from the second monitoring trial and carried out the job themselves.

When a community is doing monitoring or research, it is best to ensure that all the materials needed can be maintained and replaced easily. Use local materials. Expensive tools and equipment can create conflict. Make sure that all data remain with the community and that they understand how to collect—and especially analyze—the data. Working out who should hold the data and how those data should be

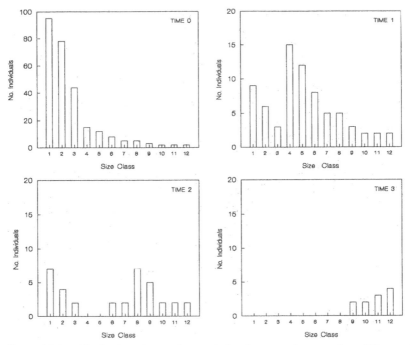

Figure 15.1. Monitoring change in nontimber-forest-product species: different size class distributions over time. This pattern indicates lack of survival of seedlings (fewer individuals in small size classes), thus a dim future for the species in this forest. (From Peters 1994: 20; courtesy of the Biodiversity Support Program & World Wildlife Fund US)

displayed and discussed is important. In chapter 16, we examine how community monitoring data can be used in environmental education.

Community monitoring can also identify and track social indicators. Examples from BCN exercises include the number of liquor shops, the number of people wearing watches, the number of marriages among clans, the number of savings accounts and the amounts in those accounts, and the percentage of species that can be identified according to age group. Community measures of habitat and socioeconomic change are abundance of key species, microclimatic variation, human and animal behavior change, fallow time, and perceived returns to labor (see, e.g., Hambly and Angura 1996; Nazarea et al. 1998). These indicators may vary by gender, generation, caste, or level of education. Community-level indicators should be elicited in a series of focus group discussions.

These indicators help track social change that can occur rapidly in even the most isolated localities. The exercise of drawing out community indicators is an enlightening one for all concerned because it indicates changes in status and role within the community, the creation of new "classes" or strata of people, and problems that emerge with commodification (see chapters 3, 5, and 6). Here outsiders can play a role by helping local people understand the implications of common transformations that occur in society with increased commercialization and "modern" education: intensification of production, change in status and roles, generational conflict, and shifts in power relations between the genders.

From Static to Dynamic Mapping

Biological monitoring of key species can be compared to community monitoring, and more in-depth ecological studies can show how depletion or an increase in the population of key species affects other species and soil composition. Thus, community mapping and monitoring are important methods for conservation that can be linked to biodiversity assessments. The ecological data collected by scientists can be presented to local people in the context of their own classifications. Note, however, that often scientists choose to monitor species other than those selected by communities because these are critical to ecosystem function or are endangered.

The remainder of this chapter discusses trends that can be associated with specific areas at or near a conservation site. These trends can be measured using a combination of action research and scientific methods in a participating learning process. Assessing trends helps conservation initiatives address future as well as current threats to biodiversity, and provides important information to local planners.

- *Is intensification of resource use taking place?* Intensification means that more cash and/or more labor is being used on a piece of land or water to produce or harvest the same amount or more of the resource. For example, a farmer may increase the use of soil management techniques (terracing, mounding, and mulching), chemical inputs, irrigation, animals or machines for planting, spraying, or harvesting. A fisher may use finer-mesh nets to catch more fish. Note that intensification in agriculture through organic/agroforestry methods can have conservation value. Intensification can occur in one area or for one crop while not occurring in other areas of a farmer's field.

   In this case, measure the changes in the frequency and area of chemical applications; the area of land under irrigation; the area of land under "high yielding" or hybrid varieties; changes in crop diversity; the cost of technology; the number of people using more intensive technology; the amount and size of hunters', fishers', or collectors' catches; the distance to harvesting or collection areas; the size of catch per trip; and the size of individuals harvested or caught.

- *"Extensification" can also be taking place.* More land is farmed with the same or fewer inputs. Fields increase in size, but yields stay the same or decline, while soil fertility may decline and erosion may increase. Extensification and intensification can occur in the same locale on different fields or in different households.

  In this case, measure changes in size of fields, person-hours per task (particularly weeding), changes in crop yields, and crop diversity.

- *Is intensification leading to resource degradation?* Intensification can lead to better management and conservation of resources when restorative and organic methods are used and when intensification of harvest is coupled with conservation of adjacent lands. In many cases, however, intensification leads to resource depletion. But the impact can be assessed by measuring changes in water quality and quantity, erosion and siltation, yields of "sensitive" crops (those that require fertile soil), catch per unit effort, and change in number of species harvested.

- *Measuring other development activities indicates change.* Land can be used for nonagricultural, nonforest use, such as construction, roads, mining, or gravel pits. The effects of these development activities are felt far beyond the construction area.

  In this case, measure the area of land being used and the transportation infrastructure and its surrounding area (roads, airstrip, and so on). Note that roads, mines, and other construction can have impacts far beyond the immediate area by spreading chemicals or impacting soils.

- *Measuring efforts to regenerate.* Efforts can be made to increase forest cover, increase the number of valued species, and restock or regenerate an area. There can be a mix of species or monocropped planting, such as plantation of fast-growing trees after a natural disaster; trees can be planted in the forest or in fallow/degraded areas.

  In this case, measure the area planted, the mix of species replanted, and harvesting rates. Note whether species are native or introduced and whether they are designed to cover an area quickly and/or provide some nutritional or economic benefit to local people.

- *Measuring conservation.* Certain areas can be set aside from exploitation for a given period of time, either to let key species build up after overharvesting or to preserve the habitat or mix of species. Conservation can be locally initiated and highly localized or very large scale and initiated by national or international organizations and authorities. Conservation of a species or taxa within an overall loss or decline of species and degradation of soil fertility and water quantity and quality arguably does not constitute conservation. An actual conservation area may be quite different in size and composition than that envisioned by planners (see the case study concerning the reserve forest in Cameroon).

  In this case, measure the number of users of the area, changes in technology around area (guns, traps, and so on), settlements (permanent or temporary), the number and area of agricultural plots, the amount of product taken out of the area, and fire incidences (natural or human induced).

- *Measuring local responses to change in ecology and economy.*
  1. *Differentiation.* Some households are intensifying production or harvesting, while others are losing land or staying with less intensive practices because of the introduction of new crops or practices. In this case, measure the number of households adopting intensive practices, the range in land area associated with households, out-migration, and the number of families with no land.
  2. *Diversification.* New crops, types of fields, or management practices may appear along with the old ones. Diversification can position the family against the odds in a declining economy or can result from new cash-earning opportunities. In this case, measure the number of crop species per hectare or other appropriate measure and investigate changes in technology and in the number of cash-earning activities per household.
  3. *Innovation.* People adopt or invent new technologies or try new ways to use resources. For example, they may experiment with different soil types or tree species, develop new harvesting techniques, or work together in new ways. In this case, interview people who the community turns to as innovators (see the reference to India's Honey Bee Network under "Community-Based Natural Resource Management/Collective Action" in the Resources section). The responses of local people indicate more profound changes in the area, such as the growth of a new class of educated people or an increase in landlessness.

This is a key focus of participatory research: scaling up local innovation.

Action research is a pathway to empowerment and thus an important tool for community-focused conservation. There are several innovative approaches that involve documenting and validating local knowledge. But action research alone is not always the best way to get high-quality information about behavior and institutions. Using other methods, such as ethnography and surveys, combined with action research, can enhance both the quality of the research and empowerment. Remember that high-quality research is important to local partners not just to build their capacity as researchers but because they use the information for planning and management. Communities are complex and changing: understanding lines of power and authority and how to support better governance and management takes time.

16

Learning and Communicating

This chapter covers topics concerning what are considered the final stages of the research: how to monitor, analyze, and communicate results and research findings. But are these really the final stages? It is hoped that they lead toward the development of new programs and approaches and the refinement of existing ones.

Keeping an Eye on Change

Measuring variables or indicators over time is called monitoring. Two key aims of monitoring are for basic research and for evaluation. We can also distinguish between scientific monitoring and community-based monitoring discussed in the previous chapter. These aims and forms affect how monitoring is structured and what instruments are used.

Scientific monitoring for research aims to measure changes in a population over time. For example, we can count the number of people who use guns to hunt in a region over a ten-year period and study the trends. If the region is large and there are no records, we can do base-line and monitoring surveys in villages in the region. Scientifically valid monitoring has to employ representative sampling.

The aim may change if an initiative to ban guns for hunting has started in a few villages in the region and authorities want to know whether the project is working. The sampling strategy is no longer random. Some or all of the villages where the project is located will be surveyed and monitored, while non–project villages chosen to match the project villages in some key criteria can be a control group.

Monitoring by the Numbers

Monitoring sets up a process of measurement, data collection, and periodic review:

- People have to be identified to collect data and review it.
- Information has to be reviewed before activities are programmed.
- The information has to be presented in a public forum so that it is discussed and used.

A formal instrument for monitoring is composed of indicators collected as part of a baseline survey and at least one other time period (for an overview of surveys, see chapter 14). The baseline survey can consist of the whole population or a representative sample of the population. But do you survey the whole region or the intended target population? Our recommendation is to carry out as wide a baseline survey as possible because the data can be used to make later comparisons within localities, keeping in mind that surveys may raise expectations.

Monitoring of indicators has to be complemented by contextual data, such as those related to market, climate, or population, in order to interpret changes. For example, in order to monitor revenue from conservation enterprises or other conservation activities, commodity prices, taxation levels, and demographics may affect the viability of new revenue-generating activities. As discussed in chapter 5, commodity prices may rise, but taxes and the cost of living can rise faster. Another key issue is the heavy emphasis on choosing indicators and formal monitoring in donor-funded projects, which often generate the fear that monitoring can result in a loss of funding. We talk about how this emphasis can distract us from understanding monitoring as a learning tool.

Table 16.1 shows how common indicators tie together baseline surveys and monitoring surveys in an analysis of the impact of conservation enterprises on conservation success.

Do It Again and Again

The sample created for the monitoring survey can be derived from the sample that was used for the baseline. Therefore, using the same survey instrument or selected questions from it, certain households or individuals that were surveyed for the baseline will be asked the same questions for the monitoring survey. Cluster samples (see chapter 10) can also be used for monitoring because they are time and cost efficient, interviewing everyone in one geographic zone or cluster.

Table 16.1. Monitoring Impacts of Conservation Enterprises

Baseline:
Number of households at site divided into significant subpopulations
Number of households in each subpopulation participating in main
    revenue-generating activities
Number of households deriving income from conservation area or from
    species to be conserved

Socioeconomic monitoring:
Number of households in each subpopulation participating in conservation
    initiative
Number of households deriving income from conservation initiative
Number of households significantly using conservation area
Number of women elected to councils that make rules for resource use

Enterprise:
Profit or loss in conservation enterprise for each year
Number of local households by subpopulation participating in management
Number of local households by subpopulation owning or sharing ownership
    of enterprise
Number of women at the management level of the enterprise

Conservation success (not biophysical measures):
Number of households by subpopulation using destructive practices before
    activity and x years later
Number of people by subpopulation caught and fined for breaking the rules
    before and after initiative
Number of men and women participating in biological monitoring activities

If monitoring is restricted to conservation sites, some of the households or individuals of these populations may or may not have been included in the original baseline survey. However, when the baseline used a representative sample, data from the monitoring survey can still be meaningful with regard to conservation impact and behavioral changes of a wider population.

Alternatively, if significant patterns emerge from analysis of the baseline data, you may wish to stratify the monitoring sample in order to query certain types of respondents. These data may help explain the emerging trend. For example, you can stratify the sample to resurvey poorer or female-headed households.

When

Resurvey respondents every year at the same time. Qualitative monitoring procedures can be conducted with greater frequency; key

informants can be reinterviewed monthly, and focus groups can be reinterviewed quarterly.

In order to estimate the time needed in the field, divide the amount
of time it took to do the baseline by the proportion of respondents who
will be resurveyed from the original sample. For example, if it took ten
weeks to do the baseline and the monitoring survey includes one-fifth
of those households, then it should take two weeks.

Survey monitoring is a highly rigorous method that can be participatory when local enumerators are trained to share results with the whole
community. Some necessary elements of success include the following:

1. Understanding the synergy between baselines and monitoring
   surveys
2. Crafting an instrument based on local categories
3. Choosing unambiguous indicators, including indicators to measure short- and long-term conservation processes
4. Creating rapport with the community
5. Identifying local partners or trained community members who
   will conduct monitoring after the outside partners leave the area

It is difficult to line up all these elements and consistently monitor.
Even institutions with excellent research capacity have a difficult time
with monitoring because of staff turnover, interview fatigue, and other
priorities. It is a sad fact that people often do not want to continue a monitoring protocol that someone else has set up; hence, locating monitoring
in an institutional framework is critical. The best way to accomplish the
work is to use local institutions, such as schools and teacher training institutes, and to train local people to resurvey and keep records. Provide
incentives for this work, such as training or equipment. In some places,
community-based monitoring is recognized formally by governments
because people have been trained in appropriate data collection.

Monitoring is time consuming, and many local people and nongovernmental organizations (NGOs) are unsure why or for whom they
are collecting the information (Mahanty and Russell 2002). When monitoring is essential to the management plan and built into it, then the
need is seen. The activities cannot proceed without monitoring. We feel
strongly that local people must be involved in the collection and review of information even if the monitoring is not "participatory" or
community based.

Indicating Change

Many individual, household, and community characteristics, as
well as conservation impact and behavioral changes, are hard to mea-

sure. Proxies are used to measure these phenomena when direct measurement is not possible. For example, household income is difficult to ascertain directly, so proxies, such as important purchases, housing features, number of children in school, or number of animals owned, are used. These proxies for household income may be used as indicators or signs of social and economic status or well-being of the household.

There are several types of indicators: those that refer to the unit of analysis, such as the household or individual; temporal indicators that delineate time relations and the order of events; and topical indicators that refer to the variables being measured or studied. Indicators can help you compare your area with others if they are widely used. Indicators to characterize households and to compare them across a community include major sources of income, access to credit, number of hectares of land (owned, leased, rented, or borrowed), number of animals, size of household, or reliance on forest products.

Monitoring as a Learning Tool

Monitoring becomes a learning tool if you select indicators that are relatively simple to measure. Assess them periodically to determine whether they resonate with local understanding of change and are the most powerful measures of impact and change. Hold community or focus group meetings to identify and agree on indicators to measure conservation impact with regard to behavioral change (participation and benefit sharing) and long-term impact (resource sustainability and enterprise viability).

Focus groups can comprise significant sectors of the community, such as elders, women, harvesters, and managers. Ask key questions, such as What will show that things are going well? What changes will show that things are going poorly? What changes will indicate increasing disharmony or unity? How can we best record these changes? Document the dynamics of these discussions, noting who proposed or blocked ideas. Apart from resurveying a subset of the original baseline sample, other methods can also be used to monitor conservation impact. Some involve record keeping, such as keeping hunting records, while others are participatory exercises (for a review of community monitoring, see chapter 15).

Using ongoing monitoring information in classrooms, community meetings, and action campaigns makes the information much more immediate and interesting. Relate monitoring information to people's daily lives—what they eat, how they get shelter, and how they make a living (see box 16.1). It may be possible to use monitoring information to put a spotlight on destructive behaviors. For example, if there are conservation or tabu areas, infractions could be monitored.

Box 16.1. Monitoring Ideas

Develop community indicators of resource quality and use them in
   government reports
Ask local colleges and schools to collect data periodically in the community
Integrate monitoring activities and data into the classroom
Monitor trends in prices of key commodities and consumer items by periodically
   interviewing traders and market women
Work with the government and research institutions to share data and ideas
Create research stations at sites and train people to collect data—turn them
   into research assistants

However, do not be surprised if there is resistance. What if monitoring reveals the extractive or illegal activities of some actors? If these
actors are powerful, they could impede the process. Others may opt out
because of fear of confrontation or conflict. Therefore, there may be a
need for compromise and conflict management around choice of indicators and communication of results. Do not put people in danger by
having them collect potentially explosive information and then not supporting them in the process. Think through the implications (for more
information, see "Monitoring and Evaluation" in the Resources section).

Learning across Sites

Cross-site analysis is necessary when your organization or a wider
partnership is working in different areas and sites and you want to
compare and contrast these sites. This comparison may help identify
successful ways of working or common bottlenecks to conservation
and community development. There are three basic ways of going
about cross-site analysis: participatory, quantitative, and qualitative.

Analyzing Together across Sites

Participatory cross-site analysis involves getting partners together
from the different sites, areas, or projects to discuss issues and situations
in a workshop setting. An example is the Asia Forest Network's workshop on "Working with Government," which brought together many
groups working in community forestry in Asia and came up with a set
of lessons and recommendations (Asia Forest Network 1997). This approach works best when you want the lessons to feed back directly to

resource users and decision makers. Choice of representatives for cross-site trips is often difficult; take the time to discuss and plan for diversity.

Doing the Numbers across Sites

Quantitative cross-site analysis involves choosing indicators that will be measured across all sites, collecting the data and analyzing them in a central location, constructing models, and the subsequent testing of those models using further data (see box 16.2). The aim of this type of analysis is scientific rigor. An example of a very detailed and long-term analytical framework comes from the Workshop on Political Theory and Policy Analysis at Indiana University (see its website under "Institutions for Natural Resource Management" in the Resources section). This group

---

Box 16.2.   Sample of BCN Cross-Site Analysis Questions

The "ultimate" BCN question: Is a conservation enterprise generating sustainable benefits that lead to changes in practices that promote conservation?

1. Enterprise sustainability analysis
   a. Did the enterprise make a profit?
   b. If not a profit, did it at least cover its costs?
   c. If it did not cover its costs, what subsidies were applied, and how long will they continue?
2. Benefit analysis
   a. How many people receive benefits from the enterprise?
   b. What proportion of household revenue of beneficiaries is coming from the enterprise?
   c. What kinds of noncash benefits are involved, and how are they distributed?
   d. What proportion of benefits goes to nonlocal stakeholders?
3. Stakeholder analysis
   a. Is there a stakeholder group or groups involved in the enterprise?
   b. What percentage of the local population is represented by these stakeholder groups?
   c. What percentage of the local population is involved in mapping or monitoring activities?
   d. What is the overlap between enterprise or monitoring stakeholders and community decision makers?
4. Institutionalization
   a. Enterprise turns a profit or covers cost for three or more years.
   b. Monitoring is continued by community after the project ends, and the data are used by decision makers.
   c. Management rules are followed and sanctions implemented.

has been analyzing data from many areas and situations concerning the use of common-property resources.

Comparing the Cases

Case Studies

This kind of analysis involves the preparation of detailed case histories or case studies. A case study should be focused on one or a few related themes. Quantitative data can and should be used in case studies, but these data are embedded in narrative (on the use of ethnography in case studies, see chapter 13). The aim of the case study is to show how certain factors relate to the overall context and situation of the case. For example, in comparing the role of stakeholder groups at BCN sites, the case studies focused on a few key factors (community participation, representation, and roles in project-funded enterprise and resource management). These factors were compared across sites but were also seen within their contexts at each site (Mahanty and Russell 2002).

A series of case studies can use the same instrument(s) to gather data or the same framework of questions. In the case of the stakeholder study mentioned previously, the same instruments were employed when possible, but conditions at some sites impeded the use of some of the instruments. At one site, no group meetings were held, while at another it was difficult to gather key informant information.

Case studies that are very short might more aptly be called case histories. For the BCN stakeholder study, case histories of almost all the stakeholder groups at the sites were prepared, but detailed case studies of selected groups were prepared for only four sites. Time, resources, and logistics obviously played a big role in this decision.

What's Working and What's Not

A good example of cross-site lessons on "what works and what does not" can be found in the BCN report *Stories from the Field* (Biodiversity Conservation Network 1997, 1998). These stories detail the successes and challenges of the partners at all twenty BCN sites. Another example is this book, which is a compilation of experiences on how to do social research in conservation from many different sites and countries.

The collection of lessons can be participatory at a community workshop. An excellent example of combining process lessons at the community level with policy implications is the Philippines Working Group, or PWG (Asia Forest Network 1997). This group of government officials, NGO members, and academics meets regularly at different community conservation sites in the Philippines. The lessons are gathered and synthesized for high-level policy action. In 1997, the PWG met with Department of Environment and Natural Resources (DENR) Secretary Victor Ramos and presented him with ten recommendations for changes to DENR policies culled from the series of PWG consultations. The involvement and voice of the local communities are strengthened as a result of this process.

A Scaly Question: Integration across Scales and "Scaling Up"

As part of the analysis process, it is often necessary to integrate levels and scales of information. This can be part of the process of scaling up village-level activities. If the work starts at a small scale and you want to increase impact over a wider area, we suggest a few ways to accomplish this task.

The Bottom-Up Approach

Digitize community maps and insert them into "official" maps if the community gives permission to do so. Often the community maps are more detailed than official maps but in other ways might not be as accurate as government maps. You can map several communities and integrate the maps into a larger map. Make sure that permissions are obtained and that the process is participatory. This facilitates larger-scale land use planning. Keep in mind that the larger the scale, the greater the chance that marginalized peoples and subpopulations will be omitted from the planning process.

Similarly, community monitoring can be integrated into national networks and scaled up by creating networks of monitors within a region that report to a central location. An NGO, government extension agency, local university, or research institute could facilitate this network. In Fiji, community monitors from one county were asked to train others across the country. Donors funded this scaling-up process in part, but the government also provided support. Landcare, a movement for grassroots environmental management, is another example of grassroots-level scaling up (see "Landcare" in the Resources section). It spread within Australia and New Zealand and then to the Philippines. Land trusts are another community-based form of conservation and environmental management that, like Landcare, draw on government, private-sector, and NGO assistance. Joint forest management spread quickly in India, while community forest users groups in Nepal now have national assemblies to promote their views and visions. These alliances show how civil society can take the lead in conservation and environment.

Using a Regional Framework

If you are at the beginning of your work, start with a regional analysis using the methods suggested in chapter 11. This will provide a framework for choosing sites and integrating information. It is critically important for local resource managers to obtain regional level information. Thus, at the outset of regional-level research, a dissemination strategy should be devised as part of an institutional inventory and partnership selection. In the case of ecoregional planning, the challenge may be "scaling down" to identify and mobilize appropriate social institutions.

Land use planning or conservation research that uses a top-down approach is unlikely ever to be effective over the long term because it will lack buy-in by local resource owners and users. Even land use planning that involves local officials, leaders, and researchers will not be effective if it does not engage the grassroots.

CASE STUDY

TRANSECTS: THE BENCHMARK APPROACH

The International Institute of Tropical Agriculture's Humid Forest Station in Cameroon uses a benchmark area to compare and contrast different localities within a region. The benchmark area runs from north of the capital, Yaoundé, to the southern border of the country. The natural resource management system (social and agro-ecological dimensions) is fundamentally the same along the transect; however, differences lie in infrastructure, population density, level of commercialization of agricultural production, and level of deforestation as measured by satellite images. Within the benchmark area, several villages have been chosen for long-term study.

Nonspatial Scaling Up

The value of working with provincial government and government agencies with regional mandates has to be assessed on the basis of how they are perceived by local people and the representativeness of the government. If leadership is freely elected to regional office, this presents a different case than if regional officials are appointed or if there is a one-party or de facto one-party system that brooks no competition. Some conservation and development groups are learning that it is important to get their representatives elected to local government. It is often necessary to keep regional officials in the loop, but having them carry out research or implement activities can create more problems than it solves. If they are already engaged, evaluate how local people perceive their actions. How does participation change when officials take part? Agricultural extension agents may be used if they are respected. Conservation officials tend to be feared.

When it comes to crafting regulations and rules, if local rules and regulations are not approved at the regional or national level, they may have no legitimacy and can be overruled. On the other hand, local people may have little knowledge of national-level laws, which may have little scope or usefulness in isolated areas.

Local groups often come together to create coalitions and alliances around issues such as development, human rights, education, or religion. Some examples were given previously and in chapter 9. These efforts can be a focus for wider conservation action. But again, take care that these coalitions have an authentic base and that they are not just a group of city-based elites who attempt to speak for the people back home.

Religious groups are probably the best way to reach and motivate large numbers of people. Many conservation groups are presently working with them to integrate notions of stewardship into the congregation and to spread messages through existing religious publications and venues. But religious groups have their own agendas, and it may not always be appropriate to collaborate with them. Markets and traders are another way to reach wider audiences. One conservation group in the Congo put its cartoon-based messages in school notebooks that are sold in the market. The notebooks sell very well, covering costs of production, and they even get sponsorship from the local private sector. Traders can also serve as information disseminators out to rural areas. Newspapers are likely to be limited to urban populations, and even radio may have limited scope in very poor countries. Newsletters created by projects tend not to last past the first few issues and usually are highly limited in distribution.

Taking Stock

Evaluations can take place at any level and at any time after the initial stages of implementation of a research or conservation initiative. There is an enormous literature on evaluation methodologies and a hoard of evaluation professionals. We look briefly at three types of evaluation, key questions in evaluation, and follow-up to evaluation through scenario building. Monitoring is closely linked with evaluation in that information needed by evaluators is partly obtained through looking at trends derived from measuring indicators over time. For any kind of evaluation, the process needs to be separated from the collection of "success stories." Success stories are important to garner funding, boost morale, and provide concrete lessons and models, but evaluations need to look at both successes and failures. Be honest and up front about mistakes and weaknesses and document carefully the measures taken to improve.

Informal, Internal, and Self-Evaluation

The BCN's "Lessons from the Field" (see box 16.3) are a series of self-evaluations that provide some good examples of how conservation initiatives learned from mistakes and in many cases went on to make significant improvements.

Box 16.3.   Examples from BCN's *Lessons from the Field* (1999)

As a motivational tool, no number of workshops or other typical project activities could compare with the direct economic benefit of having a registered community forest with a management plan that allows for collection of royalties (Nepal).

The rush to claim success can contribute to problems as rivalries and jealousies develop (India).

We believe that benefit generation is a focal point in determining whether an enterprise-based approach can work in a community-based conservation project (Indonesia).

Religion strikes a powerful chord among the populace, and when religious symbolism is married to "sustainable management," the combination can be a potent force for conservation (India).

The biggest challenge is to work with reality and not be confined by the prism of project accomplishments that have a short lifetime (Philippines).

A leader must be a fighter, an orator, a property owner, and a distributor of wealth (Papua New Guinea).

Often, organizations and initiatives choose self-evaluation because they feel they are the experts about their own work. They may hire a facilitator to lead them through the process, but the staff and/or partners do the work and make the recommendations. If there is commitment to hear divergent viewpoints and truly consider recommendations, significant change can result, but in-house evaluations can also be employed to actually stifle dissent by forcing consensus. An informal or self-evaluation can take a day or as long as weeks when there are serious issues to be resolved. Appreciative inquiry and participatory rural appraisal (PRA) are methods that are often employed in self-evaluation (see chapter 15). Srinivasan (1990) provides some exercises and tools for participatory evaluation.

Another approach to informal evaluation is to allow a researcher to carry out participant observation within the organization, at the site, and among the partners. This approach can be unobtrusive and flexible and result in nuanced and useful recommendations. Anthropologists and other social scientists working in the corporate world often use this approach when asked to make recommendations about how to improve a company.

Formal Evaluation: It May Be Needed

Self-evaluation and informality are not always possible or acceptable, however, particularly when the organization or initiative has to account for donor or public funds. Formal evaluations take time, money, and effort on the part of staff, partners, and the evaluators. The evaluators must become familiar with the organizations and the context of the initiative and must get to know staff and partners—and they must do this in a very short period of time. They must be able to probe without alienating the folks who give them the information. Typically, a team of professionals from different disciplines is employed. The following case study looks at an example of BCN's midterm evaluation (Mellor et al. 1996). Note that participatory methods such as appreciative inquiry can be used in formal evaluations.

Participatory Evaluation: Moving Forward Together

Truly participatory evaluation is hard to carry off but is necessary if the initiative is committed to empowerment. Leaving out or stifling elements of the community or partnership can result in repercussions down the road. Important issues to be resolved include leveling the playing field between staff, community, and other actors and providing a safe space to discuss issues.

BCN'S MIDTERM EVALUATION

A heavy-hitting team from Washington, D.C.— including a botanist, two economists, and a social scientist—evaluated the BCN program by visiting four BCN-funded project sites and carrying out numerous interviews. Some key findings included the following:

1. BCN was technically on track in terms of the program plan.

2. The monitoring systems used were too complex and not generating good information.

3. BCN needed to understand the community-level issues better.

4. The sustainability of the resources used in the enterprises was a critical issue.

5. The program did not have enough time to accomplish its goals. The BCN staff acted primarily on item 2 and made visits to most of the twenty project sites to help with monitoring plans within six months of the monitoring team's findings. In some cases, extensive technical assistance was provided to projects. Nevertheless, the monitoring efforts remained uneven because many project partnerships were struggling with their own issues and the project-supported enterprises were trying to get off the ground. In retrospect, an earlier external review of monitoring could have assisted BCN to be more realistic about monitoring and more helpful to the grantees.

Key Questions for Conservation Initiative Evaluation

Evaluations of conservation initiatives should use all information available (donors, private voluntary organizations, NGOs, governments, other partners, research, and monitoring) to look at the extent to which the initiative-strengthened institutions take action against threats and make positive investments.

The following questions focus on some of the social and institutional factors in a conservation initiative. Tools for getting information are suggested for each question.

- *Niche/relevance.* How does the initiative fit with others in the area? Does it meet a locally felt need, or is it attuned to distant constituencies? Does it provide unique services, skills, and resources, or does it duplicate other efforts? *Tools:* Interviews with other organizations, SWOT (strengths, weaknesses, opportunities, and threats) analysis, and customer surveys (see chapter 8).
- *Partnerships.* Do different groups working together see a common purpose? How do they complement each other? *Tools:* Partnership appraisal, key informant interviews, and focus groups.
- *Population and institutions.* Have the appropriate social groups been targeted? Are key institutions working with the initiative? Look at the social groups and benefit distribution, types of institutions, and the evolution of institutions in chapter 6. *Tools:* Review of census and surveys of target areas and rapid rural appraisal of groups and institutions.
- *Social trends.* Is factionalism on the rise? How are conflicts being managed? What kinds of new choices are families facing? Is there an increase in inequality? Look at different types of families and groups in relation to benefits and participation in activities. *Tools:* Focus groups of leaders, resurvey of households, wealth ranking, and gender analysis.
- *Trends in the local economy.* What kinds of pressures and opportunities are being experienced in the target area? How do these trends affect incentives to conserve? Characterize features of local economy and trends using guidance in chapter 5. *Tools:* Focus groups, government reports, oral histories, and monitoring prices and market trends.
- *Trends in resource use.* What is the impact of new or continuing pressures on resource use? Are local people able to measure these and understand the implications? Measure and map trends discussed in chapter 4. *Tools:* Natural resource management survey and community mapping.
- *The bigger picture.* Is the initiative addressing the social, political, and economic issues that shape resource use practices? Is it helping to build institutional capacity for sound resource management? Look critically at initial assumptions and at trend data. *Tools:* Trend analysis, SWOT analysis, customer service survey, focus groups, and ongoing participant observation.

The Crystal Ball

Evaluation assesses a project or situation as it is happening or after it has happened. Scenario building looks ahead to see what adjustments might be necessary in the future. It is based on the premise that although we cannot predict, we can envision certain likely pathways to change. Each pathway needs a strategy. Every action has a reaction, indeed, many reactions. Some reactions can be anticipated on the basis of knowledge and information, while other reactions are totally unanticipated.

On the basis of the knowledge accrued in research and evaluation, create likely scenarios of change and responses to those scenarios. Scenario building is becoming more important as the world changes ever more rapidly. In many countries, situations of instability force conservation initiatives to build scenarios and a high degree of flexibility into their strategies:

Example 1: More cash is coming into the community from an enterprise supported by the conservation initiative. Who will manage the cash? What will people use it for? Discuss likely avenues for investment and conflicts that could emerge.

Example 2: Local partner staff are burning out, and the dropout rate is high. Discuss what will happen if key staff leave. How can the pressure be eased up? How can their knowledge be retained? What are the underlying causes of the pressure?

Example 3: Conflict between two ethnic groups has made it impossible to reach an important conservation site. International staff have been evacuated. How can local staff be supported? What plans can be made, given that the duration and intensity of the conflict cannot be known?

Getting the Word Out

Analyze data in the field with partners, verify, and present immediately. Once you have left, it can take months or even years to finish your study, and communities will lose out. Research results are intellectual property, but in a community-focused conservation initiative they are also common property. When you are doing research for and with local partners, the results need to be in the hands of those who can use them, not just in academic journals that very few people have access to.

Identify the key audiences for research and tailor your research products to these audiences. Be clear about approach and methods used when presenting research. Explain why the research does not have all the answers and that it was not a perfect process. Describe the limitations (cost, staff, and time). For example, what are the differences in results using community-based monitoring versus scientific monitoring?

Design the communication strategy together with the research strategy: Who will get the information, and how will they get it? Who "owns" information and analyses? What format will be needed to present information to nonliterate partners? In a household survey in Fiji, analysis was done with local people and the findings presented at a council meeting.

Analyze what methods were more or less successful. Did research and monitoring change conservation objectives? Did partners adopt methods or use findings? For example, the previously discussed BCN mid-term evaluation discovered that monitoring advice was too complex and leading to confusion of partners.

Think about innovative means for communicating findings, such as through the use of skits, fables, songs, visual representations, and other artistic media. Integrate pictures and other visual materials into write-ups. Wan Smolbag Theater in Vanuatu, South Pacific, uses theater to display messages about conservation and to give people pride in their natural resource and traditional storytelling heritage.

Disseminate findings into ongoing cultural and political activities, such as church group meetings, trade fairs, and social action meetings. Fiji Library Day presented a showcase of community monitoring results that drew a big crowd. To accomplish these goals, you will need to set aside adequate time and funds for translation and dissemination of findings to community groups. A national NGO in Mindanao, the Philippines, took care to translate research findings and government reports into the local language, Binukid. This greatly strengthened local ownership and understanding of the initiative.

Discuss what will happen to sensitive information, such as maps, locations of harvesting or hunting, and illegal activities. Recheck findings and conclusions with key informants and community members. Triangulate and factor in minority views. A baseline survey verification process in Palawan involved verifying information with both indigenous and nonindigenous populations.

Different Folks Need Different Messages

Here are some different ways to organize data and present back to different audiences.

Back to the Community

Create pictographs using data collected by either survey or PRA:

- Proportion of people getting products from the forest
- Proportion of people with water quality problems
- Proportion of people with a bank account or in a savings group

Use surveys and monitoring:

- Number of people getting cash benefits from participation in conservation initiative

Use censuses and mapping:

- Age pyramids (the number of people in each age-group) in relation to total area available for crops can show what will happen when the children grow up. Will there be enough land for them? What can be done?

Use focus groups and surveys:

- Returns to labor for different activities and how these activities use resources. What do these activities do to the resource base?

Use detailed surveys, weighing, and price trends:

- Average returns for logging, commodities, wage labor (trends in wage rates), effort/benefit analysis (e.g., catch per unit effort)

Use media:

- Videos of their experiences and the experiences of others, role plays and dramas, and oral histories from different sites or sectors of the community

To the NGO Partners

- Customer service survey: Are we targeting the right groups in the community? Show from which sectors of the community the participants come. What about gender balance?

- Analysis of household survey results: Are the benefits from conservation enterprises competitive with other benefits?
- PRA/survey/focus group/customer service survey: Do people have ideas that have not been incorporated into the initiative?

To Donors or Potential Donors/Government

- PRA or census: Highlight community problems and proposed solutions
- Survey: Characterize socioeconomic level of community (education, health, water)
- Socioeconomic monitoring: Proportion of community participating in and/or benefiting from the initiative
- Surveys and focus groups: Comparative risks and benefits of different activities
- PRA/focus groups: Lessons learned for better program design
- Policy changes needed

Box 16.4 shows where community-based conservation research results can be published.

Box 16.4. Publication Venues for Research on Community-Based Conservation

Agriculture and Human Values
Common Property Digest
Cultural Survival Quarterly
Development and Change
Development in Practice
Honeybee Network

Human Ecology
Indigenous Knowledge and Development Monitor (online)
Journal of Sustainable Forestry
ODI Gatekeeper Series
PLA Notes
Society and Natural Resources
See also Resources section

The Last Word

We have been on a long journey, from a tour of human behavior covering concepts used by social scientists studying humans in nature through a variety of planning and research approaches to ideas about evaluation and communication of research findings. There is a wealth of additional information to be found on these topics in the Resources section. The points we want you to remember from reading this book are the following:

- Human behavior is complex and messy; it is not easy to understand, nor is it easy to deal with humans. Do not fall for simplistic answers or think that you can make significant progress using quick-and-dirty research.
- Research *on* humans involves research *with* humans: learn ethics and good practice.
- Draw deeply on the history and culture of a place.
- Be informed about a wide variety of methods and approaches.
- Take the time to formulate good research questions at appropriate scales. From the start, link micro- and macro-scales.
- Work in partnership. Partnership is not easy or simple: It requires careful analysis and reflection.

Our partnership on this book is now over, but we treasure both that partnership and our future one with you, our readers.

Resources

Biodiversity Conservation Network (BCN)

A program funded by the United States Agency for International Development that supported conservation activities, enterprises, and monitoring at twenty sites in seven Asia-Pacific countries. The BCN was designed to help conservation planners evaluate the effectiveness of enterprise as a conservation tool. The program extended from 1994 through 1999 and generated several important publications as well as a website: www.bcnet.org. Publications are now available from the World Wildlife Fund (U.S.):

Biodiversity Conservation Network. *Annual reports 1996–98.* Washington, DC: World Wildlife Fund.

———. *Stories from the field 1997–98.* Washington, DC: World Wildlife Fund.

———. 1999. *Evaluating linkages between business, the environment, and local communities: Final stories from the field.* Washington, DC: World Wildlife Fund.

Biodiversity Support Program (BSP)

Until December 31, 2001, BSP was a consortium of the World Wildlife Fund (U.S.), The Nature Conservancy, and the World Resources Institute. Funded by the United States Agency for International Development, it was the parent program for BCN. The BSP's publications, many of them cited here, can be found at www.bsponline.org. Resources are now available from the World Wildlife Fund (U.S.):

Biodiversity Support Program. 1998a. *Lessons from the field: Keeping watch: Experiences from the field in community-based monitoring.* Washington, DC: Biodiversity Support Program.

———. 1998b. *Lessons from the field: If I only knew then what I know now: An honest conversation about a difficult conservation and development project.* Washington, DC: Biodiversity Support Program.

———. 1999a. *Lessons from the field: Doing business in Borneo.* Washington, DC: Biodiversity Support Program.

———. 1999b. *Lessons from the field: Linking theory and practice in biodiversity conservation.* Washington, DC: Biodiversity Support Program.

———. 2000. *Shifting the power: Decentralization and biodiversity conservation.* Washington, DC: Biodiversity Support Program.

Salafasky, N., and R. Margoulis. 1999. *Greater than the sum of their parts: Designing conservation and development programs to maximize results and learning. A practical guide for program managers and donors.* Washington, DC: Biodiversity Support Program.

Anthropology and Environment

Agrawal, A., and C. C. Gibson. 2001. *Communities and the Environment: Ethnicity, Gender, and the State.* New Brunswick, NJ: Rutgers University Press.

Crumley, C. L., ed. 2001. *New directions in anthropology and environment: Intersections.* Walnut Creek, CA: AltaMira.

Human and Political Ecology

Agroforestry Systems: www.wkap.nl/prod/j/0167-4366

Alternatives to Slash-and-Burn (ASB) program and links to a multitude of related sites: www.asb.cgiar.org/Links.shtm

Human Ecology: www.wkap.nl/prod/j/0300-7839

Human Ecology Review: www.humanecologyreview.org

Journal of Political Ecology: Case Studies in History and the Social Sciences; www.library.arizona.edu/ej/jpe/jpeweb.html

Society for Human Ecology: www.societyforhumanecology.org

Greenberg, J., and T. Park. 1994. Political ecology. *Journal of Political Ecology* 1, no. 1: 1–12.

Machlis, G. E., J. E. Force, and W. R. Burch. 1997. The human ecosystem. Part 1: The human ecosystem as an organizing concept in ecosystem management. *Society and Natural Resources* 10, no. 4: 347–367.

Moran, E. F., ed. 1990. *The ecosystem approach in anthropology.* Ann Arbor: University of Michigan Press.

Netting, R. M. 1986. *Cultural ecology.* 2nd ed. Prospect Heights, IL: Waveland.

Rhoades, R., ed. 2001. *Bridging human and ecological landscapes: Participatory research and sustainable development in an Andean agricultural frontier.* Dubuque, IA: Kendall/Hunt Publishing Co.

Vayda, A. P. 1999. Against political ecology (with Bradley B. Walters). *Human Ecology* 27, no. 1: 167–179.

University Programs in Human Ecology

ACT (Anthropological Center for Training and Research on Global Environmental Change): Cornell University: www.human.cornell.edu

Indiana University: www.indiana.edu/~act/home.html

Michigan State University: www.he.msu.edu

Rutgers University/Cook College: aesop.rutgers.edu

University of Georgia, Ecological and Environmental Anthropology: anthro.dac.uga.edu, also SANREM (Sustainable Agriculture and Natural Resource Management) at University of Georgia.

University of Minnesota College of Human Ecology: www.che.umn.edu

Institutions for Natural Resource Management

Cornell University: ciifad-iap.cornell.edu/iap/index.html

International Association for the Study of Common Property (IASCP): www.indiana.edu/~iascp

Workshop on Political Theory and Policy Analysis, Indiana University: www.indiana.edu/~workshop

Berkes, F., and C. Folke, eds. 2000. *Linking social and ecological systems: management practices and social mechanisms for building resilience.* Cambridge, UK: Cambridge University Press.

Berry, Sara. 1989. Social institutions and access to resources. *Africa* 59, no. 1: 41–55.

Ostrom, E. 1990. *Governing the commons: The evolution of institutions for collective action.* Cambridge: Cambridge University Press.

———. 1992. The rudiments of a theory of the origins, survival and performance of common-property institutions. In *Making the Commons Work,* edited by D. W. Bromley and D. Feeny. San Francisco: ICS Press.

Uphoff, N. T. 1986. *Local institutional development: An analytic sourcebook with cases.* West Hartford, CT: Kumarian Press.

——. 1998. Community-based natural resource management: Connecting micro and macro processes, and people with their environments. International Workshop on Community-Based Natural Resource Management: Plenary Presentation. Washington, DC: World Bank.

Environmental Governance

Environmental governance at World Resources Institute: www.wri.org/wri/governance/program.html

Global environmental governance at Yale: www.yale.edu/envirocenter/research/geg.html

Perverse Incentives

Economics, Trade, and Incentives: Convention on Biological Diversity. Includes case studies and OECD workshop report: www.biodiv.org/programmes/socioeco/incentives/

Subsidies and Sustainable Development: Key issues and reform strategies. Institute for Research on Public Expenditure, Oranjestraat 8, 2514 JB, The Hague, Netherlands; www.ecouncil.ac.cr/rio/focus/report/english/subsidies

Action Research

Clark University: www.clarku.edu/departments/idce/research/ (note that they are specialists in integrating geographic information systems into development using IDRISI)

Community Research Network—Loka Institute: www.loka.org

Indigenous Knowledge and Development Monitor: www.nuffic.nl/ik-pages/index.html

Innovative Resources Management: www.irmgt.com

International Institute for Environment and Development: www.iied.org

Spirituality, Ethics, and Values in Conservation

About biophilia: arts.envirolink.org/interviews_and_conversations/ EOWilson.html

Bibliography on conservation and ethics: ecoethics.net/bib/tl-205-a. htm

Congo River Baptist Community: Program on peace, justice, and nature conservation (CBFC): www.open.org/~noyesusa/CBCO_USA. html or through CARPE office (carpe-drc@ic.cd)

Encyclopedia of religion and nature: www.religionandnature.com/ about.htm

Harvard University Forum on religion and ecology: environment. harvard.edu/religion

Huxley College of Environmental Studies, Western Washington University, Supplementary Bibliography on Environmental History and Ethics by Gene Myers, Ph.D., and John C. Miles, Ph.D. This page provides lists of published materials in environmental history and ethics. In addition, there are links to several other important bibliographies and other Internet resources:www.ac.wwu.edu/~gmyers/ehebib.html

Links on religion and ecology from the Boston Theological Institute Program: www.bostontheological.org/rae/re_links.htm

Orion Society: www.orionsociety.org

SWIFT (Solomon Islands program for sustainable timber sponsored by the United Church): www.bajazzo.com/swift/info.html (in Dutch)

Toward a world conservation ethics by M. S. Swaminathan: www. unesco.org/courier/2000_05/uk/doss33.htm

Berkes, F., 1999. *Sacred ecology: Traditional ecology knowledge and resource management*. Philadelphia: Taylor and Francis.

Chapple, C., and M. E. Tucker. 2000. *Hinduism and ecology: The intersection of earth, sky, and water*. Religions of the World and Ecology series. Cambridge, MA: Harvard University Press.

Deb, D., K. Deuiti, and K. C. Malhotra. 1997. Sacred grove sites as bird refugia. *Current Science* 73, no. 10: 815–817.

Decher, J. 1997. Conservation, small mammals, and the future of sacred groves in West Africa. *Biodiversity and Conservation* 6: 1007–1026.

Dorm, A.C., O. Ampadu-Agyei, and P. G. Veit. 1991. *Religious beliefs and environmental protection: The Malshegu sacred grove in northern Ghana*. Washington, DC: World Resources Institute and African Center for Technology Studies.

Fujiki, N., and D. R. J. Macer, eds. 2000. *Bioethics in Asia*. Science City, Japan: Eubios Ethics Institute. www.biol.tusukuba.ac.jp/~macer/ EJAIB.html

Kellert, S. R., and E. O. Wilson, eds. 1993. *The biophilia hypothesis. Part 6: Ethics and political action.* Washington, DC: Island Press. For information on biophilia: http://arts.envirolink.org/interviews_and_conversations/EOWilson.html.

Norton, B. G., and E. F. Stevens, eds. 1996. *Ethics on the Ark: Zoos, animal welfare and wildlife conservation.* Washington, DC: Smithsonian Institution Press.

Ramakrishnan, P. S. 1996. Conservation of the sacred: from species to landscapes. *Nature and Resources* 32, no. 1: 11–19.

Rappaport, R. 1979. *Ecology, meaning and religion.* Richmond, CA: North Atlantic Books.

Salim, A., et al. 2001. In search of a conservation ethic. In *People managing forests: The links between human well being and sustainability,* edited by C. J. P. Colfer and Y. Byron. Washington, DC: Resources for the Future and Center for International Forestry Research.

Participatory Development

Beyond fences: Sourcebook on community participation in conservation: www.iucn.org/themes/spg/beyond_fences/bf_publication.html

Institute of Development Studies: www.ids.ac.uk/ids

International Institute of Environment and Development (*PLA Notes* and other publications on participatory development): www.iied.org/bookshop/pubs

Source book for customer service: www.usaid.gov/pubs/sourcebook/usgov/cf.html

United States Agency for International Development. Global Participation Network (GP-Net) E-Mail group: www.usaid.gov/about/part_devel/gpnet.html; source book for customer service: www.usaid.gov/pubs/sourcebook/usgov/cf.html

Cernea, M., ed. 1985. *Putting people first: Sociological variables in rural development.* New York: Oxford University Press.

Goulet, D. 1989. Participation in development: New avenues. *World Development* 17: 165–178.

Holland, J., and J. Blackburn, eds. 1998. *Whose voice? Participatory research and policy change.* London: Intermediate Technology Publications.

Lai, C. K., D. N. Yabut, J. C. Fernandez, and W. H. Libuao. 2001. Participatory methods for uplands systems research and development: Highlights from a training course in the Philippines. International Centre for Research in Agroforestry/Southeast Asia Programme (www.icraf.cgiar.org/sea) and Southeast Asia Regional Center for Graduate Study and Research in Agriculture (SEAMO/SEARCA: www.searca.org).

Narayan, D. 1995. *The contribution of people's participation: Evidence from 121 rural water supply projects*. Washington, DC: World Bank.

Oakley, P., and D. Marsden. 1984. *Approaches to participation in rural development*. Geneva: International Labor Office.

Uphoff, N. T. 1992. *Learning from Gal Oya: Possibilities for participatory development and post-Newtonian social science*. Ithaca, NY: Cornell University Press.

World Bank. 1996. *The World Bank participation sourcebook*. Washington, DC: World Bank.

Sustainable Use of Natural Resources

International Institute for Bamboo and Rattan; headquarters in China; sustainable development organization: www.inbar.int/

IUCN sustainable use initiative: iucn.org/themes/ssc/susg/index.html

CIFOR and IUCN manual on sustainable use of nontimber forest products: www.cifor.cgiar.org/publications/pdf_files/books/incomes.pdf

Convention on Biodiversity; case studies of benefit sharing in biodiversity conservation: www.biodiv.org/programmes/socio-eco/benefit/case-studies.asp

Non-Wood News (Food and Agricultural Organization, Rome) www.fao.org/forestry/fop/fopw/nwfp/newsle-e.stm

People and Plants handbook: www.rbgkew.org.uk/peopleplants

People and Plants sustainable use network: www.rbgkew.org.uk/peopleplants/handbook/handbook5/networks.htm

Clay, Jason W. 1994. Generating income and conserving resources: Twenty lessons from the field. Paper prepared for the workshop on "Non-Timber Tree Product Market Research," Annapolis, MD, December 12–14.

Honey, M. 1999. *Who owns paradise? Ecotourism and sustainable development*. Washington, DC: Island Press.

Peters, C. M. 1994. *Sustainable harvest of non-timber plant resources in tropical moist forest: An ecological primer*. Washington, DC: Biodiversity Support Program.

Plotkin, M., and L. Famolare, eds. 1992. *Sustainable harvest and marketing of rain forest products.* Washington, DC: Conservation International and Island Press.

Wolvekamp, P., ed. 1999. *Forests for the future: Local strategies for forest protection, economic welfare and social justice.* London: Zed.

Market Analysis and Conservation Enterprises

Conservation International, conservation enterprises: www.conservation.org/xp/CIWEB/programs/conservation_enterprises/cons_enterprise_dev.xml

EnterpriseWorks International: www.enterpriseworks.org

Intermediate Technology Development Group: www.itdg.org

Technoserve: www.technoserve.org

Certification

Forest Stewardship Council UK: www.fsc-uk.demon.co.uk

Forest Stewardship Council US: www.fscus.org

SmartWood: www.smartwood.com

Sustainable Forestry and Certification Watch: sfcw.org

Higman, S., S. Bass, N. Judd, J. Mayers, and R. Nussbaum. 1999. *The sustainable forestry handbook: A practical guide for tropical forest managers on implementing new standards.* London: Earthscan.

Community-Based Natural Resource Management (CBNRM)/Collective Action

Action for Community and Ecology in Central America (looks at relationships among free trade, ecology, and local communities): www.acerca.org

Asia Forest Network: socrates.berkeley.edu/~cseas/research.html

CBNRM database for Africa: FRAME: www.frame-web.org

CBNRM links from International Development Research Centre: www.idrc.ca/cbnrm/documents/CBNRM_Toolkit/websites6.htm

Common Property Digest: www.indiana.edu/~iascp/aboutcpr.html\

Community-based wildlife management; CAMPFIRE: www.campfire-zimbabwe.org

Community logging in Mexico: srdis.ciesin.org/cases/mexico-010. html

Cultural Survival and *Cultural Survival Quarterly:* www.cs.org

Decentralization of forest management in Africa: www.cifor.cgiar.org/ polex/01November05.htm

Forest, Trees and People: www.trees.slu.se

Honeybee Network, India (disseminates information about innovations that come from rural people; newsletter sent out in local languages to millions of people): www.sristi.org/honeybee.html

Indigenous Knowledge and Development Monitor: www.nuffic.nl/ ik-pages/index.html

International Network of Forests and Communities: www. forestsandcommunities.org

Joint Forest Management (India): www.iifm.org/databank/jfm/ jfm.html; see also www.teriin.org/jfm/jfm.htm

Native Forest Network: www.nfn.org.au

Regional Community Forestry Training Center for Asia and the Pacific (RECOFT) Thailand: www.recoftc.org/courses.html

South Pacific Regional Programme on the Environment: Landowners' rights recognition in provincial bylaws (Fiji, Solomon Islands), Community Marine Parks (Palau, Micronesia) and community fisheries (Samoa): www.sprep.org.ws

Testing sustainable forest indicators in community forestry in Mexico: www.fs.fed.us/institute/mexican_lucid/english_summary.htm

World Wildlife Fund publications on partnership with indigenous people: www.panda.org/resources/publications/sustainability/ indigenous/ip_publications.htm

Associates in Rural Development. 1992. *Decentralization and local autonomy: Conditions for achieving sustainable natural resource management.* Washington, DC: USAID/Center for Development Information and Evaluation.

Blumenthal, D., and J. Jannink. 2000. A classification of collaborative management methods. *Conservation Ecology* 4, no. 2: 17–26.

Bromley, W., and D. Feeny, eds. 1992. *Making the commons work.* San Francisco: ICS Press.

Colchester, M. 2000. Self-determination or environmental determinism for indigenous peoples in tropical forest conservation? *Conservation Biology* 14, no. 5: 1365–1367.

Gambill, David. 1999. Intentionally sustainable: How community-based resource management enables and encourages the sustainable use of resources. Washington, DC: DevTech Systems, Inc., and WID-STRAT Project/USAID Office of Women in Development.

Hobbley, M. 1996. *Participatory forestry: The process of change in India and Nepal.* London: Overseas Development Institute.

International Centre for Integrated Mountain Development. 1995. Community forestry: The language of life. Report on the First Regional Community Forestry Users' Group Workshop. Kathmandu: International Centre for Integrated Mountain Development.

Read, T., and L. Cortesi/Biodiversity Support Program. 2001. *Stories at the forest edge: The KEMALA approach to crafting good governance and sustainable futures.* Washington, DC: Biodiversity Support Program.

Shah, Anil C. 1998. *Participatory process of organizing effective community-based groups.* International Workshop on Community-Based Natural Resource Management. Washington, DC: World Bank.

Singleton, S., and M. Taylor. 1992. Common property, collective action and community. *Journal of Theoretical Politics* 4: 309–324.

Stevens, S., ed. 1997. *Conservation through cultural survival: Indigenous people and protected areas.* Washington, DC: Island Press.

Western, D., and R. M. Wright, eds. 1994. *Natural connections: Perspectives in community-based conservation.* Washington, DC: Island Press.

World Bank. 1998a. *Community-managed programs in forestry: A synthesis of good practices.* Prepared by Environment Sector Management Unit, East Asia Region.

———. 1998b. Series of papers from the International Workshop on Community-Based Natural Resource Management. Washington, DC: World Bank.

Landcare

www.icraf.org/sea/landcare/landcare.htm (Philippines)

www.landcareaustralia.com.au

www.landcaresa.org.au (South Australia)

www.landcareweb.com (general information and resources on Australian and other country landcare efforts)

www.landcare.cri.nz (New Zealand: Manaaki Whenua)

Campbell, A. 1994. *Landcare: Communities shaping the land and the future.* St. Leonard's: Allen & Unwin.

Catacutan, D. 2001. Technical innovations and institution-building for sustainable upland development: Landcare in the Philippines. Paper presented at the International Conference on Sustaining Upland Development in Southeast Asia: Issues, Tools and Institutions for Local

Resource Management. Sustainable Agriculture and Natural Resource Management Collaborative Research Support Project (SANREM-CRSP), Makati City, Philippines, May 27–30.

Critiques of Community-Based/ Sustainable Use Approaches

Oates, J. 1999. *Myth and reality in the rain forest: How conservation strategies are failing in West Africa.* Berkeley: University of California Press.
Redford, K. H., and S. E. Sanderson. 2000. Extracting humans from nature. *Conservation Biology* 14, no. 5: 1362–1364.
Soulé, M., and G. Lease, eds. 1995. *Reinventing nature? Responses to postmodern deconstruction.* Washington, DC: Island Press.
Terborgh, J. 1999. *Requiem for nature.* Washington, DC: Island Press.
Wunder, S. 2001. Poverty alleviation and tropical forests: What scope for synergies? *World Development* 29, no. 11: 1817–1833.

Partnership

Ashman, Darcy. 2000. Strengthening North-South partnerships: Addressing structural barriers to mutual influence. *IDR Reports* 16, no. 4. Boston: Institute for Development Research.
Brown, L. D. 1991. Bridging organizations and sustainable development: Strengthening civil society as a sector: A Selection of IDR Reports 1997. Boston: Institute for Development Research.
Brown, L. D., and D. Ashman. 1996. Participation, social capital, and intersectoral problem solving: African and Asian cases in promoting civil society-government cooperation: A selection of IDR Reports 1997. Boston: Institute for Development Research.
Brown, L. D., and R. Tandon. 1992. Multiparty cooperation for development in Asia. *IDR Reports* 10, no. 1. Boston: Institute for Development Research.
Central Africa Regional Program on the Environment. 2001. *Private sector partnerships: Wildlife Conservation Society–Compagnie International du Bois Partnership in Central Africa Regional Program on the Environment (CARPE). 2001. Phase 1 Results and Lessons Learned.* Washington DC: Biodiversity Support Program. http://carpe.umd.edu
Edwards, M., and D. Hulme, eds. 1995. *Non-governmental organisations: Performance and accountability beyond the magic bullet.* London: Earthscan.

Fowler, A., ed. 2000. Questioning partnership: The reality of aid and NGO relations. *IDS Bulletin* 31, no. 3. Sussex: Institute for Development Studies.

Gray, B. G. 1989. *Collaborating: Finding common ground for multiparty problems.* San Francisco: Jossey-Bass.

Kalegaonkar, A., and L. D. Brown. 2000. Intersectoral cooperation: Lessons for practice. *IDR Reports* 16, no. 2. Boston: Institute for Development Research.

Jones, R. F. 1993. Choosing partnership: The evolution of the Katalysis model. Stockton, CA: Katalysis North/South Development Partnerships. www.katalysis.org

Save the Children USA. 1996. Partnership and institutional development. U.S. Working Paper Series. www.savethechildren.org

United States Agency for International Development. 1997. *New partnerships initiative: A strategic approach to development partnering (NPI Resource Guide).* Vol. 1. Washington, DC: United States Agency for International Development. www.dec.org

Waddell, S. 1997a. Fostering intersectoral partnering: A guide to promoting partnerships between government, business and civil society actors. *IDR Reports* 13, no. 3. Boston: Institute for Development Research.

———. 1997b. Market–civil society partnership formation: A global status report on activity, strategies, and tools. *IDR Reports* 13, no. 5. Boston: Institute for Development Research.

World Bank Group. 1998. Consultative meeting on partnerships: Joining hands with government and non-government development organizations and local communities. www.worldbank.org

Research Guides

Research guides: www.researchresources.net

Agresti, A., and B. Finlay. 1997. *Statistical methods for the social sciences.* 3rd ed. Upper Saddle River, NJ: Prentice Hall.

Babbie, E. R. 1997. *The practice of social research.* 8th ed. Belmont, CA: Wadsworth.

Bernard, R. 2001. *Research methods in anthropology: Qualitative and quantitative approaches.* 3rd ed. Walnut Creek, CA: AltaMira.

Chevalier, J. 2001. Stakeholder analysis and natural resource management: An alternative to itchy and scratchy. Ottawa: Carleton University. An excellent Web resource for applied research: www.carleton.ca/~jchevali/STAKEH.html

Devereux, S., and J. Hoddinott, eds. 1993. *Fieldwork in developing countries.* Boulder, CO: Rienner.

Gladwin, C. H. 1989. *Ethnographic decision tree modeling: Qualitative research methods series 19.* Walnut Creek, CA: Sage.

Munck, V. C., and E. J. Sobo. 1998. *Using methods in the field: A practical introduction and casebook.* Walnut Creek, CA: Sage/AltaMira.

Murphy, D., M. Scammell, and R. Sclove, eds. and comps. 1997. *Doing community-based research: A reader.* Amherst, MA, and Knoxville, TN: Loka Institute and Community Partnership Center of the University of Tennessee.

Schensul, J. J., M. D. Le Compte, R. T. Trotter II, E. K. Cromley, and M. Singer. 1999. *Mapping social networks, spatial data and hidden populations.* Ethnographer's Toolkit 4. Walnut Creek, CA: AltaMira.

Wax, Rosalie. 1971. *Doing fieldwork: Warnings and advice.* Chicago: University of Chicago Press.

Whyte, W. F. 1997. *Creative problem solving in the field: Reflections on a career.* Walnut Creek, CA: Sage/AltaMira.

Wolcott, H. 1995. *The art of fieldwork.* Walnut Creek, CA: Sage/AltaMira.

Regions and Ecoregions

Center for the Study of Institutions, Population and Environmental Change: www.cipec.org/index.html

Characterization of ecoregions in Africa (Yale and International Institute of Tropical Agriculture): www.geology.yale.edu/%7Esmith/africa_project.html

Hotspots (Conservation International): www.conservation.org/xp/CIWEB/strategies/hotspots/hotspots.xml

Wildlife Conservation Society, Living Landscapes: wcs.org/5675/livinglandscapes

World Wildlife Fund, Global 200: www.worldwildlife.org/science/global200.htm

Olson, D. M., et al. 2001. Terrestrial ecoregions of the world: A new map of life on Earth. *BioScience* 51, no. 11: 933–938.

The Nature Conservancy. 2000. *Designing a geography of hope: A practitioner's handbook to ecoregional conservation planning.* Vols. 1 and 2. Arlington, VA: The Nature Conservancy.

———. 2001. *Conservation by design: A framework for mission success.* Arlington, VA: The Nature Conservancy.

Resources on Geomatics for Indigenous Management

Center for the Support of Native Lands: www.nativelands.org
Environmental Science for Social Change, Manila: www.essc-asia.
com/sparkDB
Innovative Resources Management: www.irmgt.com
Eghenter, C. 2000. *Mapping peoples' forests: The role of mapping in planning community-based management in conservation areas in Indonesia.* Washington, DC: Biodiversity Support Program.
Jones, A. 2001. Participatory mapping resources compiled April–May 2001 by Andrew Jones, Middlebury College. http://community.middlebury.edu/~ajones
Liverman, D., E. F. Moran, R. R. Rindfuss, and P. C. Stern, eds. 1998. *People and pixels: Linking remote sensing and social science.* Washington, DC: National Academy Press.

Rapid Rural Appraisal

Comparisons between rapid rural appraisal and other rapid methods: www.unu.edu/unupress/food2/UIN08E/uin08e0x.htm
iisd1.iisd.ca/casl/CASLGuide/RapidRuralAppraisal.htm
See also www.usaid.gov/about/part_devel/docs/pdiwksp1.html
www.csu.edu.au/research/crsr/ruralsoc/v4n3p30.htm
Food and Agriculture Organization of the United Nations. 1991. *Wood fuel flows: Rapid rural appraisal in four Asian countries (Philippines, Thailand, Nepal, Indonesia).* Bangkok: Regional Wood Energy Development Programme in Asia. www.rwedp.org/fd26.html
Grandstaff, S. W., and T. B. Grandstaff. 1987. Semi-structured interviewing by multidisciplinary teams in RRA. In *Proceedings of the 1985 International Conference on Rapid Rural Appraisal.* Rural Systems Research and Farming Systems Research Projects. Khon Kaen University, Thailand.
Messerschmidt, Donald E. 1995. *Rapid appraisal for community forestry: The RA process and rapid diagnostic tools.* London: International Institute for Environment and Development.
Ogle, B. Rapid rural appraisal (RRA): A useful approach for exploring linkages between forestry and food security? *Forests, Trees and People,* no. 11. Rome: Food and Agriculture Organization of the United Nations.

Participatory Action Research

Chambers, R. 1983. *Rural development: Putting the last first.* London: Longman.

———. 1994a. The origins and practice of participatory rural appraisal. *World Development* 22: 953–969.

———. 1994b. Participatory rural appraisal (PRA): Analysis of experience. *World Development* 22: 1253–1268.

———. 1994c. Participatory rural appraisal (PRA): Challenges, potentials and paradigm. *World Development* 22: 1437–1454.

———. 1999. Relaxed and participatory: Appraisal notes on practical approaches and methods. Institute for Development Studies Research. www.ids.ac.uk/pra/main.html

Cornwall, A., S. Musyokie, and G. Pratt. 2001. In search of a new impetus: Practitioner's reflections on PRA and participation in Kenya. IDS Working Paper no. 131. Sussex: Institute of Development Studies. (critique of PRA as practiced)

Freire, P. 1970. *Pedagogy of the oppressed.* London: Penguin.

Appreciative Inquiry

Training in appreciative inquiry: www.taosinstitute.org

Elliott, C. 1999. *Locating the energy for change: An introduction to appreciative inquiry.* Winnipeg: International Institute for Sustainable Development. www.iisd.org

GEM Initiative. *Appreciative inquiry in action: A practitioner's manual.* Washington, DC: GEM Initiative. www.geminitiative.org

Hammond, S. A. 1996. *The thin book of appreciative inquiry.* Lima, OH: CSS Publishing. www.csspub.com

Watkins, J. M., and B. J. Mohr. 2001 *Appreciative inquiry: Change at the speed of imagination.* Hoboken, NJ: Jossey-Bass/Wiley.

Surveys

An excellent survey research bibliography: www.ucalgary.ca/~newsted/survrefs.htm

Review of survey software: www.fas.harvard.edu/~stats/survey-soft/survey-soft.html

Software for surveys: www.princeton.edu/~abelson/xpractic.html
BRIDGE (Development-Gender). 1994. Annotated bibliography on statistical methodologies for the collection, analysis and presentation of gender-disaggregated data. Bibliography no. 2. Briefing prepared for the British Council Regional Office for West Africa, September. Brighton: Institute of Development Studies.

Ethnography Resources

Anthropak, Ethnograph, and other anthropology research software at Cultural Systems Analysis Software; also Laboratory of Applied Ethnography and Community Action Research, University of Maryland: www.bsos.umd.edu/anth/cusag/cusag3.html
APFT, an anthropologically informed conservation program of the European Union (Forest Peoples Conservation Program, or Appui pour les populations en forêt tropicale): lucy.ukc.ac.uk/Rainforest (ttrefon@ulb.ac.be)
Culture and Agriculture (see especially the fall 1999 issue on anthropology and the environment): csbs3.utsa.edu/culture&agriculture/index.htm
Ethnoquest: An interactive multimedia simulation for cultural anthropology: www.prehall.com/anthropology
References on the American Indian use of fire in ecosystems: wings.buffalo.edu/anthropology/Documents/firebib.txt
What is culture? This is an excellent overview: www.wsu.edu:8001/vcwsu/commons/topics/culture/culture-index.html#top
Comaroff, J., and J. Comaroff. 1992. *Ethnography and the historical imagination.* Boulder, CO: Westview.
Croll, E., and D. Parkin, eds. 1992. *Bush base: Forest farm. Culture, environment and development.* New York: Routledge, Chapman and Hall.
Descola, P., and G. Palsson. 1996. *Nature and society: Anthropological perspectives.* London: Routledge.
Ellen, R. 1982. *Environment, subsistence and system: The ecology of small-scale social formations.* New York: Cambridge University Press.
Netting, Robert M. 1993. *Smallholders, householders: Farm families and the ecology of intensive, sustainable agriculture.* Stanford, CA: Stanford University Press.
Vayda, A., ed. 1969. *Environment and cultural behavior: Ecological studies in cultural anthropology.* Garden City, NY: American Museum Sourcebooks in Anthropology.
Wilk, R. 1996. *Economies and cultures: Foundations of economic anthropology.* Boulder, CO: Westview.

Language and Biodiversity

Terralingua (partnerships for linguistics and biodiversity): www. terralingua.org

Land History

Agrarian studies program at Yale University: www.yale.edu/ agrarianstudies/real/ashome.html
Journal of Agrarian Change: www.blackwellpublishers.co.uk/ journals/JAC/descript.htm
Boston University. 1993. Papers from History of Land Use Workshop, African Studies Association annual meetings, Boston, December 3–7.
Orlove, B. S., and D. W. Guillet. 1985. Theoretical and methodological considerations on the study of mountain peoples: Reflections on the idea of subsistence type and the role of history in human ecology. *Mountain Research and Development* 5, no. 1: 3–18.
Vansina, J. 1990. *Paths in the rainforests: Toward a history of political tradition in Equatorial Africa.* Madison: University of Wisconsin Press.

Ethnobotany

Ethnobotany links: www.rbgkew.org.uk/peopleplants/links.htm
Healing Forest Conservancy: www.shaman.com/Healing_Forest.html
Alexiades, M. N. 1996. *Selected guidelines for ethnobotanical research: A field manual.* Bronx: New York Botanical Garden Press.
Balick, M., and P. A. Cox. 1996. *Plants, people and culture: The science of ethnobotany.* New York: Scientific American Library.
Cunningham A. B. 2001. *Applied ethnobotany: People, wild plant use and conservation.* London: Earthscan.

Conservation Monitoring and Evaluation

Foundations of Success (adaptive management tools): www. FOSonline.org
IUCN monitoring and evaluation initiative: www.iucn.org/themes/eval
Salafsky, N., R. Margoluis, and K. Redford. 2001. Adaptive management: A tool for conservation practitioners. Biodiversity Support

Program Analysis and Adaptive Management Program: www.
bsponline.org/issues/3rd_level/adaptive.html
World Conservation Monitoring Centre: www.unep-wcmc.org

Sustainability Indicators

Centre for International Forestry Research (CIFOR): www.cifor.org/
CimatWeb/ie4/c_i_mainpage_toolbox.htm
International Institute for Sustainable Development: Compendium
of Sustainable Development Indicator Initiatives and Publications:
www.iisd.org/measure/compindex.asp
NASA: Measuring, monitoring and evaluation for biodiversity conservation at the ecoregional and site levels: www.earth.nasa.gov/
outreach/biodiversity/section_d1.html
Tropenbos sustainable forest monitoring: www.etfrn.org/tropenbos/
stortebeker.pdf
Hambly, H., and T. O. Angura, eds. 1996. *Grassroots indicators for desertification: Experience and perspectives from Eastern and Southern Africa.*
Ottawa: International Development Research Centre. www.idrc.ca

Participatory Evaluation

Abbot, J., and I. Gujit. 1998. Changing views on change: Participatory
approaches to monitoring and evaluation. SARL Discussion Paper
no. 2. London: International Institute for Environment and Development.
Ashby, J. A. 1990. *Evaluating technologies with farmers: A handbook.* CIAT
(International Tropical Agriculture Center) Publication no. 187. Obtain from CIAT, Apartado Aereo 6713, Cali, Colombia. www.ciat.
cgiar.org
Carter, J. 1996. *Recent approaches to participatory forest resource assessment.*
Rural Development Forestry Study Guide 2. London: Overseas Development Institute. www.odi.org.uk/publications
Feuerstein, M. T. 1986. *Partners in evaluation: Evaluating development and
community programmes with participants.* London: Macmillan.
Fox, J. 1989. Diagnostic tools for social forestry. *Journal of World Forest
Resource Management* 4: 61–77.

References

Aalbersberg, W. I. Korovulavula, J. Parks, and D. Russell. 1997. The role of a Fijian community in a bioprospecting project. Case study prepared for the Convention on Biodiversity website, www.biodiv.org/programmes/socio-eco/benefit/case-studies.asp (accessed January 3, 2002).

Abram, D. 1996. *The spell of the sensuous: Perception and language in a more-than-human world.* New York: Vintage.

Aburrow, Y. 1994. *The sacred grove: Mysteries of the forest.* Capall Bann Publishing.

Acheson, J. 2000. Clearcutting Maine: Implications for the theory of common property resources. *Human Ecology* 28, no. 2: 145–169.

Adams, J. S., and T. O. McShane. 1992. *The myth of wild Africa: Conservation without illusion.* Berkeley: University of California Press.

Agrawal, A. 1995. Dismantling the divide between indigenous and scientific knowledge. *Development and Change* 26: 413–439.

Agresti, A., and B. Finlay. 1997. *Statistical methods for the social sciences.* 3rd ed. Upper Saddle River, NJ: Prentice Hall.

Alcorn, J. B. 2000. *Borders, rules and governance: Mapping to catalyse changes in policy and management.* IIED Gatekeeper, no. 91. London: International Institute for Environment and Development

Alcorn, J. B., and A. G. Royo, eds. 2000. *Indigenous social movements and ecological resilience: Lessons from the Dayak of Indonesia.* Washington, DC: Biodiversity Support Program.

American Anthropological Association. 1998a. Statement of ethics. *Anthropology Newsletter* 38, no. 10.

———. 1998b. Statement on race. *Anthropology Newsletter* 39, no. 6: 3.

Appleby, G. 1976. Export monoculture and regional social structure in Puno, Peru. In *Regional analysis,* edited by C.A. Smith. New York: Academic.

Asia Forest Network. 1997. Linking government with community resource management: What's working and what's not. Report of the Fifth Asia Forest Network Meeting. Research Network Report 9. Berkeley, CA: Asia Forest Network.

Associates in Rural Development. 2001. Information about the Philippines governance and local democracy (GOLD) project, www.ardinc.com/htm/projects/p_gold.htm (accessed January 3, 2002).

Atlanta Journal-Constitution. 2000. Lowe's to stop selling products from endangered forests. August 8, p. D1.

Bachrach, P., and M. S. Baratz. 1970. *Power and poverty: Theory and practice.* New York: Oxford University Press.

Bahuchet, S., ed. n.d. APFT Pilot Report. *The situation of indigenous peoples in tropical forests,* lucy.ukc.ac.uk/Sonja/RF/Ukpr/Report_c.htm (accessed January 3, 2003).

Bennagan, P. L., and M. L. L. Fernan. 1996. *Consulting the spirits, working with nature, sharing with others: Indigenous resource management in the Philippines.* Manila: Sentro Para sa Ganap na Pamayanan.

Berlin, B. 1992. *Ethnobiological classification: Principles of categorization of plants and animals in traditional societies.* Princeton, NJ: Princeton University Press.

Bernard, R. 2001. *Research methods in anthropology: Qualitative and quantitative approaches.* 3rd ed. Walnut Creek, CA: Sage/AltaMira.

Berry, Sara. 1985. *Fathers work for their sons: Accumulation, mobility and class formation in an extended Yoruba community.* Berkeley: University of California Press.

Bhatt, S. 1998. *Stakeholder institutions for forest management in Garhwal, India.* Washington DC: Biodiversity Conservation Network/World Wildlife Fund.

Bikié, Henriette, et al., eds. 2000. *An overview of logging in Cameroon: A Global Forest Watch Cameroon report.* Washington, DC: World Resources Institute.

Biodiversity Conservation Network. 1997. *Getting down to business: Biodiversity Conservation Network annual report.* Washington, DC: Biodiversity Conservation Network/World Wildlife Fund.

———. 1998. *Biodiversity Conservation Network annual report.* Washington, DC: Biodiversity Conservation Network/World Wildlife Fund.

———. 1999. *Evaluating linkages between business, the environment, and local communities: Final stories from the field.* Washington, DC: Biodiversity Conservation Network/World Wildlife Fund.

Biodiversity Conservation Network and Institute of Environmental Science for Social Change. 1997. *Report on indigenous people's savings and credit workshop in Philippines.* Quezon City: Institute of Environmental Science for Social Change, Ateneo de Manila University.

Biodiversity Support Program. 1998a. *Lessons from the field. Keeping watch: Experiences from the field in community-based monitoring.* Washington, DC: Biodiversity Support Program.

———. 1998b. *Lessons from the field. If I only knew then what I know now: An honest conversation about a difficult conservation and development project.* Washington, DC: Biodiversity Support Program.

Bohannan, P. and L. Bohannan. 1968. *Tiv economy.* Evanston, IL: Northwestern University Press.

Borrini-Feyerabend, G., ed. 1997. *Beyond fences: Seeking social sustainability in conservation.* Gland: World Conservation Union.

Bowen, E. S. [pseud.]. 1964. *Return to laughter.* New York: Doubleday.

Brechin, S., P. Wilshusen, C. Fortwangler, and P. West. 2002. Beyond the square wheel: Toward a more comprehensive understanding of biodiversity conservation as social and political process. *Society and Natural Resources* 15: 41–65.

Brondízio E. S., E. F. Moran, P. Mausel, and Y. Wu. 1996. Changes in land cover in the Amazon estuary: Integration of the thematic mapper with botanical and historical data. *Photogrammetric Engineering and Remote Sensing* 62, no. 8 (special issue): 921–929.

Brondízio E. S., E. F. Moran, A. D. Siqueira, P. Mausel, Y. Wu, and Y. Li. 1994. Mapping anthropogenic forest: Using remote sensing in a multi-level approach to estimate production and distribution of managed palm forest (*Euterpe oleracea*) in the Amazon estuary. *International Archives of Photogrammetry and Remote Sensing* 30, no. 7a: 184–191; Proceedings of the ISPRS Commission VII Symposium Resource and Environmental Monitoring, Rio de Janeiro.

Brosius, P. 2001. The politics of ethnographic presence: Sites and topologies in the study of transnational environmental movements. In *New Directions in Anthropology and Environment: Intersections,* edited by C. Crumley. Walnut Creek, CA: AltaMira Press.

Brosius, J. P., and D. Russell. 2003. Conservation from above: An anthropological perspective on transboundary protected areas and ecoregional planning. *Journal of Sustainable Forestry* 17, no. 1–2: 39–65.

Brosius, J. P., A. L. Tsing, and C. Zerner. 1998. Representing communities: Histories and politics of community-based natural resource management. *Society and Natural Resources* 11: 157–168.

Brown, M. 1999. The implications of participatory mapping: The CARPE experience in Cameroon, www.irmgt.com (accessed January 3, 2003).

———. 2000. Emerging coalitions and sustainable development in the commons: Developing frameworks and tools for negotiating development space in the new millennium. Paper presented at the Eighth Conference of the International Association for the Study of Common Property. Bloomington, IN, May 31–June 2.

Brown, M., and B. Wyckoff Baird. 1996. *Designing integrated conservation and development projects.* Washington, DC: Biodiversity Support Program.

Brunson, M. 1998. Social dimensions of boundaries: Balancing cooperation and self-interest. In *Stewardship across boundaries,* edited by R. L. Knight and P. B. Landres. Washington, DC: Island Press.

Burch, William R. 1964. *A new look at an old friend—Observation as a technique for recreation research.* Portland, OR: Pacific Northwest Forest and Range Experiment Station, U.S. Department of Agriculture Forest Service.

Burns, T. J., E. L. Kick, and D. A. Murray. 1994. Demography, development and deforestation in world-system perspective. *International Journal of Comparative Sociology* 35: 221–239.

Bushmeat Crisis Task Force. 2000. *Bushmeat: A wildlife crisis in West and Central Africa and around the world.* Washington, DC: Bushmeat Crisis Task Force. Available at www.bushmeat.org (accessed August 4, 2002).

Butzer, Carl. 1990. A human ecosystem framework for archaeology. In *The ecosystem approach in anthropology,* edited by E. Moran. Ann Arbor: University of Michigan Press.

Byers, B. 2000. *Understanding and influencing behavior: A guide.* Washington, DC: Biodiversity Support Program.

Campbell, A. 1994. *Landcare: Communities shaping the land and the future.* St. Leonard's: Allen & Unwin.

Catacutan, D. 2001. Technical innovations and institution-building for sustainable upland development: Landcare in the Philippines. Paper presented at the International Conference on Sustaining Upland Development in Southeast Asia: Issues, Tools and Institutions for Local Resource Management. Sustainable Agriculture and Natural Resource Management Collaborative Research Support Project (SANREM-CRSP), Makati City, Philippines, May 27–30.

Central Africa Regional Program on the Environment. 2001. Private sector partnerships: Wildlife Conservation Society-Compagnie International du Bois partnership in Central Africa Regional Program on the Environment (CARPE). 2001. Phase 1: Results and lessons learned. Washington, DC: Biodiversity Support Program. Available at http://carpe.umd.edu (accessed January 3, 2002).

Chambers, R. 1994a. The origins and practice of participatory rural appraisal. *World Development* 22: 953–969.

———. 1994b. Participatory rural appraisal (PRA): Analysis of experience. *World Development* 22: 1253–1268.

———. 1994c. Participatory rural appraisal (PRA): Challenges, potentials and paradigm. *World Development* 22: 1437–1454.

———. 1996. *The power of participation: PRA and policy.* IDS Policy Briefing No. 7, 1–6. Sussex: Institute for Development Studies.

———. 1999. Relaxed and participatory: Appraisal notes on practical approaches and methods. Sussex: Institute for Development Studies. Available at www.ids.ac.uk/pra/main.html (accessed January 3, 2002).

Chao-Beroff, R. 1999. Self-reliant village banks, Mali (case study), http://nt1.ids.ac.uk (accessed January 3, 2002).

Chapin, M., and B. Threlkeld. 2001. *Indigenous landscapes: A study in ethnocartography.* Washington, DC: Center for the Support of Native Lands.

Cincotta, R. P., and R. Engleman. 2000. Nature's place: Human population and the future of biological diversity. Report for Population Action International, Washington, DC.

Colburn, T., D. Dumanoski, and J. P. Myers. 1996. *Our stolen future: How we are threatening our fertility, intelligence and survival—a scientific detective story.* New York: Dutton.

Community Research Network Conference. 1996. *Report of the 1996 Community Research Network Conference: Building a community research network.* Amherst, MA: Loka Institute.

———. 1999. *The 1999 Community Research Network Conference report.* Amherst, MA: Loka Institute.

Connor, R., B. Gerehe, L. Paia, D. Russell, and G. Saemane. 1998. Analysis of the Makira Island (Solomon Islands) household surveys. Conservation International South Pacific, Auckland, New Zealand, September.

Cronon, W., ed. 1995. *Uncommon ground: Toward reinventing nature.* New York: Norton.

Cumming, David H. M. 1999. *Study on the development of transboundary natural resource management areas in southern Africa—Environment context: Natural resources, land use, and conservation.* Washington, DC: Biodiversity Support Program.

De Waal, F. 2001. *The ape and the sushi master: Cultural reflections of a primatologist.* New York: Basic.

Diamond, J. M. 1997. *Guns, germs and steel: The fates of human societies.* New York: Norton.

Dinerstein, E. Wikramanayake, and M. Forney. 1995. Conserving the reservoirs and remnants of tropical moist forest in the Indo-Pacific region. In *Ecology, conservation and management of Southeast Asian rainforests,* edited by R. B. Primack and T. F. Lovejoy. New Haven, CT: Yale University Press.

Dove, M. R. 1993. A revisionist view of tropical deforestation and development. *Environmental Conservation* 20, no. 1: 17–24.

Dugatkin, L. 1999. *Cheating monkeys and citizen bees: The nature of cooperation in animals and humans.* New York: Free Press.

Ehrenfeld, D. 2000. War and peace and conservation biology. *Conservation Biology* 14, no. 1: 105–112.

Elphick, C. 2000. Functional equivalency between rice fields and seminatural wetland habitats. *Conservation Biology* 14, no. 1: 181–191.

Fairhead, J., and M. Leach. 1996. *Misreading the African landscape: Society and ecology in a forest-savanna mosaic.* Cambridge: Cambridge University Press.

Fiji Government. 2000. 31st October, 2000: The Minister for Local Government, Housing and Environment Ratu Cokanauto Tu'uakitau yesterday said he will soon be tabling the National Biodiversity Strategy and Action Plan (NBSAP) for Cabinet's endorsement, www.fiji.gov.fj/press/2000_10/2000_10_31-03.shtml (accessed July 21, 2002).

Forest, Trees and People Newsletter. 1995. Participatory rural appraisal methods. *Forest, Trees and People Newsletter,* no. 26/27, 9. Rome: Food and Agriculture Organization.

Fox, J. 1992. The problem of scale in community resource management. *Environmental Management* 16, no. 3: 289–297.

Franzel, S., R. Coe, P. Cooper, F. Place, and S. J. Scherr. 2001. Assessing the adoption potential of agroforestry practices in sub-Saharan Africa. *Agricultural Systems* 69: 37–62.

Gadgil, M. N.d. Documenting diversity: An experiment. Center for Ecological Science, Indian Institute of Science, Bangalor. Manuscript.

Gallagher, W. 1993. *The power of place: How our surroundings shape our thoughts, emotions, and actions.* New York: Poseidon.

Galvin, K. A., P. K. Thornton, and J. Roque de Pinho. 2001. Integrated modeling and assessment for balancing food security, conservation and ecosystem integrity in East Africa. Paper presented at the American

Anthropological Association meetings, November 28–December 2, Washington, DC.

Gezon, Lisa. 1997. Institutional structure and the effectiveness of integrated conservation and development projects. *Human Organization* 56, no. 4: 462–470.

Giles-Vernick, T. 2001. Rethinking migration and indigeneity in the Sangha River Basin of Equatorial Africa. In *Producing Nature and Poverty in Africa,* edited by Vigdis Broch-Due and Richard Schroeder. Uppsala: Nordic Africa Institute and Transaction Press.

Gladwin, C. H. 1989. *Ethnographic decision tree modeling.* Qualitative Research Methods, no. 19. Walnut Creek, CA: Sage Publications.

Graham, E. 1998. Save the rainforest? The last terrestrial frontier population and conservation past present and future. Paper presented at the annual meeting of the American Anthropological Association.

Gujit, I., and M. K. Shah, eds. 1998. *The myth of community.* London: Intermediate Technology Publications.

Guyer, J., and P. Richards. 1996. The invention of biodiversity: Social perspectives on the management of biological variety in Africa. *Africa* 66, no. 1: 1–13.

Hardin, G., and J. Baden, eds. 1977. *Managing the commons.* San Francisco: Freeman.

Hardin, R. 2000. Translating the forest: Tourism, trophy hunting, and transformation in forest use in Southwestern Central Africa. Ph.D. diss., Yale University.

Harshbarger, C. 1995. Farmer-herder conflict and state legitimacy in Cameroon. Ph.D. diss., University of Florida.

———. 1996a. Guidelines for partnership appraisal and formation: The CARE-International Zambia model. August 1996. Atlanta, GA: CARE-USA.

———. 1996b. Interviews with Michael Drinkwater at CARE-International Zambia, August.

———. 1997. Partnership guidelines for the Greater Horn of Africa, CARE East Africa Unit.

———. 1998. Interviews with staff at Centro Maya, Guatemala, April 1998.

———. 2001. Interview with Dr. James Booth, Department of Statistics, University of Florida, Gainesville, Florida, December 2001.

Hart, T., and J. Hart. 1997. Conservation and civil strife: Two perspectives from central Africa. *Conservation Biology* 11, no. 2: 308–314.

Hart, T. B., J. A. Hart, and J. S. Hall. 1996. Conservation in the declining nation state: A view from eastern Zaire. *Conservation Biology* 10, no. 2: 685–686.

Honey, M. 1999. *Who owns paradise? Ecotourism and sustainable development.* Washington, DC: Island Press.

Hughes, D. M. 2001. Rezoned for business: How eco-tourism unlocked Black farmland in eastern Zimbabwe. *Journal of Agrarian Change* 1, no. 4: 575–599.

Jones, R. F. 1993. *Choosing partnership: The evolution of the Katalysis model.* Stockton, CA: Katalysis North/South Development Partnerships.

Kaiser, C., and H. Lisa. 1998. *Baseline socioeconomic status of communities participating in the project community-based forest management of buffer zone forests at Gunung Palung National Forest West Kalimantan.* Cambridge, MA: Harvard University Press.

Kaplan, H., and K. Hill 1992. The evolutionary ecology of food acquisition. In *Evolutionary ecology and human behavior*, edited by E. A. Smith and B. Winterhalde. New York: Aldine de Gruyter.

Kellert, S. R. 1996. *The value of life: Biological diversity and human society.* Washington, DC: Island Press.

Kennebeck Highlands Project, www.kennebechighlands.org (accessed Janurary 3, 2002).

Khotari, A., S. Suri, and N. Singh. 1995. People and protected areas: Rethinking conservation in India. *The Ecologist* 25, no. 5: 188–194.

Knight, R. L., and P. B. Landres, eds. 1998. *Stewardship across boundaries.* Washington, DC: Island Press.

Korten, D. 1995. *When corporations rule the world.* West Hartford, CT: Kumarian Press.

Krumpe, E., and S. Ham. N.d. Belief-centered approach to environmental education. University of Idaho. Slides.

Kuper, A. 1988. *The invention of primitive society: Transformations of an illusion.* New York: Routledge.

Lal, R., ed. 2000. *Integrated watershed management in the global ecosystem.* Boca Raton, FL: CRC Press.

Lambin, E., and J. Guyer. 1994. The complementarity of remote sensing and anthropology in the study of complex human ecology. History of Land Use Working Papers in African Studies no. 175. Boston: Boston University, African Studies Center.

Lansing, J. S. 1991. *Priests and programmers: Technologies of power in the engineered landscape of Bali.* Princeton, NJ: Princeton University Press.

Liverman, D. T., E. F. Moran, R. Rindfuss, and P. Stern, eds. 1998. *People and pixels: Linking remote sensing and social science.* Washington, DC: National Academy Press.

MacGaffey, J., with Vwakyanakazi Mukohya. 1991. *The real economy of Zaire: The contribution of smuggling and other unofficial activities to national wealth.* Philadelphia: University of Pennsylvania Press.

Mahanty, S., and D. Russell. 2002. What's at stake? Stakeholder groups in the Biodiversity Conservation Network. *Society and Natural Resources* 15: 175–184.

Manning, R. 1993. *Hunters and poachers: A cultural and social history of unlawful hunting in England, 1485–1640.* Oxford: Clarendon.

Marcus, G., and M. Fischer. 1986. *Anthropology as cultural critique: An experimental moment in the human sciences.* Chicago: University of Chicago Press.

Margoluis, R., C. Margoluis, K. Brandon, and N. Salafsky. 2000. *In good company: Effective alliances for conservation.* Washington, DC: Biodiversity Support Program.

Martin, G. J. 1995. *Ethnobotany: A methods manual,* www.rbgkew.org.uk/peopleplants/manuals/index.html (accessed January 3, 2002).

McCay, B. J. 1998. Co-managing the commons. International Workshop on Community-Based Natural Resource Management: Plenary Presentation. Washington, DC: World Bank.

————. 2000a. Going global: A regional approach. Common Property Resource Digest no. 52. Bloomington: Indiana University, International Association for the Study of Common Property, March.

————. 2000b. Post-modernism and the management of natural and common resources. Common Property Resource Digest no. 54. Bloomington: Indiana University, International Association for the Study of Common Property, September.

McCay, B. J., and S. Hanna. 1998. Co-managing the commons: Creating effective linkages among stakeholders—Lessons from small-scale fisheries. International Workshop on Community-Based Natural Resource Management: Plenary Presentation. Washington, DC: World Bank.

McCracken, Stephen D., et al. 1999a. Land-use patterns on an agricultural frontier in Brazil: Insights and examples from a demographic perspective. In *Patterns and processes of land use and forest change in the Amazon,* edited by C. Wood et al. Gainesville: University of Florida Press.

————. 1999b. Remote sensing and GIS at farm property level: Demography and deforestation in the Brazilian Amazon. *Photogrammetric Engineering and Remote Sensing* 65, no. 11 (November): 1311–1320.

McDermott, Melanie Hughes. 2000. Boundaries and pathways: Indigenous identities, ancestral domain, and forest use in Palawan, the Philippines. Paper presented at the meeting of the International Association for the Study of Common Property, Bloomington, IN, May 31–June 4.

Mellor, J., C. M. Peters, S. Malik, et al. 1996. *Midterm evaluation of the Biodiversity Conservation Network.* Washington, DC: Mellor and Associates.

Mintz, S. 1985. *Sweetness and power: The place of sugar in modern history.* New York: Viking.

Moran, E., ed. 1990. *The ecosystem approach in anthropology.* Ann Arbor: University of Michigan Press.

Moran, E. F. 1993. Minimum data for comparative human ecological studies: Examples from studies in Amazonia. *Advances in Human Ecology* 2: 191–213.

Moran, E. F., et al. 1994. Integrating Amazonian vegetation, land-use, and satellite data: Attention to differential patterns and rates of secondary succession can inform future policies. *BioScience* 44, no. 5: 329–338.

Mount Cameroon Project. 1998. Proceedings of a participatory land use training workshop, http://carpe.umd.edu (accessed January 3, 2002).

Nash, J. 1981. Ethnographic aspects of the world capitalist system. *Annual Review of Anthropology* 10: 393–423.

Nazarea, V. S. 1998. *Cultural memory and biodiversity.* Tucson: University of Arizona Press.

Nazarea, V., R. Rhoades, E. Bontoyan, and G. Flora. 1998. Defining indicators which make sense to local people: Intra-culture variation in perceptions of natural resources. *Human Organization* 57, no. 2: 159–170.

————, ed. 1999. *Ethnoecology: Situated knowledge, local lives.* Tucson: University of Arizona Press.

Neumann, R. 1998. *Imposing wilderness: Struggles over livelihood and nature preservation in Africa.* Berkeley: University of California Press.

——. 2000. Primitive ideas: Protecting area buffer zones and the politics of land in Africa. In *Producing nature and poverty in Africa,* edited by V. Broch-Due and R. Schroeder. Uppsala: Nordiska Afrikainstitutet.

New Zealand Overseas Development Association. 1998. *Proceedings of the Pacific ecotourism workshop.* Wellington: New Zealand Overseas Development Association and Tourism Research Consultants.

Nyerges, E. A., and G. M. Green. 2000. The ethnography of landscapes: GIS and remote sensing in the study of forest change in West African Guinea Savanna. *American Anthropologist* 102, no. 2: 1–19.

Oelschlager, M. 1991. *The idea of wilderness: From prehistory to the age of ecology.* New Haven, CT: Yale University Press.

Olson, D., and E. Dinerstein. 1997. *Ecoregion-based conservation planning: Identifying priority sites and activities within ecoregions.* Washington, DC: World Wildlife Fund, Conservation Science Program.

Olson, M. D. 2001. Development discourse and the politics of environmental ideologies in Samoa. *Society and Natural Resources* 14: 399–410.

Orstrom, E. 1998a. Coping with the tragedy of the commons. Paper presented at the Annual Meeting of the Association for Politics and the Life Sciences, Boston, September 3–6.

——. 1998b. How communities beat the tragedy of the commons. International Workshop on Community-Based Natural Resource Management. Washington, DC: World Bank.

——. 1998c. Self-governance and forest resources. International Workshop on Community-Based Natural Resource Management: Plenary Presentation. Washington, DC: World Bank.

Panos Institute. 1997. *People and parks: Wildlife, conservation and communities.* Media Briefing, no. 25 (June), http://panos.org.uk/briefing/cites.htm (accessed August 4, 2002).

Parks, J. 1997. *Ngali nut* (Canarium indicum) *monitoring training for landowners on Makira Island, Solomon Islands.* Washington, DC: Biodiversity Conservation Network.

Peluso, N. 1992. *Rich forests, poor people: Resource control and resistance in Java.* Berkeley: University of California Press.

Peters, C. M. 1996. Beyond nomenclature and use: A review of ecological methods for ethnobotanists. In *Selected guidelines for ethnobotanical research: A field manual,* edited by M. N. Alexiade. Bronx: New York Botanical Garden Press.

——. 1999. *A protocol for participatory inventories of timber and non-timber forest products in Cameroon II: Refining the methodology.* New York: Institute of Economic Botany, New York Botanical Garden.

Peters, P., ed. 1996. Who's local here? *Cultural Survival Quarterly* 20, no. 3 (special issue).

Poole, P. 1995. *Indigenous peoples, mapping and biodiversity conservation: An analysis of current activities and opportunities for applying geomatics technologies.* Washington, DC: Biodiversity Support Program.

Posey, D., and W. Balée, eds. 1989. *Resource management in Amazonia: Indigenous and folk strategies.* Bronx: New York Botanical Garden Press.

Pottier, J., ed. 1993. *Practising development: Social science perspectives.* London: Routledge.

Powerdemaker, H. 1966. *Stranger and friend: The way of the anthropologist.* New York: Norton.

Price, M. F. 1996. People in biosphere reserves: An evolving concept. *Society and Natural Resources* 9: 645–654.

Raffles, H. 1999. Exploring the anthropogenic Amazon: Estuarine landscape transformations in Amapá, Brazil. In *Várzea: Diversity, development, and conservation of Amazonia's whitewater floodplains,* edited by C. Padoch et al. Bronx: New York Botanical Garden Press.

Rappaport, R.A. 1979. *Ecology, meaning and religion.* Richmond, CA: North Atlantic Books.

Rempel, H., J. Harris, and M. Todaro. 1970. Rural-to-urban labour migration: A tabulation of the responses to the questionnaire used in the migration survey. University College Discussion Paper no. 92. Nairobi: Institute for Development Studies.

Rhoades, R., 1998. Participatory watershed research and management: Where the shadow falls. Gatekeeper Series no. 81. London: International Institute for Environment and Development.

Rhoades, R., and J. Stalling, eds. 2001. *Integrated conservation and development in tropical America: Experiences and lessons in linking communities, projects, and policies.* Athens, GA: SANREM (Sustainable Agriculture and Natural Resource Management Collaborative Support Project).

Roosevelt, A. 1989. Resource management in Amazonia before the conquest: Beyond ethnographic projection. In *Resource management in Amazonia: beyond indigenous and folk strategies,* edited by D. Posey and W. Balée. Bronx: New York Botanical Garden Press.

Russell, D. 1983. Reassessing *The Forest People:* A systems approach to Mbuti economic strategies. Unpublished paper, Boston University.

———. 1989a. Liberalization and the local economy in Zaire: Evidence from Kisangani's rice trade. African Studies Center Working Paper no. 139. Boston: Boston University.

———. 1989b. Women farmers in Bandundu. Washington, DC: International Institute for Research on Women.

———. 1991. Food supply and the state: The history and social organization of the rice trade in Kisangani, Zaire. Ph.D. diss., Boston University.

Russell, D., and J. Stabile. In press. Ecotourism in practice: Trekking the highlands of Makira, Solomon Islands. In *Tourism in the Pacific,* edited by J. Harrison. London: Cognizant Press.

Russell, D., and N. Tchamou. 2001. Soil fertility and the generation gap: The Bene of Cameroon. In *People managing forests: The links between human well being and sustainability,* edited by C. Colfer and Y. Byron. Washington, DC: Resources for the Future and Center for International Forestry Research.

Ruttan, L. M. 2000. Games and the CPR Toolkit. *Common Property Resource Digest,* no. 55 (December). Bloomington: Indiana University, International Association for the Study of Common Property.

Salafsky, N., and R. Margoluis. 1998. *Measures of success: Designing, monitoring and managing conservation and development projects.* Washington, DC: Island Press.
———. 1999. *Greater than the sum of their parts: Designing conservation and development programs to maximize results and learning. A practical guide for program managers and donors.* Washington, DC: Biodiversity Support Program.
Sauni, Samasoni, et al. 1999. A socio-economic baseline survey of Ucunivanua Village, Verata Tikina. Suva, Fiji: South Pacific Action Committee for Human Ecology and Environment. Submitted to Biodiversity Conservation Network and Verata Tikina, June 22.
Save the Children USA. 1996. Partnership and institutional development. Save the Children, U.S. Working Paper Series, www.savethechildren.org (accessed January 3, 2002).
Sayer, J. N.d. Get the forest people on your side. Unpublished manuscript, Center for International Forestry Research, Bogor, Indonesia.
Schensul, J. J., M. D. Le Compte, R. T. Trotter II, E. K. Cromley, and M. Singer. 1999. *Mapping social networks, spatial data and hidden populations.* Ethnographer's Toolkit 4. Walnut Creek, CA: AltaMira Press.
Schwartzmann, S., A. Moreira, and D. Nepstad. 2000a. Rethinking tropical forest conservation: Perils in parks. *Conservation Biology* 14, no. 5: 1351–1357.
Schwartzmann, S., D. Nepstad, and A. Moreira. 2000b. Arguing tropical forest conservation: People vs. parks. *Conservation Biology* 14, no. 5: 1370–1374.
Scott, James. 1998. *Seeing like a state: How certain schemes to improve the human condition have failed.* New Haven, CT: Yale University Press.
Shambaugh, J., J. Oglethorpe, R. Ham, and S. Tognetti. 2001. *The trampled grass: Mitigating the impacts of armed conflict on the environment.* Washington, DC: Biodiversity Support Program.
Sinha, F., and N. Verma. 1997. Socioeconomic conditions and village institutions in a hill valley: A baseline survey of the Akash Kamini Valley. Project report. Gurgaon, Haryana, India: EDA Rural Systems.
Smith, C. A., ed. 1976. *Regional analysis.* 2 vols. New York: Academic Press.
Social Development Research Center. 1995–1996. *Pag-le-teg: Socioeconomic monitoring report for Campung Ulay and Kayasan.* Vol. 1. Manila: De la Salle University, Social Development Research Center.
Srinivasan, L. 1990. Tools for community participation. Technical series. Distributed by PACT.
Stuckey, J. 1994. Institutional partnering: Perspectives and lessons from the PACA project. CARE USA, ANR Technical Report series no. 5, 1994, www.care.org (accessed January 3, 2002).
Sunderland, T. C. H., L. E. Clark, and P. Vantomme, eds. 1999. *Non-wood forest products of Central Africa: Current research issues and prospects for conservation and development.* Rome: FAO.
Sunderlin, W. D., O. Ndoye, H. Bikié, N. Laporte, B. Mertens, and J. Pokam. 1999. Economic crisis, small-scale agriculture and forest cover change in southern Cameroon. *Environmental Conservation* 27, no. 3: 284–290.
Taussig, M. 1980. *The devil and commodity fetishism in South America.* Chapel Hill: University of North Carolina Press.

The Nature Conservancy. 1996. Designing a geography of hope: Guidelines for ecoregion-based conservation in the Nature Conservancy, www.tnc.org (accessed January 3, 2002).

———. 2000. *Designing a geography of hope: A Practitioners handbook to ecoregional conservation planning*. Vols. 1 and 2. Arlington, VA: The Nature Conservancy. Available at www.tnc.org (accessed July 22, 2002).

Thompson, E. P. 1975. *Whigs and hunters: The origins of the black act*. London: Allen Lane.

Trefon, T., and L. Defo. 1999. Can Rattan Help Save Wildlife? *Development* 42, no. 2: 68–70.

Tsing, A. L. 1993. *In the realm of the diamond queen: Marginality in an out-of-the-way place*. Princeton, NJ: Princeton University Press.

United States Agency for International Development. N.d. Guide to customer service: Quality standards for working with USAID's customers and partners, www.usaid.gov.

Uphoff, N. T. 1986. *Local institutional development: An analytic sourcebook with cases*. West Hartford, CT: Kumarian Press.

Van der Linde, H., J. Oglethorpe, T. Sandwith, D. Snelson, and Y. Tessema. 2001. *Beyond boundaries: Transboundary natural resource management in sub-Saharan Africa*. Washington, DC: Biodiversity Support Program.

Van Noordwijk, M., T. Tomich, and B. Verbist. 2001. Negotiation support models for integrated natural resource management in tropical forest margins. *Conservation Ecology* 5, no. 2: 21. Available at www.consecol.org/vol5/iss2/art21c.

Vayda, A. P. 1995a. Failures of explanation in Darwinian ecological anthropology: Part I. *Philosophy of the Social Sciences* 25, no. 2: 219–249.

———. 1995b. Failures of explanation in Darwinian ecological anthropology: Part II. *Philosophy of the Social Sciences* 25, no. 3: 360–375.

West, P. 2001. Environmental non-governmental organizations and the nature of ethnographic inquiry. Paper presented at the annual meeting of the American Anthropological Association, Washington, DC, November 28–December 2.

Wilkie, D. S., and J. T. Finn. 1996. *Remote sensing for natural resources monitoring: A guide for first time users*. New York: Columbia University Press.

Williams, G. W. 1994. References on the American Indian use of fire in ecosystems, http://wings.buffalo.edu/anthropology/Documents/firebib.txt (accessed January 3, 2002).

Wilmsen, E. 1989. *Land filled with flies: A political economy of the Kalahari*. Chicago: University of Chicago Press.

Wilhusen, P., S. Brechin, C. Fortwrangler, and P. West. 2002. Reinventing a square wheel: Critique of a resurgent "protection paradigm" in international biodiversity conservation. *Society and Natural Resources* 15: 17–40.

World Bank. N.d. Girls' education yields significant environmental benefits: Education increases women's ability to manage natural resources efficiently and raises the likelihood that they will adopt new, more effective, technolo-

gies which are environmentally friendly, www.girlseducation.org/PGE_
active_pages/GirlsEdResources/main.asp?DirectoryName=EconAnd
SocialDev%2F (accessed January 3, 2002).

World Wildlife Fund. 1995a. Draft report: Workshop II of the ICDP review: Local knowledge and social organization: Foundations for biodiversity conservation. Puerto Princesa, Philippines, November 12–18.

———. 1995b. *Review of integrated conservation and development projects,
1985–1996. Workshop II: Local knowledge and social organization: Foundations for
biodiversity conservation.* Washington, DC: World Wildlife Fund.

———. 1996. Final draft report: Workshop III of the ICDP review: The enabling
environment for ICDPs: Policies, institutions, and ethical dilemmas at local,
national, and international levels. Syria, VA, May 5–9.

———. 1997a. *Final draft report: Lessons from the field: A review of World Wildlife
Fund's experience with integrated conservation and development projects.
1985–1996.* Washington, DC: World Wildlife Fund.

———. 1997b. *Summary report: Review of integrated conservation and development
projects, 1985–1996.* Washington, DC: World Wildlife Fund.

World Wildlife Fund for Nature—South Pacific Programme. 1998. *Survey skills
workshop for collection of baseline data.* Suva, Fiji: World Wildlife Fund for
Nature—South Pacific Programme.

Index

Page numbers in italics indicate a box, photo, or table.

Abram, David, 23, 52
accountability and social impact of conservation, 113–14
action research: advantages of, 235–36; appreciative inquiry (AI) in, 238, *238*, 239–41; biological monitoring in, 253–56; community monitoring in, 250–51, *251*, 252, *252*, 253; definition of a community in, 237; mapping land use zones and resource use in, 248–49; participatory rural appraisal (PRAs) in, 241, *242*, 243, *243*, 244, *245*; social realities of, 236–38
Adams, J. S., 30
Africa, "registered farms" in, 55
agriculture, cropping systems of, 42, 45–46, *46*, 47–48
agroforestry, practices of, 46, *46*, 47
almaciga resin, 45
American Anthropological Association (AAA), 111

analysis: cross-site analysis in, 262–63, *263*, 264–65; merging different units of, 4–5; units in social research for, 152–56
animals, managing domestic and/or wild, 50–51, *51*, 52
anthropogenic forests, 30
Anthropological Center for Training in Global Environmental Change, 177
anthropology, critical perspective in, 8. *See also* ethnographic research
Appleby, G., 184
appreciative inquiry (AI): approach of empowering communities with, 117, 147; in community-owned research, 238, *238*, 239–41; Four-D model in, 239–40; phases in community work using, 118–20, *120*
appreciative planning and action (APA), 241
archaeology, land history studies with, 217–19
Asia, case study of project planning in, 3

Asia Forest Network, 35, 80, 262
assumptions, 122, *122*, 123, *123*, 124
authoritarian political systems, 93

Bachrach, P., 94
Baden, J., 33
Bahuchet, Serge, 30
Baratz, M., 94
barter and informal markets, 61, 73
baseline instruments, 231–32
baseline surveys, 229, 230–31
beneficiaries, as unit of analysis in social research, 156
benefit distribution, 120–21, *121*, 122
Berlin, Brent, 109, 212, 221
Berry, Sara, 107
"big man," political system of, 92
biodiversity: case studies in conservation of, 54, 219; conservation areas of, 53–55; national biodiversity strategy action plan (NBSAP) in, 132; "no-man's-land" of, 53, 54; partnerships in conservation of, 125
Biodiversity Conservation Network (BCN): on challenges in developing partnerships, 125, 134, 135, *135*, 136; common indicators in monitoring by, 258, *259*; ethical guidelines for research by, *112*; evaluation and monitoring of programs in, 10, 122, 251; questions for cross-site analysis by, *263*; sampling designs by, 162, *163*; survey

principles of, *230*; testing claims of NTFPs enterprises by, 49
Biodiversity Support Program, 10
biological resources, 40–41
birthrates, 18–19
boundaries and territoriality, 17
bribes and transaction costs, 69–70, *70*
bridewealth, 57, 59
bubble sheets, 233
Buddhism, 108
bureaucratic/nation-state political systems, 93
bushmeat, 51, *51*, 84, 172–73

Cameroon: beliefs and norms in, 107; benchmark approach in monitoring in, 266; invisible husbands in, 81
CAMPFIRE program, 35, 52
CARE, 79, 128
CARE International-Zambia, 137–38
carrying capacity, 248
case studies: of beliefs and norms, 107; on benchmark approach in monitoring, 266; on communicating conservation in village meetings, 204; on communication in interdisciplinary teams, 5; of conservation of biodiversity areas, 54; contrasting AI and conventional approaches, 118; on credit groups in Cameroon, 60; on "Dayak" rubber tappers, 62; of debt and dependency in the rattan trade, 97; on developing

baseline questions, 232; on differentiation, 100; on ethnobiology fieldwork in Cameroon, 214; on evaluations of BCN-funded projects, 270; on evolving traditions, 203; of factionalism in the Philippines, 96; on forbidden barter in the Congo, 62; on "forest markets" in the Congo, 61; of forest users' groups, 86; on gossip affecting initiatives, 105; of health consequences with conservation, 6; on identifying skills of a population in Fiji, 63; of "incursion" in conservation, 249; of intensification in rural Africa, 55; on invisible husbands in Cameroon, 81; on labor markets of men and women in India, 63; of the Lumad and Dumagat in the Philippines, 83; of *mataqalis* in Fiji, 98; on Mayan garbage and biodiversity, 219; of migration issues in the U.S., 99; on *ngali* nuts as subsistence or cash crop, 59; of out migration in Fiji, 99; of patronage networks in the Philippines, 96; on policies of perverse incentives, 25; on politics of a saving mammals program, 4; of poor project planning in Asia, 3; on population around Lore Lindu National Park, Indonesia, 79; on population *versus* environment, 19; on preparation for interviews, 194; of religious sects and community members, 98; on researching existing literature, 117; in sampling choices and field realities, 161; of savings and investment systems, 65; on scaling up in Somalia, 131; on social economy and logging in New Guinea, 60; on social identities of conservationists, 90; on stakeholders in the Kalahan Educational Foundation (KEF), 84; on stratification in Nigeria, 100; of subvillage formations, 80; of transmigration in Indonesia, 56; on transport and economic development, 64; on urban consumers of bushmeat, 84; on using census data in fieldwork, 227; on using genealogies in ethnographic research, 216; on using local knowledge in interviews, 197; on using RRA in regional study in the Congo, 179; on valuable nontimber forest products (NTFPs), 66; on working with focus groups, 205

cash crops, 47–48
caste, definition of, 82
catchment, as unit of analysis in social research, 155
cattle ranching, 19
Cauley, Hank, 141
census surveys, 3, 226–28
Center for the Support of Native Lands, 247
central place theory, 183–84, *184*
Centro Maya, 129
Chambers, Robert, 180

Chao-Beroff, R., 73
Chapin, Mac, 247
charitable organizations, institutions of, 89
chiefly political systems, 92–93
Christianity, 108
CIONG, 131
civil institutions, 89
clan: definition of, 81–82, *82;* as unit of analysis in social research, 153
cluster sample, *160,* 161–62
coalitions, networks of, 188
Cold War, 22
collectivités, 171
commodification, 66–67
commodities: regional market studies of, 184–85; and role in conservation, 30–34
commodity extraction, 4
Common Property Resource Digest, 35
common-property resource scale, 151
communal ownership of land, *44*
communication, challenges in, 2–5
"community," definition of, 79
community-based organization (CBO), 129
community-level indicators, 253
community management of resources: challenges in, 36–37; ethics in choosing a site and partners, 114–15; examples of, *35;* motivations for, 34–37
community management plans, 244–46, 247–52, *252,* 253–56
community mapping, 245, 246, 247–50
community monitoring, 250–51, *251, 252, 252,* 253

community-owned research: advantages of, 236; appreciative inquiry (AI) in, 238, *238,* 239–41; biological monitoring in, 253–56; community monitoring in, 250–51, *251,* 252, *252,* 253; definition of a community in, 237; mapping land use zones and resource use in, 248–49; participatory rural appraisal (PRAs) in, 241, *242,* 243, *243, 244, 245;* social realities of, 236–38
competition of resources, 16–17
CONGAD, 130
Congo: "Congo Basin Wilderness Area" in, 178; hidden taxation and social costs in, *70;* impact of Christian groups on conservation in, 108; regional analysis of the Tshopo in, 171–72, *172,* 173–74; using RRA in regional study in, 179
conservation: historical elements of, 27–34; holistic definition of problems in, 5; as a social process, 5–7
conservation biology, 11
conservation institutions, 89
Conservation International (CI), 120, 149
consumerism, 19–20
convenience sample, 159, *159*
Convention on Biodiversity, 24
Convention on International Trade in Endangered Species, 24
cooperative social life, 16–17
cooperative strategies, 20–21
cooperatives, institution of, 88

Cooperrider, David, 238
coping strategies in economic
    systems, 71, 72
corporate ownership of land, 44
cost-effectiveness in partnerships,
    131–32
costs of doing business, 69–70, 70
"countermapping," 247
credit and savings systems, 64,
    71–72, 72, 73, 74
critical perspective, 7–9
cross-site analysis, 262–63, 263,
    264–65
cultural diversity, 23–24
culture, behavior of, 17–18
culture brokers, 103, 135–36
"custom feasts," 59
 "customary land," 55
"customary" tenure of land, 44
customer service surveys, 115

database, 144
de facto tenure/control of land,
    44
debtor–creditor relationships, 97
Department of Environment and
    Natural Resources (DENR),
    265
development, balance of
    conservation and, 21–22
differentiation, 99–100
disease, risks with "progress," 24
diversity, 23–24
Domaines de Chasse, 51
dowry, 20, 57, 59

economic incentives, 28
economic institutions, 88–89
economic systems, 57–76
ecoregion scale, 149–50, 155–56
ecotourism, 100

egalitarian political system, 91
Ehrenfeld, David, 38
ejido, 44
elite dominance, 94
"emotional intelligence," 10
EnterpriseWorks International,
    187
enumerators, 144, 179, 226, 233
environmental governance, 24–25
ethics in research: BCN
    guidelines for, 112; in
    choosing sites and partners,
    114–15; implementation of, 11;
    principles for field research
    in, 111–12, 112, 113–14
ethnic groups, definition of,
    81–82, 82
ethnicity, role in cooperative
    strategies, 20–21
ethnobiology, 109–10, 213, 213,
    214–15
ethnobotany, 129
ethnographic research: agrarian
    studies in, 220; kinship and
    genealogy studies in, 216–17,
    218; language and linguistics
    in, 220–21; "mini-
    ethnographies" in, 222–23;
    multisite ethnographies in,
    221–22; participant observation
    in, 208–9, 209, 210–12; study of
    land history in, 217–20
ethnology, 222
ethnotaxonomies, 212–13, 213,
    214–15
evaluations: formal evaluations
    in, 269; informal, internal, and
    self-evaluations in, 268, 268,
    269; key questions for
    conservation initiatives in,
    270–71; participatory

evaluations in, 269; scenario building in, 272
extended household, as unit of analysis in social research, 153
extinction, rates in nonhuman species, 28–30

factionalism, 95–96
Fairhead, James, 30
faith-based conservation, 107–8
Fathers Work for Their Sons (Berry), 107
"fees" and transaction costs, 69–70, *70*
feudal political systems, 93
Fiji: community management programs in, 35; community monitoring in, 250; fishing management practices in, 53; hidden taxation and social costs in, *70; mataqalis* in, 98; out migration in, 99; skills in a population on, 63; *Turaga ni Koros* in, *165*
fines and transaction costs, 69–70, *70*
Finn, J., 175
fishing, resource management of, 52–53
fission, 97
focus groups, 115, 204–6
food crops, 47
foraging, 41–42
"forest markets" in the Congo, 61
Forest Stewardship Council (FSC), 75–76, 141
Forest, Trees and People, 35
forests: anthropogenic forests in, 30; exploitation of, 48–50; forest users' groups and, 86; multistory agroforestry,

practices of, 37, 46, *46;* nontimber forest products (NTFPs) from, 49–50
formal interviews, 195
Four-D model, 239–40
freshwater and marine subsistence, 42–43
"Futa Wino ya Leta," *70*

gender, 106–7, 212
generational dynamics, 107
geographic information systems (GIS), 7, 156, 173, 175–77
geomatics, 175–77
global commodity trends, 4
Global Excellence in Management (GEM), 238, *238*
Global Forest Watch, 155, 178
global positioning systems (GPS), 175, 248
global scale, 149
globalization, impact of, 73–76
gossip, 104–5
Graham, Liz, 30
Greenpeace, 141

habitat scale, 150
Ham, Sam, 103
Hardin, G., 33
heuristic regions, 171
hidden assumptions, 122, *122,* 123, *123,* 124
hidden economy, 4, 94
Hinduism, 108
households: definition of, 79–81; suggested questions for interviews of, *198;* survey unit of, 228–29, *230;* as unit of analysis in social research, 153
"How Beliefs Can Be Used in Communication Programs to

Affect Local Conservation
Practices" (Krumpe and Ham),
103
human behavior, conservation as,
15–26
human ecology, 12
human evolution, role in
conservation, 15–26
human reproduction, 18–19
hunting, of wildlife resources, 51,
51, 52
hypothesis, *144*

incentives and sanctions in
initiatives, 28–29, 120–21, *121*,
122
India: community management
of forests in, 34, 35; Forest
Department in, 86, 87; labor
markets of men and women in,
63
*Indigenous Knowledge and
Development Monitor*, 35
indigenous peoples: domains of
land by, *44*; indigenous
knowledge of, 108–9
individual: as unit of analysis in
social research, 152; views and
concepts of, 102–3
Indonesia: "Dayak" rubber
tappers in, 62; hidden taxation
and social costs in, *70*;
multistory agroforestry in, 46,
46; population around Lore
Lindu National Park in, 79
informal markets and barter, 61, 73
Innovative Resources
Management, 247
Institute of Environmental
Science for Social Change
(ESSC), 83, 128

institutions: definition of, 33–34;
evolution of, 85, *85*; forms and
types of, 83–85, *85*, 86–90;
partnerships with, 129; of
resource management, 12
integrated conservation and
development projects (ICDPs),
3
International Institute of Tropical
Agriculture, 266
International Monetary Fund, 75
interviews: attitude adjustments
for, 191–95; building rapport
for, 190–91; confidentiality of,
192; field instruments for,
195–99; focus groups in, 204–6;
introduction protocols and
setting up of, 189–90, *190*, 191;
open-ended and closed-choice
responses in, 196, *196*;
questions and topics for,
196–97, *197*, 198, *198*, 199; role
of oral history in, 201–2;
topical guides in, *195*;
translators and translation
needs in, 192; working with
group interviews, 203–4
irrigated agriculture, 42
Islam, 108

Kalahan Educational Foundation
(KEF), 84
Kennebeck Highlands, 155
Kenya, hierarchy of status in, *91*
key informant interviews:
expertise provided by,
199–200, *200*, 201; needs
assessment of, 115; and role in
conservation buy-in, 2; in
selecting partners, 133; using
questions for, *198*

kinship/kinship groups: definition of, 81–82, *82;* in ethnographic research, 216–17, *218;* institution of, 87; social networks of, 188

knowledge systems and conservation, 108–10, 129

Krumpe, Edwin, 103

labor, division of, 3

labor markets, 62–63

land: agricultural practices on, 45–46, *46,* 47–48; conserving with land trusts, 265; expropiation of, 4; forms of control over, 43, *44,* 45; land speculations and "land use planning" of, 28, 32; plants and trees in the "wild" of, *45;* resource of, 43–48

land histories in ethnographic research, 217–20

Landcare, 265

landowners associations, 87

landscape scale, 150

language, in ethnographic studies, 220–21

Leach, Melissa, 30

League of Women Voters, 89

legal institutions, 87–88

life plans, 103–4

lineage: definition of, 81–82, *82;* as unit of analysis in social research, 153

"local economy": economic institutions in, 88–89; goals and strategies of, 58–65; social economy of, 57–60; trends in and tracking changes of, 65–76

local knowledge in partnerships, 129

local systems and abilities to manage resources, 9

logging, 19, 24, 48–49

long-term cost effectiveness in partnerships, 131–32

Makira conservation initiative, *120*

Managing the Commons (Hardin and Baden), 33

maps/mapping: community mapping in, 245, 246, 247–49; in regional studies, 175–78; social mapping in, 2

marine and freshwater subsistence, 42–43

market capitalism, 23–24

markets: economic institutions in, 88–89; functions of, 61–65; and trading network surveys in regional studies, 183–84, *184,* 185–88

marriage, institution of, 87

mataqalis, 98

materialism, 19–20

McDermott, Melanie Hughes, 17

McShane, T. O., 30

memorandum of understanding (MOU), 136

"memory banking," 47

micro-approach, 9

Micronesia, community management programs in, 35

migration: ethnographic studies of, 188; impact on territories and boundaries, 17, 19, 28; sociopolitical systems of, 97–99

military camps, 90

"mini-ethnographies," 222–23

mining, 19, 24

"mining" of resources, 58

monitoring: biological
monitoring in action research,
253–56; in community-owned
research, 250–51, *251*, 252, *252*,
253; definition of, 257; of the
impact of conservation, *259*; of
indicators, 258–59, *259*, 260–62,
262; as a learning tool, 261–62,
262; scales and scaling up in,
265–67; scientific monitoring
in, 257; timing and consistency
of, 259–60
Moran, Emilio, 17, 19, 38, 177
Mount Cameroon Project, 246–47
multistory agroforestry, 42, 46, *46*,
47
mutual capacity building, 129

nation: definition of, 78; as unit of
analysis in social research, 155
national biodiversity strategy
action plan (NBSAP), 132
natural regions, 171
natural resource management
(NRM) surveys, 232–33
natural resources, management
systems for, 40–56
The Nature Conservancy (TNC),
10, 79
Nazarea, Virginia, 47
needs assessment, 114–15, 127
Nepal, community management
of forests in, 34, 35
networks, 183–88
New Partnerships Initiative
(NPI), 126
NGAAD, 131
ngali nuts as subsistence or cash
crop, 59, 67
Nigeria, stratification in, 100
"no-man's-land," 53, 54

nomadic pastoralists, 42
nongovernmental organizations
(NGOs), 89, 114, 126
nonhuman species, rates of
extinction of, 28–30
nonprobability sampling, 158–59,
159, 160, *160*
nonspatial scaling up, 267
nontimber forest products
(NTFPs), 49–50, 66
norms, 106–7

Oelschlager, M., 30
"optimal foraging," 145
oral history, role in interviews,
201–2
ownership of land, forms of, 43,
44, 45

Palau, community management
programs in, 35
Panos Institute, 54
Papua New Guinea, 54
paradigms in conservation
projects, 122, *122*, 123, *123*,
124
Parks, John, 251
participant observation:
considerations in project
planning with, 8; in
ethnographic research, 208–9,
209, 210–12; role in
conservation buy-in, 2
participants, as unit of analysis in
social research, 156–58
participatory action research
(PAR), 241
participatory cross-site analysis,
262–63
participatory learning and action
(PLA), 241

participatory methods, appraising partnerships with, 136–38, *138*, 139

participatory monitoring and evaluation (PM&E), 241

participatory rural appraisals (PRAs): in action research, 241, *242*, 243, *243*, 244, *245*; empowering communities with, 147, 180; in social research, 6

partnerships: accountability by professionals in, 127; appraisal of, 136–38, *138*, 139; conservation of biodiversity with, 125; corporate and private-sector partnerships in, 141–42; criteria for and creation of, 126–28; features of, 128; goals and outcomes of, 128–32; memorandum of understanding (MOU) for, 136; mobilization and rights of local groups in, 127, 139–41; "primary-secondary partner model" in, 131; strategies and criteria for selecting partners in, 132–35, *135*, 136

pastoralism, 42

"pathways," 17

patronage relations, 96–97

"Peace, Justice and Stewardship of Nature," 108

permits and transaction costs, 69–70, *70*

perverse incentives, 25, 69

pet theories in conservation initiatives, *11*

Peters, Charles, 214

Philippines: community management of forests in, 34, 35; debt and dependency of the rattan trade in, 97; Department of Environment and Natural Resources (DENR) of, 25; factionalism in, 96; Kalahan Educational Foundation (KEF) in, 84; Lumad and Dumagat in, 83; patronage networks in, 96; value of domestic animals in, 50

Philippines Working Group (PWG), 264–65

plantations, 48

political ecology, 12

political institutions, 87–88

political systems: categories and structures of, 91–92, *92*, 93–95; considerations in project planning, 3

polygon/vector images, 175

Poole, Peter, 177

population: definition of, 78; and reproductive strategies, 18–19; and social systems, 77–101

potlatches, 20

prestige, definition of, 20

private ownership of land, *44*

private-sector partnerships, 141–42

private voluntary organizations (PVOs), 126

probability sampling, 160, *160*, 161–62

projects: approaches for, *116*; incentives and sanctions in, 120–21, *121*, 122; paradigms for conservation projects, *123*; planning strategies for, 115–16, *116*, 117–20, *120*

protected areas (PAs), 54–55

protocols and rules of societies, 105–6
province, as unit of analysis, 155
purposive sample, 159, *159*

qualitative and quantitative methods: in cross-site analysis, 263, *263*, 264–65; in research, 157, *157*, 158

Ramos, Victor, 265
Ramsar Convention on Wetlands Important as Waterfowl Habitat, 54
rapid research, 7
rapid rural appraisal (RRA), 178–81, *181*, 182–83
raster-based images, 175–77
reciprocity, 73
redistribution, 73
redistributive political systems, 92
refugee camps, 90
regional studies: defining regions for, 170–72, *172*, 173–74; geomatics in, 175–77; landscapes and watersheds in, 174–75; "natural" and "heuristic" regions in, 171; rapid rural appraisal (RRA) in, 178–81, *181*, 182–83; surveys of markets and trading network in, 183–84, *184*, 185–88; using maps in, 177–78
"registered farm," 55
religion, 23, 107–8
remote sensing images, 175
research ethics, 111–24
research in conservation: advance considerations and thinking in, 143–44;

collaboration in the field of, 162; debriefing in, 167; developing a hypothesis for, 146–47; formal and informal models of, 144–46; literature review for, 117, 147–48; multidisciplinary teams in, 164–65; organizing a project in, 143–68; pilot testing field instruments in, 166; planning of, 165, *165*, 166; qualitative and quantitative methods in, 147, 157, *157*, 158; research management, system of, *167*, 168, *168*; scales and research units in, 148–51; social research and social units in, 151–57; survey sampling in, 158–62; teams and team leaders in, 163–65
research results: audiences and tailoring messages to, 273–75, *275*; as common property, 272; communicating strategies for, 272–75, *275*
Resident's Development Committee (RDC), 137–38, *138*, 139
resource extraction, 30–34
resource management: changes in systems of, 56; definition of, 40–41; history of, 27–28; sociopolitical realities affecting, 95–101
resource-user group, 154
rites and rituals, 106
role, definition of, 90–91, *91*
rotary clubs, 89
rules and protocol in social interaction, 104–6
rural development, 11

rural sociology, 11
Russell, Diane, 171

sampling procedures, 158–62
sanctions and incentives in initiatives, 120–21, *121*, 122
satellite maps, 175–77
Save the Children, 128, 129, 131
savings and credit systems, 64, 71–72, *72*, *73*, *74*
scales and research units, 149
scaling up, 130–31, 265–67
scenario building in evaluations, 272
schools, institutions of, 89
Schwartzmann, S., 30, 53
scientific knowledge, 108–9
self-evaluations, 268, *268*, 269
seminomadic pastoralists, 42
semistructured interviews, 195
services and trade labor markets, 63
settled pastoralists, 42
settlements or villages, definition of, 79
shame and embarrassment, controlling with, 104
Sierra Club, 99
simple random sample, *160*, 161
sites and partners, ethics of choosing, 114–15
small-scale logging, 48–49
Smartwood, 76
social economy, 4, 58–60
social forestry, 11
"social impact" scales, 77
social institutions, 89
social mapping, role in conservation buy-in, 2
social research: challenges in, 37–39; critical issues in, 33–34;

model-driven approaches in, 38–39; quality of projects in, 7; role in project planning, 121, *121*, 122; social units in, 151–56
social systems and populations, 77–101
social welfare institutions, 89
societies, definition of, 78
soli, 70
Solomon Islands: community management programs in, 35; community monitoring in, 251–52; differentiation in, 100; fishing management practices in, 53; impact of Christian groups on conservation in, 108; knowledge of species or habitat in, 109; Makira conservation initiative in, *120*; religious sects and community members in, 98, role of social research in projects in, 122
Solomon Islands Development Trust, 120
The Spell of the Sensuous (Abram), 52
spirituality and conservation, 107–10
Srinivasan, L., 269
stakeholders: definition of, 82–83; priorities of, 6; as unit of analysis in social research, 154–55
"state," 78, 93–95
state ownership of land, 44
status, definition and hierarchy of, 20, 90–91, *91*, *92*
Stories from the Field (BCN), 135, 264
stratification, 100
stratified sample, *160*, 161–62

Stuckey, J., 133
subsectors, 186
subsistence farming, 58
subsistence strategies, 41–43
surveys: baseline instruments in, 231–32; baseline surveys in, 229, 230–32; census of study areas in, 226–28; interviewing a household in, 228–29, 230; managing data from, 233–34; methods and approaches of, 224–26; natural resource management (NRM) surveys in, 232–33
sustainability in partnerships, 130
swidden agriculture and multistory agroforestry, 42
systematic sample, 160, 161

"target groups," ethics in choosing of, 114–15
taxation and rents, 69–70, 70, 94
technology, impact of demand on resources, 22–23, 28
Technoserve, 187
tenure institutions, 87–88
"terms of trade," 67–68, 68
Terralingua, 221
territoriality, 17
township, as unit of analysis in social research, 155
trade and services labor markets, 63
"tragedy of the commons," 32, 32, 33
transaction costs, 69–70, 70
transboundary conservation, 170
transportation systems, 64
tribes/tribal councils, 81–82, 82, 87
Tropical Forest People's Program (APFT), 84
Turaga ni Koros, 165

"umbrella organizations," 130
"underground economy," 65, 94
United States Agency for International Development (USAID), 10, 126
unit of analysis, 144
Uphoff, Norman, 34
use/access rights of land, 44

Venn diagrams, 145
village or settlement, definition and unit of analysis of, 79, 154
"voluntary simplicity," 75

Wan Smolbag Theater, 110, 273
warfare, 28, 31, 90
water, resource management of, 52–53
watershed scale, 150–51, 155
"wilderness," 30
wildlife management areas (WMAs), 51
Wilkie, D., 175
William, G. W., 30
Workshop on Political Theory and Policy Analysis, 263
World Bank, 18, 75
"world park," 55
World Resources Institute, 10, 178
World Trade Organization (WTO), 75
World Wide Fund for Nature-South Pacific Program, 230
World Wildlife Fund (WWF), 10, 128, 141, 149

Zaire. See Congo
Zimbabwe: community management programs in, 35; wildlife programs in, 52
"zones," 171

About the Authors

Diane Russell's interests include community-based conservation, human ecology, economic anthropology, agrarian studies, research methods, and international development. Diane received a Ph.D. in anthropology from Boston University in 1991 with a dissertation on the rice trade around Kisangani, Zaire (now Democratic Republic of Congo). From 1995–1998, she was senior program officer and social scientist for the Biodiversity Conservation Network, based in Manila and Fiji. Diane is currently team leader for Advancing Innovation and Impact at the World Agroforestry Centre (ICRAF), Nairobi, Kenya. In 2001, she was awarded a master's in Environmental Management from Yale University School of Forestry and Environmental Studies. She lives in Nairobi with her family.

Camilla Harshbarger is an applied anthropologist who specializes in program design, evaluation, and organizational and community capacity building. She has consulted in international development throughout sub-Saharan Africa, Central America, and the United States, working with a wide range of institutions, including corporations, small businesses, community-based organizations, cooperatives, governments, local and international nongovernmental organizations (NGOs), and donors. Her work focuses on organizational effectiveness, democracy and governance, gender, household nutrition and food security, field methods for NGOs, and partnership and regional strategies for West and Southern Africa.

Dr. Harshbarger received her Ph.D. in anthropology in 1995 from the University of Florida. She has conducted research in Latin America, Africa, and the United States. Her work addresses diverse topics, including state legitimacy and dispute resolution of land conflicts in Cameroon, agricultural credit in Costa Rica, social impact assessment of federal construction projects on Native Americans in the western United States, stigmatized subpopulations in Chicago, and Japanese nonverbal communication for Americans conducting business in Japan.

Currently, Dr. Harshbarger is a behavioral scientist working on HIV/AIDS prevention in Atlanta, Georgia. She is working on a strategy to diffuse effective HIV prevention interventions into communities across the United States.